Intellectual Property and Ethics

Australia
LBC Information Services
Sydney

Canada and USA
Carswell
Toronto

New Zealand
Brooker's
Auckland

Singapore and Malaysia
Thomson Information (S.E. Asia)
Singapore

Intellectual Property and Ethics

Edited by Lionel Bently and Spyros M. Maniatis

Perspectives on Intellectual Property Series
General Editor: Professor James Lahore

Editorial Board
Chairman: Hugh Brett
Professor Gerald Dworkin
Alison Firth
Geoffrey Hobbs Q.C.
Mary Vitoria Q.C.

In association with the I.P. Unit, Queen Mary & Westfield
College, University of London

LONDON ● SWEET & MAXWELL ● 1998

Published in 1998 by
Sweet & Maxwell Limited
100 Avenue Road
Swiss Cottage
London NW3 3PF
Typeset by LBJ Typesetting Ltd
of Kingsclere
Printed and bound in Great Britain
by Arrowhead Books Ltd, Reading

No natural forests were destroyed
to make this product only farmed
timber was used and replanted.

A CIP catalogue record for this book
is available from the British Library

ISBN 0 421 624 40X

Introduction

Introduction

Writing on intellectual property law has traditionally been doctrinal in nature: dry and technical legal elaborations of complicated rules. Recently, however, the emphasis has changed and we have witnessed a proliferation of valuable interdisciplinary studies of intellectual property. Primarily, the subject has been viewed through the eyes of economics.[1] Other studies employed the insights and techniques of cultural studies[2] or looked at the social and historical roots of intellectual property.[3] Furthermore intellectual property terminology and concepts have indicatively been used in politics,[4] cultural theories,[5] or theories on consumerism.[6]

Rarely, however, has the interaction between the domains of intellectual property and ethical discourse formed the subject of inquiry or scholarship. One reason that ethical dimensions of intellectual property law have not been extensively explored during this century is undoubtedly the pervasiveness of positivism throughout the western academy.[7] There are also other reasons more specific to intellectual property law. In particular, the history of the development of intellectual property law is very much a history of legal attempts to capture and render certain the evanescent notions of creativity and genius. This has involved a reduction of intellectually illusive (and elusive) concepts to manageable and protectable properties through a variety of legal techniques (the idea expression dichotomy, the drafting of patent specification and claims, design representations). Each technique attempts to limit the scope of interpretation and role of judgment in the evaluation of the intangible contribution or mental labour expended in the making of the work and thus to effect a closure of the property.[8] The persistent attempt to exclude

---

[1] See for example Sterling (ed.), *Intellectual Property and Market Freedom*, (Vol. 2.) Perspectives on Intellectual Property (Sweet & Maxwell, London, 1997) and Palmer, "Intellectual Property: A Non-Posnerian Law and Economics Approach", 12 *Hamline Law Rev.* 261.

[2] Saunder, *Authorship and Copyright* (Routledge, London, 1992); Gaines, *Contested Culture: The Image, the Voice and the Law* (BFI, London, 1992); Sherman & Strowel, *Of Authors and Origins: Essays on Copyright Law* (OUP, Oxford, 1994).

[3] Firth (ed.), *The Pre-History and Development of Intellectual Property Systems*, (Vol. 1) Perspectives on Intellectual Property (Sweet & Maxwell, London, 1997).

[4] Leonard, *Britain™* (Demos, London, 1997).

[5] Lury, *Cultural Rights, Technology, Legality and Personality* (Routledge, London, 1993).

[6] Gabriel & Lang, *The Unmanageable Consumer* (Sage Publications, London, 1995).

[7] Douzinas, Goodrich & Hachamovitch, in "Politics, ethics, and the legality of the Contingent" in Douzinas, Goodrich & Hachamovitch, *Politics, Postmodernity and Critical Legal Studies* (Routledge, London, 1994), at p. 16:

> "The defining feature of modernist legality was the separation of legality and morality: a wholly positivized conception of juridical phenomena was predicated upon the exclusion of ethics, morality, value and indeed substance from questions of law, legality, validity and form".

[8] "Any contamination of law by value will compromise its ability to turn social and political conflict into manageable technical disputes about the meaning and applicability of preexisting public rules."; *ibid.*, p. 17.

judgement, in part explains the failure of modern intellectual property law to explore ethical issues which would otherwise prevail in an intellectual property discourse.

Despite the occasional recognition of important inter-relations between ethics and law of intellectual property, there has been no sustained or focused reflection on the relationship between these two domains. This collection of essays attempts to initiate the task of exploring in a more thorough-going and reflective manner.

Why should we consider that the intersection between intellectual property and ethics be worth exploring? In part, because ethical issues are already finding their way on to the intellectual property law agenda: most evidently, through the issue of the patenting of biotechnology (explored in part in the papers by Dhadda and Sherman and Bently), but also in the revival of interest in the general justification for intellectual property rights. The intersection between ethics and intellectual property has also formed part of much of the broader discussion on the "theoretical justification" for intellectual property legislation or from a different perspective the processes of its legitimation.[9] In addition, ethical issues have been raised in discussions relating to the grounds of the obligation of confidentiality, the transfer of technology, and the legitimacy of using intellectual property rights to divide up markets. Further issues are clearly implicated by the way that intellectual property law is colonising new geographies—a colonisation that often presents a clash of cultures.

In part, too, the domain looks to be a rich one because ethics has become fashionable again as a focus of intense debate in the light of a proliferation of new approaches extending beyond the traditional debate between universalism and conventionalism. Indeed, the domain of ethics has now been shifted to encompass more than theoretical explorations of notions of right and good (whether they be determined by divinity, reason or consequences). Indeed recent discussion of "ethics" has embraced a number of strands, some of the most prominent of which are the "discourse ethics" associated with Jurgen Habermas, the "ethics of alterity" associated with the work of Emmanuel Levinas, feminist ethics associated with Carol Gilligan, as well as Michel Foucault's conception of ethics as the techniques, sources and ends of the "self acting upon the self". Furthermore, considerable literature has developed in various fields of applied ethics which may usefully be employed in examinations of intellectual property law—such work ranging from business ethics,[10] organisational ethics, institutional ethics (as opposed to individual ethics), environmental ethics, bioethics as well as ethics and international affairs.[11]

The essays collected in this volume cover a wide range of ethical theories and draw on a variety of issues in intellectual property law.

---

[9] See Hettinger, "Justifying Intellectual Property", (1989) 18 Phil. & Pub. Affs 31.
[10] e.g. Lippke, *Radical Business Ethics* (Lanham, Maryland, Rowman & Littlefield, 1995).
[11] See, for example, the series Ethics and International Affairs.

There are, unsurprisingly, questions of justification of intellectual property rights (Hughes), as well as explorations of the ethical underpinnings of familiar legal concepts (Kamperman Sanders), and the treatment of ethically controversial areas by intellectual property law (Dhadda, Sherman and Bently). But there are also essays which explore the implications of the colonising operations of intellectual property, that is, the ethical dimensions of the encounter between intellectual property law and new geographies (Burrell), new spaces (Bowrey) and new cultures (Barron).

The more traditional notions of ethics are employed in the papers by Hughes, Kamperman Sanders and Burrell. Hughes's paper, written as an intervention in the topical debate over the harmonisation of the artists resale royalty right in Europe, draws on traditional ethical notions of "equality", "fairness" and "consistency" to support in principle the adoption of such a right in the United Kingdom. While the concept of "equality" is not explored theoretically,[12] the central tenet of Hughes's essay is that groups of legal subjects should be entitled to equal treatment before the law, but that such treatment does not demand that these groups be given the same formal legal rights. Rather, artists, who benefit poorly from remuneration based on exploitation of the "reproduction right", should be given an economic equivalent such as the *droit de suite*.[13]

Kamperman Sanders adopts an innovative approach in attempting to explore the ethical norms which lie hidden behind and supplement the dominant economic discourse in which unfair competition law is couched and legitimised. He does so by arguing that the economic specificities are necessarily mediated into socially operative norms through the employment of "ethical criteria". In particular, Kamperman Sanders sees unfair competition law as based around and dependent upon a notion of "unjust enrichment", a concept that finds its ethical basis in the lengthy tradition of corrective justice.[14]

Burrell's paper explores the techniques employed to expand recognition of intellectual property rights outside their origins in the western legal systems. In particular, he argues that while economic motives explain such legal imperialism, the ethical dimensions of such strategies demand reflection. Employing a variety of understandings of ethics, Burrell argues that many of the United States actions in relation to China can be criticised as unethical in that they lack "integrity". Moreover, drawing on consequentialist approaches, Burrell points out that the United States refusal to engage with the existing structures of Chinese administration have caused the United States to advocate changes in China's law which are ethically objectionable—most notably, in that they render copyright infringement potentially a capital offence.

---

[12] See, for example, Dworkin, *A Matter of Principle* (Harvard University Press, Cambridge Mass, 1985).

[13] See also Gordon, "An inquiry into the Merits of Copyright: The Challenges of Consistency, Consent and Encouragement Theory", (1989) 41 Stan L. Rev. 1343, comparing copyright with copyprivilege.

[14] See Aristotle, *Nicomachean Ethics* (Ross trans.) (Oxford University Press, Oxford, 1980).

The papers of Dhadda, Tadros, Barron and Bowrey draw on the possibilities for exploration of intellectual property law presented by the recent proliferation of ethical theories which define "ethics" beyond discourse about how we ought to live, (that is moral principles, norms, obligations, ways of thinking and interdictions that rule, regulate and structure human behaviour or guide actions of particular groups).

More specifically, Dhadda draws on the work of Jacques Derrida to examine recent debates over the patenting of genetic products. She argues that the debates reveal ethical concerns which go much deeper than questions of consent or remuneration. For Dhadda the project itself (rather than issues of patenting) is the source of the ethical contest. She employs the concept of "différance" as a tool for determining the validity of information arising from biotechnology and argues against the preconceptions which once more deny the alterity. She argues that the role of the human genome project, though it is in the constitution of notions of human identity, reinforces the categories of primitive and modern.

In contrast with Dhadda, Sherman and Bently treat the debate over patenting life from a historical viewpoint, as marking a critical point for laws' re-encounter with ethics. For Sherman and Bently, the modern legal system has attempted to exclude from its domain questions of moral and aesthetic judgement and other matters perceived to be subjective in nature. What is at stake in the debate over patenting the products of biotechnology is thus the purity of law, and any meaningful response to the calls for the incorporation of morality into law implies a thorough renegotiation of existing structures and practices.

Tadros' focus is different still. He employs the work of Foucault and Heidegger to explore the "ethics of authorship". Here, Tadros uses the extended notion of ethics employed by Foucault as referring to the "selfs working on the self".[15] Tadros argues that the models of writing embodied in copyright discourse operate to construct, constitute, reinforce and reflect particular ethics: authorship norms embody an ethic of self reflection, soul-searching and confession. However, when a right is assigned to a text it becomes mobilised and the ethic of authorship is replaced by a market dominated by desire. In place of this, Tadros argues for the development of a different ethic of writing, one which focuses on the constitution of ethical subjects, and thus emphasises not the novelty of writing but its quality.

Bowrey's essay draws on the burgeoning literature on "cyberspace" to outline and dissect the various ethical issues raised by the new communication technologies, in particular, the "internet". While acknowledging problems of categorisation of these writings many of which are premised on ideas of radical transformation and destabilisation of existing intercourse, Bowrey analyses the ethical issues raised by the internet as falling into three categories: those concerning access to technology, those

---

[15] Rabinow, *The Foucault Reader* (Penguin, Harmondsworth, 1986) p. 352; Davidson, "Archaeology, Genealogy and Ethics" D. Hoy, *Foucault: A Critical Reader* (Basil Blackwell, London, 1986).

concerning control of information and those pertaining to relationships. Intellectual property questions, which primarily fall into the middle category, are thus placed within the full panoply of transformative possibilities heralded by the new social space.

Finally, Barron draws on the work of Foucault, Bourdieu and Levinas, in an examination of the way in which Australian copyright law has treated questions of aboriginal art. In particular, she employs Levinas' "Totality and Infinity"—rejecting existing ethical discourse for its privileging of epistemology—to develop the thematic of otherness.[16] Using a case decided by the Federal Court of Australia in 1991, *Yumbulul v. Reserve Bank of Australia*, she offers an account of the construction of the Aboriginal artist as author-in-law which aims to historicise that construction and, at the same time, to expose it to ethical interrogation. This excavates the links between the emergence of this figure and the emergence of the Aboriginal artist as an aesthetic personality, and explores how both of these constructions have operated to deny the alterity of Aboriginal creative practices. She suggests, finally, how this alterity might be mobilised within and against the apparently necessary and self-evident form of copyright's author.

The essays collected here illustrate the potential vitality of interdisciplinary research and writing in general, and its particular relevance for intellectual property. The collection marks a tentative first step. There is ample scope for further work: institutional ethics, professional ethics and a comprehensive deontological analysis of intellectual property rights developed in parallel with their economic analysis property are but a few examples of the areas demanding further research and publications. This volume of *Perspectives* can be seen as a contribution to the recognition of this need and the establishment of a basis for more exploration.

Lionel Bently
King's College, London

Spyros M. Maniatis
Queen Mary & Westfield College, London

---

[16] See Levinas, "Totality and Infinity and Commentaries" in Peperznak (ed.), *Ethics as a First Philosophy* (Routledge, New York, 1995). For Levinas, the ethical regard is one that resists encompassing the other as part of the same, that resists recognising the other solely within the already spoken codes of a universalizing vision of humankind. The notion is one of infinite respect for an alterity that always evades complete comprehension. Morality is a recognition of and vulnerability to alterity, and ethical relations must not homogenize humanity but rather be nontotalizing. For a discussion of Levinas in a legal setting see C. Douzinas & R. Warrington, *Justice Miscarried: Ethics, Aesthetics and the Law* (Harvester Wheatsheaf, Hemel Hempstead, 1994) Chap. 4 and Chap. 6 for application; see also M. Schapiro, *Violent Cartographies: Mapping Cultures of War* (Un. of Minnesota Press, Minneapolis, 1977), Chap. 6, "The Ethics of the Encounter: Unreading, Unmapping the Imperium".

Contents

TABLE OF CASES

TABLE OF NATIONAL LEGISLATION

TABLE OF UNITED KINGDOM LEGISLATION

TABLE OF EUROPEAN LEGISLATION

TABLE OF INTERNATIONAL LEGISLATION

1. Ethical Boundaries and Internet Cultures

Kathy Bowrey

Lecturer in Law, at Macquarie University, Sydney, Australia. B.A., LL.B. SJD. Her dissertation, "Don't Fence Me In: The Many Histories of Copyright", explores cultural and legal responses to the development of reproductive technologies, from medieval times to the present. Her academic interests include not only writing about new technologies, but also using them, exploring their potential for interdisciplinary legal education and new methods of critical analysis. She has written, with Terry Libesman, a multimedia introduction to legal studies, Pickle Street: Dispute Resolution and Legal Studies CD ROMs (Board of Studies NSW, 1996) and is in the process of producing a CD Rom entitled "Copy, Not Copy" with artist Lloyd Sharp. She also operates a website: http://www.ozemail.com.au/~copy.

Ethical Boundaries and Internet Cultures*

Introduction: Disabling Metaphors

Terms used to describe the internet such as: "the electronic frontier"; "information superhighway"; "cyber-space"; "virtual community"; "being Wired"; and "the Net" are loaded with cultural expectation, attitude and values. It is difficult not to use and implicitly endorse such descriptors. Science fiction has greatly contributed to the internet and its cultures, inspiring scientific enhancements of it, future possibilities and assisting understandings of our interactions within the internet. Cultural studies, alongside deconstructive readings of the internet, have also proselytised it. Further both cultural studies and science fiction have contributed to a perception that the internet is for the bold, an uncharted destiny, emphatically different from what those who have been left behind are familiar with. The avowed revolutionary nature of the internet contributes to the difficulty of realistically addressing questions about the ethical implications of internet technologies.

Writings about the ethical implications of the internet are difficult to summarise. Writers adopt very different points of entry, informed by diverse moral values and visions. Even thematically related materials often embrace irreconcilable assumptions about the role of internet technologies and the nature of the activities involved, the character of the internet community, the relationship between real and virtual communities, and the relationship between ethics, laws and law reform. Further there is a high emotivity present in much of the writing. We have seen interminable moral panics displayed in print media, radio and television—about the possibility of corruption of innocents by online predatory opportunists, alarm at the limitations of applying intellectual property rights in cyberspace, anarchy and ruin brought about by "hacking" at the institutions of respectable society, new and extreme levels of social alienation because a keyboard and terminal mediates interactions. Exuberant testimonials to the internet are also commonplace, with technologies having made possible previously impossible friendships and romances, connecting communities based upon a philosophy of sharing and nurturing a creative ethos, giving us a safe place spiritually within the world but away from the inhospitable realities of city life, somewhere playfully serious where we are unhindered by maladroit bodies.

* With thanks to Kathe Boehringer, Marie Bowrey and Lloyd Sharp.

Broadly speaking, questions of ethics relate to three themes—(1) access to internet technologies; (2) access to information; and (3) the impact of both technology and information upon identity and relationships. In evaluating arguments raised with respect to each of these themes I want to do more than merely describe or contrast writers' hypotheses about the problems created by the internet.

The ability of a new technology to transform society depends upon how it affects the collective imagination and whether it stimulates a desire for a different future. Technology can create a desire to change the physical and human environment, including our laws, to amplify technological dreams and with that, stimulate further innovation. Less optimistic fantasies can focus efforts to forestall such developments. Acceptance and appreciation of any technology is always uneven. In this context it is unsurprising that internet technologies have generated strong opinions for and against their development and use. Utopian and dystopian stories are part of any new technological milieu.

In order to evaluate realistically the stories being told about the internet I want to put this development into a broader context by treating it as an example of how a new communications technology disrupts the social, political and economic landscape. To help focus this study I want to refer to the impact of an earlier revolutionary communications technology—the printing press. The development of printing technology also heralded calls for more intense censorship, new monopoly rights, made possible new relationships between strangers, led to the creation of reading societies and new meeting places for self selecting groups of writers and readers. A comparison between these two communication mediums can help ground discussion, providing a measure to judge the more extravagant claims about the impact of cyberspace. Are there parallels between the early broadsheets sold on street corners and internet home pages? between pirate printers and hackers? between meetings in coffee houses and internet Newsgroups? between the "Sublime Society of Beef Steaks" and the "WELL" (Whole Earth 'Lectronic Link)? Do contemporary calls for regulation mirror those of an earlier age? Are there any fundamental similarities in the ethical issues that arise with developments in communications technology?

This paper appraises the ethical implications of the internet from a position neither within current debates or one that presumes the possibility of an objective position suspended outside of them. Rather, in exposing the internet to an historical analysis, it is hoped we can more realistically comprehend precisely what new challenges the internet involves, appreciate the precedent of contemporary calls for its regulation and, in the process, come to better understand the complex interrelationship between new technologies, ethics and law.

Dissecting Cyberculture

"The cyborg is our ontology; it gives us our politics."[1]

To separate cyberculture writings into one of three concerns—technology, information or people—is problematic. It is at odds with the view that whether we like it or not as individuals, as a society we have already embraced "technobiopower" and as a consequence, technology, information and identity are now inseparable constructs. Regardless of how we, as individuals, may feel about any of the cyber-technologies, the society we live in accepts the reality of medicinal and cosmetic implants, genetically-enhanced plant and animal species, the economic importance of high technology industries and the value of their "virtual" intellectual property, the global networking of communities, nations and humanity. In this situation technology transcends the status of being a mere tool or instrument. Technology can become an active participant in its own application. Communicating involves more than comprehending the message. Information becomes open-ended and adaptive within the parameters set by the technology. Identity is not bound by nature or biology. Nature and biology merge with the machine and its infomatics:

> "When Haraway declares that we are all cyborgs, she means it both literally—medicine has given birth to 'couplings between organism and machine,' bio- and communications technologies are 'recrafting our bodies'—and figuratively, in the sense that 'we are living through a movement from an organic, industrial society to a polymorphous, information system'."[2]

Evaluating cyberculture and its ethics by separating analyses into groups primarily interested in technology or information or identity is, not only reductive but also incompatible with the basic premise of cyberculture. However, from the perspective of where questions of ethics intersect with questions of law, this kind of categorisation makes more sense.

Questioning the conditions of access to internet technologies usually intersects with issues of public policy, the global infrastructure, democracy, government and private regulation. Who should have a right to use the internet, how, in what circumstances and for what ends? To what extent should manufacturers of technology or providers of technology based services be forced to act in the public interest? Who should establish the international standards and protocols that allow "the Net" to function, and on what terms? Is there a case for subversive application of technology to expose or perhaps redress power imbalances?

---

[1] Donna J. Haraway, *Simians, Cyborgs and Women: The Reinvention of Nature* (Routledge, New York, 1991), p. 150.
[2] Mark Dery, *Escape Velocity*, (Hodder & Stoughton, London, 1996), p. 243.

Writings that debate the issue of access to information usually also concern the ethics of intellectual property protection in cyberspace. Should information be part of a "cultural commons"? Is it "theft" to circulate information online without regard for the wishes of the person who holds rights to it? Is "theft" to be determined with respect to the nature of the use of the information? What should be done to redress the practical problems of enforcing intellectual property rights in cyberspace? To what extent should third parties, such as internet service providers, be forced to take responsibility for the intellectual property transgressions of those who make use of their services?

Concern for the effect of internet technologies on human relationships often intersects with questions of criminal law and torts such as personal injury or defamation. Should an internet user be responsible for harm caused to another in a "virtual" interaction? If one learns online of harm that was caused to another, should they track down the alleged perpetrator off line and call them to account? To what extent are internet users responsible for each other? Or to those more vulnerable?

Despite the violence done to the definition of cyberculture and the reality that the classification of particular writings may be contested, the identification of works emphasising a regulatory interest is useful. Questions of ethics are generally linked with questions of legal regulation.

By its nature legal regulation is a conservative force. Whilst it is essential that individual laws possess a degree of flexibility to cope with the unique and the unknown, in presuming its own coherence, law sets limits to its ability to accommodate the unexpected. Law can respond instrumentally to contemporary overtures and, in that way, try to extend its embrace well beyond that previously anticipated. To a degree this strategy is essential to resolve immediate conflicts before the courts. Nevertheless, however well this strategy is executed, the mismatch cannot be hidden. The legal "resolution" of a completely unanticipated problem is based upon a discriminating, reinterpretation of legal language and an insecure repositioning of legal space, language and categories. Legal meaning remains under a high degree of stress, and its extension and capacity to regulate the novel circumstances disputed. In this environment new ethical discourses proliferate, in addition to technical legal ones.

Law is a conservative force not only because of its ties with established power, but also because legal power contests change. Law always redefines contemporary developments in its own terms. This means that regardless of how revolutionary the internet is, and how inappropriate the application of current legal processes and laws may be, the internet will continue to be judged by and through these laws or reincarnations of them. Accordingly discussing the ethical implications of the internet in terms of current regulatory arrangements is also appropriate. It does not follow that any "lack of fit" will be overlooked. Rather this approach can help pinpoint the limits to legal innovation and lead to an appraisal of the role of ethics in such a situation.

Access to Internet Technologies

"Increasingly we find that the greatest shortcoming of cyberculture is not in the provision of occasionally disreputable freedoms and liberties, but in the unavailability of such facilities of participation and fulfilment to the majority; in its foreclosure to certain geographies and in the general unwillingness of the privileged to account for the unrepresented. Cyberspace, as we have seen, is not the new, free global democracy we presume and defend, but an aristocracy of location and disposition, characterized, ironically, by acute insensitivity and territorialist proclivities.

To remember that the vast majority of humanity, both outside and within the highly industrialised world, have [sic] no knowledge whatsoever of this new platform of liberties, to speak less of access to it, is to underline not only the esotericism [sic] of our discourses, but also to call our attention to the challenges of forsaken geographies and silent territories, of populations and denominations on a new margin of our own creation; those races condemned, as Gabriel Garcia Marquez ominously observes, to a hundred years of solitude with no respite on earth."[3]

The question of the right to access technology is an issue that raises questions of equality both between nations and within national boundaries. An apt companion piece to Oguibe is a Doonesbury cartoon:

"Trudeau draws a street person going to collect his e-mail at the public library, where addresses had been handed out free to the homeless. Looking for potential employers' responses to his job resume, he posts an address that puts the hype about the universal democracy built into the technoscientific information system into perspective: lunatic @ street_level."[4]

The question of access to internet technologies entails issues of responsibility for developing telecommunications infrastructure, the cost of devices and services that link individuals to the network, the level of technical mastery required as a consequence of the design of the devices and services, and the availability of an education that allows individuals to connect and use these technologies. What space is there for ethical discourses with respect to these things? How is the internet different from the press in this regard?

It is worth remembering that printing became very popular very quickly after it first emerged in 1476 despite the reality that comparatively few people were able to read, paper production was both complicated and costly, and printing equipment was expensive.[5] However the ethical issues raised by printing technology were not concerned with enabling more liberal access, but with discouraging the use of the press for purposes other than education as authorised by

---

[3] Olu Oguibe, "Forsaken Geographies: Cyberspace and the New World 'Other' ", *5th International Conference on Cyberspace*, June 6–9, 1996, Proceedings published at http://www.telefonica.es/fat/eoguibe.html
[4] Donna J. Haraway, *Modest_Witness@Second_Millennium.FemaleMan©Meets_OncoMouse* ™ (Routledge, New York, 1997), p. 6.
[5] See Elizabeth Eisenstein, *The Printing Press as an Agent of Change* (Cambridge University Press, Cambridge, 1979).

Church and State. The introduction of new technology generated a legal response that took the form of licensing presses and censoring printed literature. However despite active discouragement of popularist uses of the press, such uses still proved hard to restrain, especially after 1640 when small hand presses were developed that could be purchased for a more modest outlay and were easier to conceal.[6] Once the potential of the new technology was appreciated, popular interest in it meant that thereafter it proved very difficult to deny individuals or communities access to it.

Henry VIII actively encouraged the dissemination of "useful" information by granting patents for a set terms of years for specific titles to guarantee that a publisher had a reasonable chance of a return.[7] This practice was also followed by Elizabeth I, James I and Charles I, although only a minority of books were ever privileged in this fashion. As well as these formal printing privileges, *de facto* printing privileges developed amongst the trade, with stationers recognising amongst the members of their guild a monopoly in the first who printed the text. The Stationer's Company had been founded in 1403 from older societies of scriveners, limners, bookbinders and stationers, and in the guild tradition the Company controlled entry into the printing trade. It had applied for a company charter and formal recognition of its *de facto* publication privileges in 1534. As part of the Catholic Counter-Reformation, Mary Tudor agreed to this request in 1557, not for the benefit of the stationers, but in order to extend control over what her subjects could read. Members of the Stationer's Company were given a monopoly in the printing of works, the right made effective by entering the work into the Company Register in the name of the publisher (the latter's copy-right). In return for these personal privileges the Company's keepers of the Register were responsible for seeing that the work was appropriately approved by Church and State.[8] No books, pamphlets, newsbooks or broadsides were to be printed without such a licence.[9]

Early regulatory responses to the development of printing show a ready appreciation of the potential of the technology to disrupt the established social order. However there was no notion of a right to access print technology, even though in some quarters there was clearly a desire for free speech. The licensing of presses ceased in 1695 when regulation

---

[6] For an entertaining study of the output of such presses see Jerome Friedman, *Miracles and the Pulp Press during the English Revolution. The Battle of the Frogs and Fairford's Flies* (University College London Press, London, 1993).

[7] See John Feather, "From Rights in Copies to Copyright", (1992) 10 *Cardozo Arts & Entertainment Law Journal* 455.

[8] Michael Black, *Cambridge University Press 1584–1984* (Cambridge University Press, Cambridge, 1984) p. 28.

[9] Feather argues that this royal charter had the effect of banning provincial printing outside of Oxford and Cambridge universities because only freemen of London, normally resident there, were able to join the Stationer's Company. However this was not of immediate consequence because none of the provincial enterprises had been very successful, there being little infrastructure to support transportation and distribution of books. See John Feather, *A History of British Publishing* (Croom Helm, London, 1988) p. 31.

lapsed following years of strenuous debate about the politics of the licenser's role, the need for a free press and the creation of unfair monopolies.[10]

The point here in relation to our contemporary concern with ethics and the internet is a simple one: the right to access a technology has to be considered in the context of the political environment and regulatory practices of the day. With respect to the internet, today's political rhetoric generally supports the notion that access should ideally be democratic. However, public policy is generally directed towards defining and supporting access through "the market", not necessarily "of right":

"Everywhere, governments are preparing new laws and regulations for the digital era, but in virtually all of these debates the superiority of the market and the profit motive as the regulator of all branches of communication is taken as a given."[11]

"A market access regime favouring the material interests of the information and communication network and service users is recognised as requiring a complicated balancing of market liberalization measures and measures to ensure that the use of networks and services generates an acceptable economic return to their producers."[12]

Enabling access to technology via the market does not automatically exclude questions of ethics. However:

"The internet is not a thing: it is the interconnection of many things— the (potential) interconnection between any of millions of computers located around the world."[13]

Because there is no such thing as *the* "internet market", no possibility of a democratic "right" to access it or any other sort of overriding "internet ethic" can emerge:

"The outcome of the regime formation processes that coincide with technical change are not determined in a straightforward way by the power exercised by dominant industry actors or by the power of State actors."[14]

Shifting alignments among technology and service producers and users forestall any one party closely controlling developments. Vertical integra-

---

[10] See Raymond Astbury, "The Renewal of the Licensing Act in 1693 and its Lapse in 1695", (1978) 336 *Library* 5th series, 296.
[11] Edward S. Herman & Robert W. McChesney, *The Global Media* (Cassell, London, 1997), p. 109.
[12] Robin Mansell, "Network Governance" in Robin Mansell & Roger Silverstone (eds), *Communication by Design* (Oxford University Press, Oxford, 1996), p. 192.
[13] Michael Froomkin, "The Internet as a Source of Regulatory Arbitrage" in Brian Kahin & Charles Nesson (eds), *Borders in Cyberspace* (MIT Press, Massachusetts, 1997), p. 130.
[14] Mansell, above n. 12, p. 192.

tion of various market sectors may be a potential problem for the internet, but at this stage in its development there are many players servicing different technologies and services, and subject to various regulatory regimes. Further, the various markets that comprise the internet are governed by an array of regulatory provisions that have their precedence in different communications strategies.[15]

The internet can be loosely deconstructed into markets along the lines of historically specific regulatory interests:

- telecommunications: where market players are government-licensed private owners;
- computer hardware and software: where along with ongoing revisions to trade policy, access to operating equipment is provided for by way of incentives to manufacturers, largely through reinvigorated intellectual property laws designed to accommodate the convergence of technologies and global "harmonisation" of these laws.
- internet services: this area remains largely unregulated beyond the various consumer and financial laws that affect most businesses in any given locality. Part of the regulatory challenge here is not to provide disincentives so that services relocate interstate or offshore.
- education: the "deregulation" of universities and colleges is sponsoring a redirection of attention to the interests and needs of industry,[16] especially where research and learning relates to the perceived needs of high technology industries.

Each of these areas is continually subject to law reform initiatives that contribute to more precise definition of markets for particular internet goods or services. Ethical questions tend to arise as part of these broader debates. For example, there is a perceived need for the internet to be universal in reach so that users are able to send a message or talk to anyone. Within national boundaries, where population densities are low and there are significant distances between large centres, there might be no profit in connecting homes to electricity grids and rolling out or upgrading cables and wires. Should government force telecommunications companies to service these "disadvantaged" areas as part of their licence to service more profitable routes, or should government rely upon a technological fix, such as the development of satellite services? Is connectivity to internet services as essential as to other communications services such as the post or telephone? If so, should a "common carrier" model also be adopted for the internet?[17] Some proprietary network systems such as America Online and Compuserve have seen the

---

[15] See Ithiel de Sola Pool, *Technologies of Freedom* (Harvard University Press, Cambridge, Massachussetts, 1983), p. 233.
[16] See John McCollow & Bob Lingard, "Changing discourses and practices of academic work", (1996) 39(2) *Australian Universities Review*, 11.
[17] See generally de Sola Pool, above n. 15, pp. 237–8.

necessity for a common communications interface and have developed ways of integrating their networks with the internet. Where pressure from users does not call for such a development should government step in? Debate about the appropriate choice of model for the internet may be infused with questions of economics and debate over what is a viable return for an investment in infrastructure. Nevertheless underpinning these arguments is a moral issue: should public policy considerations, such as the "right" of anyone, anywhere, to interconnect, be structured into the internet telecommunications market?

Were a common carrier model to be adopted, this, of course, need not mean that every person could connect to anyone of their choosing. Were democratic access the general goal, along with a non-discriminatory capacity to connect to telecommunications infrastructure, it would necessitate non-discriminatory access to the essential hardware, software, services and internet know-how. However, because historically telecommunications regulation has been seen as separate from regulation of computer hardware, software and services, the regulation of access to these other things is generally treated separately to that of the internet infrastructure.[18] Technologies must converge in order to make the internet function, but from a regulatory point of view they can be disconnected and treated separately.[19] This means that even were a policy of a democratic right to access telecommunications infrastructure to be adopted, it would not result in equal access unless there were a corresponding obligation to provide access to all of the other essential components. So, for example, subsidised access to the infrastructure would need to be coupled with subsidised access to properly maintained computers and technical assistance in order for the "right" to access internet technology to be meaningful.

At some levels the intersection of previously distinct markets is recognised. As a consequence new regulatory fora and standards have emerged to negotiate the shared interests of the various network and service innovators. Beyond the more general issue of "harmonised" commercial laws that has generated quite a lot of academic attention,[20] there is the no less important issue of industry standards and protocols. These allow for the interoperability and networking of technologies:

"Each of these computers is independently managed by persons who have chosen to adhere to common communications standards,

---

[18] This is not to suggest that telecommunications is only about the provision of infrastructure. The separation of telecommunications into hardware and services is an issue of major contention in itself. Issues constantly arise over cost of installing and maintaining a communications infrastructure as opposed to that of providing services.

[19] Often this means that a number of regulatory bodies are asked to provide input into policy formation, with each uncertain as to how their role meshes with that of others. This diffusion of responsibility can work in the political interest of the Minister for Communications. The Minister can play organisations off against each other with careers of public servants affected by a judgment of how useful their organisation's policy is in the prevailing political situation.

[20] See for example, Raymond T. Nimmer & Patricia Ann Krauthaus, "Globalisation of law in intellectual property and related commercial contexts", (1992) 10(2) Law in Context 80.

particularly a fundamental standard known as TCP/IP, which makes it practical for computers adhering to the standard to share data even if they are far apart and have no direct line of communication. TCP/IP is the fundamental communication standard on which the internet has relied: "TCP" stands for Transmission Control Protocol while "IP" stands for Internet Protocol. There is no single program one uses to gain access to the Internet; instead there are a number of programs that adhere to the Internet Protocols."[21]

However despite the convergence of technologies generating a need for the establishment of common standards to enable interconnection of the various technology sectors and internet markets, this does not create a new opportunity for the development of an industry ethic. Instead corporate alliances emerge and their co-ordination and co-operation strategies are the basis for common standards and protocols. This can be seen from the following account of how and why corporate alliances arise:

"AOL (America Online) has always been open-minded about partnering with companies. . . In the case of some of the core internet technologies around the Web, we realized that although we could continue to build these ourselves, the pace of innovation was accelerating, and several companies, including Microsoft, Netscape, and Sun, were pouring in significant resources. It made sense for us to partner with one or more of these companies, as opposed to competing with or trying to replicate what they were doing. We ended up establishing alliances with all of them . .
. . . Competing with companies on one level while partnering with them at another level is an increasingly typical strategy, though it requires subtlety and finesse."[22]

Co-ordination, it turns out, is an important aspect of a competitive strategy. The new international regime of protocols and standards that has emerged is merely a further level of corporate negotiation in the face of mutual interests and problems. To the extent that an ethical issue is identified that affects all corporate and government players, it generally is restricted to concern whether recompense is owed to an innovator of an industry standard, in recognition of the loss of control over future development of its innovation, and perhaps the forfeiture of some level of monopoly protection that could have been conferred by intellectual property laws. If Java becomes the universal platform independent object oriented programming language for the internet, is its developer, Sun Microsystems, entitled to any special role in its ongoing development and licensing?[23]

---

[21] Michael Froomkin, "The Internet as a Source of Regulatory Arbitrage" in Kahin & Nesson, above n. 13, p. 130.
[22] "The States Man: Steve Case", in John Brockman, (ed), *Digerati*, (Orion, London, 1996), p. 64.
[23] Not according to Microsoft and others. See Michael Moeller, "Intel, Microsoft, Compaq, Digital ask Sun to relinquish control of Java", *PC Week Online*, Sept. 11, 1997, 6pmET. http://www.zdnet.com/pcweek/news/0908/11elett.html

In the competitive environment of large corporations there is no realistic possibility of an industry ethic developing. But individuals, organisations and private corporations are not precluded from developing or adopting their own ethic. Consider, for example, the following from the "GNU Manifesto" written by Richard Stallman, President of the Free Software Foundation and co-founder of the League for Programming Freedom:

"I consider that the golden rule requires that if I like a program I must share it with other people who like it. Software sellers want to divide the users and conquer them, making each user agree not to share with others. I refuse to break solidarity with other users in this way. I cannot in good conscience sign a nondisclosure agreement or a software license agreement. For years I worked within the Artificial Intelligence Lab to resist such tendencies and other inhospitalities, but eventually they had gone too far: I could not remain in an institution where such things are done for me against my will.

So that I can continue to use computers without dishonor, I have decided to put together a sufficient body of free software so that I will be able to get along without any software that is not free I have resigned from the AI lab to deny MIT any legal excuse to prevent me from giving GNU away."[24]

Individuals with such ethics have played a major role in fostering the development and public appreciation of the internet as a new sphere of freedom. As members of online communities and in association with like-minded organisations such as the Electronic Freedom Foundation,[25] they pressure the courts and legislature to make policy sympathetic to their beliefs. Professional organisations such as the Association for Computing Machinery (ACM)[26] host conferences, newsgroups and publish journals with a view to raising interest in ethical issues with respect to computer design and the broader relationship between computers and society. Competition does not erase optimistic ethical discourses about the internet. In some respects it invigorates this culture. However these views sit alongside the reality as seen by Bob Stein, founder of the Voyager Company:

"Whenever a new technology comes to the fore, people glom on to it and do what they can. In capitalism, the tendency over a very short period of time is for the market winners in the first year or two to be co-opted and made into businesses so there's no longer any room for the individual. First you get a Netscape—originally built as Mosaic on

---

[24] Free Software Foundation (FSF), "The GNU Manifesto—GNU Project", http://www.gnu.ai.mit.edu/gnu/manifesto.html
[25] See http://www.eff.org
[26] The specific organisation with responsibility for this is the Special Interest Group on Computers and Society (SIGCAS). See, for example, 26(4) *Computers and Society*, Dec. 1996.

a university campus for work-study money—going public for $72 million. Next we have Yahoo!, a wonderful little site on the internet, which basically kept track of all the other sites, and overnight it became a business. The window of opportunity for individuals is shorter than we'd like it to be.

Another much deeper concern in the long run is the contradiction between the technologists, who keep making and improving their technologies, without thinking about their social implications, and the rest of us, who have to live with these technologies for the next hundred generations. . . . They don't want the responsibility of having to think about the long-term implications of something as fundamental as . . . the development of new communications technologies."[27]

There may be space to consider ethics, but there is also the opportunity to not think about them or to think about ethics differently. For example, one researcher has recently argued that because people can access the Net "too cheaply", they are encouraged to "consume greedily while thinking that their actions have little effect on the overall performance of the Internet".[28]

This section began with reference to the technology needs of the poor. As Oguibe writes;

"Some would argue, perhaps, that such advanced technologies may not, after all, be of interest or indeed necessity to certain sections of society or regions of the world . . . Such arguments, however, only underline a tendency not only to create and perpetuate underclasses, but also to assume a liberal right to speak for such constituencies. Clearly, for billions of people around the world, cyberspace and connectivity are not a priority . . . but surely, a technology as versatile and increasingly domineering as that of cybercommunication holds inevitable possibilities, and consequences, for not just the minority that presently accesses and controls it, but for many others, too."[29]

Microsoft Corporation has recently embarked on schemes that seek to redress current imbalances in internet access. One program relates to enhancing access to internet technologies in India, another to "disadvantaged areas" in the USA:

" 'To be a leader in the digital economy of the twenty-first century, India must invest in basic infrastructure, education and information technology,' said Gates in a speech to the Confederation of Indian Industry. 'These are the tools which will drive the country into the future and make India an economic and software superpower.'

[27] "The Radical: Bob Stein", in Brockman, above n. 22, p. 272.
[28] Elizabeth Weise, "Going with the Flow", *Sydney Morning Herald*, Computer Section, July 29, 1997.
[29] Above n. 3.

He also urged that illiteracy, poverty, unemployment and ignorance be alleviated through the use of computers. However, this concern for the developing nation's future was not reflected in the billionaire's reported actions. Some of the world's richest man's hotel bills were reportedly paid for by the government."[30]

Microsoft's "assistance" to India was in launching the "Microsoft India Initiative" and in establishing the "University Advanced Technology Labs Program" in five universities. The investment of approximately $U.S. 1 million is designed to increase the number of Microsoft Certified Professionals who will teach Microsoft software skills and "to accelerate the use of the internet in India".[31] Comparatively speaking, the U.S. Microsoft initiative was much more generous. It involved "a $U.S. 200 million fund to port Internet access into libraries in 'disadvantaged areas'."[32] Perhaps the Doonesbury cartoon is closer to reality than, at first glance, one might think.

Do these new programs testify to Microsoft's commitment to an ethic of a right to access internet technologies? Is Bill Gates Inc. the patron of the electronic age?

In the face of declining overseas aid to less developed countries and diminution in funding for public institutions such as libraries, it would be comforting to think that civic minded private institutions are working in "the public interest" of wiring structurally disadvantaged communities. These Microsoft initiatives may attest to the glory and moral virtue of Bill Gates. In effect, however, they are more corporate sponsorship than patronage. Historically a patron spent his [sic] money in return for public admiration and respect, but he generally didn't invest in works he touted as bringing future financial return, in expectation that he would eventually be a major beneficiary. That Gates sees this as the outcome of the Indian initiative is clear from his own projections about the future importance of India's technology and information industries. His initiative enslaves the country to a broader business development strategy under the guise of "patronage". With respect to his assistance to libraries in "disadvantaged communities", one commentator suggests it is part of a bigger strategy of establishing "push" technology as *the* means of navigating the Net. Push technology is technology that guides and directs a user's access to the internet:

"the Net has everybody on there with as much to say as they want about anything they want ... This freedom of information—admittedly only available to those wealthy and politically free enough to have Net access—is what makes the Net such an explosive phenomenon. It can be likened to the Reformation in Europe, when

---

[30] Selina Mitchell, "Cultivating the Technology Backyard", *Australian Personal Computer*, Sept. 1997, p. 103.
[31] *ibid.*
[32] Jeremy Torr, "Resisting the Push", *Australian Personal Computer*, Sept. 1997, p. 52.

ordinary people first got to see books and realise that they could learn about things previously hidden from them . . .

Combine this thirst for knowledge with the perceived veracity that the computer screen gives information displayed on it, and you have a potentially dangerous situation. Especially if some smart programmer at the Push Technology Institute decides that fascists are morally indefensible and doesn't include them in the potential site index, or if the push technology search engine is skewed to favour all the sites and reports relating to one particular industrial corporation.

. . . Bill Gates has announced a $U.S 200 million fund to port Internet access into libraries in 'disadvantaged areas'. Given the hype push technology is getting from the Gates camp, I would seriously question the motives involved there."[33]

The technology "needs" of the poor are constructed in the same terms as the "needs" of investors, producers and current consumers of technology products and services. The acknowledgment of "information rich" and "information poor" communities is not accompanied by any sense of "duty" toward the potential technology creators and users who will inevitably be disabled from meaningful participation in this new sphere of "freedom" by market dynamics:

"The historical diffusion and use of electronic information services and their substructural support networks has been uneven and the prevailing network governance regime has been unsuccessful in creating incentives that would alleviate the gaps in the accessibility of advanced networks and services and the exclusionary consequences that these have engendered. Is there any reason to expect that the instability that presently characterizes the network governance regime will create conditions that will enable more inclusive participation in the production and consumption of electronic information services in the twenty-first century?"[34]

Strategies that seemingly reach out to the poor do not encompass any generalised ethic of a right to equal access to internet technology. Inequality of access is a product of the adoption of "the market" as the distribution strategy for the internet. Initiatives such as Microsoft's are designed to support, not disrupt, the market as the model for distribution of internet technologies and services.

A right of democratic access to internet technologies is advocated in many hacker communities. Further, hacking program code or electronic hardware has been viewed as political intervention, targeting commodification of information and technology, part of a broader political strategy of holding corporate power to account. As Dorothy Denning puts it:

---

[33] *ibid.*
[34] Mansell, above, n. 12, p. 190.

"Hackers say that it is our social responsibility to share information, and that it is information hoarding and disinformation that are the crimes. This ethic of resource and information sharing contrasts sharply with computer security policies that are based on authorization and 'need to know'. This discrepancy raises an interesting question: Does the hacker ethic reflect a growing force in society that stands for greater sharing of resources and information—a reaffirmation of basic values in our constitution and laws?"[35]

Denning argues that the public conception of hackers as anarchists and criminals is false to the extent that many hacker communities adhere to an ethical code, involving principles such as not erasing or modifying data. However, more recently, in a postscript,[36] she raised fresh doubts about the politics of hacking suggesting that for many hackers, it was more of a game than a reflection of a coherent political strategy. Her change of heart can be largely attributed to the view that whilst hackers advocate on behalf of their own rights, they extend no corresponding respect to the rights of people and organisation they harass.[37] She says that, but for the presence of hackers breaking into networks, a good deal of corporate security would not actually be necessary. For this reason, she now recommends against engaging with hackers in her work as a computer security expert. Amanda Chandler's article, "The Changing Definition and Image of Hackers in Popular Discourse",[38] also points to the diversity of motivation and political outlook amongst hackers. She too notes that whereas at an earlier period hackers attracted more respect for their technical ingenuity and understanding of the personal computer revolution, popular images of hackers are now predominantly negative. Although she does not claim that the negative press is always deserved, she suggests that this proliferation of negative imagery coincides with an increasing diversity of hacking practices.

Vivian Sobchack takes a different position arguing that even as constructed by its advocates hacker culture is neither progressive nor democratic. She uses the cyber-delic magazine, *Mondo 2000*[39] as reference material on hacker culture. Prominent writers featured in *Mondo 2000* include Howard Rheingold, Timothy Leary, John Perry Barlow, the virtual reality innovators Brenda Laurel and Jaron Lanier, as well as the magazine owners R.U. Sirius and Queen Mu. In analysing their work she comments that:

"The hacker/cracker/cyberpunk 'world-view' pits the individual against big government and big corporations and cannot envision

---

[35] "Concerning Hackers who break into computer systems" in Peter Ludlow (ed.), *High Noon on the Electronic Frontier: Conceptual Issues in Cyberspace* (MIT Press, Massachusetts, 1996), p. 157.
[36] *ibid* at p. 160.
[37] For an account of the pain hackers can inflict see Cotton Ward, "Revenge of the Nerds", *.net*, Issue 35, August 1997, p. 68.
[38] (1996) 24 *International Journal of the Sociology of Law* 229.
[39] *Mondo 2000* is a glossy Berkeley based quarterly. The description of it as "cyberdelic" is drawn from Dery, above n. 2, p. 22.

more than 'small group' intervention in the public sphere . . . Their ideolect is one that 'winners' in the modern world adopt and speaks to a belief in personal freedom and a faith in self-help that are grounded in privilege and the *status quo*: male privilege, white privilege.

Indeed, the rights and privilege of the 'individual' in this libertarian view of things are most openly evident in the discourse surrounding the Utopian 'public sphere' of virtual reality. Supposedly the new 'public sphere' in which people can freely—and equally—come together in consensual social interaction, the magazine's major interests in virtual reality seem to be as a 'private sphere' in which a free (from inhibition or prohibition) and (generally white) male body 'comes' in sensual—and safe—sexual intercourse with a (name the colour) female body. Thus, the increasing development (and sales) of 'cybererotic' software on this new democratic frontier."[40]

She argues that in terms of enabling access to internet technologies the hacker is profoundly self-interested. The more democratic aspects to the internet, such as email, are overwhelmed by an obsession with virtual reality and desire for a technologically-extended body. She concludes that despite its anti-establishment affectations, *Mondo 2000* culture ultimately supports libertarian individualism and corporate capital.[41]

The common co-option of hackers to work on the payroll of the institutions and organisations they once explored as unauthorised "guests" provides support for Sobchack's analysis. The mutual interest of hackers and corporations can be seen in the following example: a Swedish company, Infinit Information, hosted the "Crack a Mac" contest, giving a 10,000 kronor prize for modifying Infinit's home page and providing a description as evidence of having hacked into its server.[42] Print culture offers a precedent for the co-option strategy. The hacker's ancestor is the printing "pirate" who refused to respect the trade monopolies of the London Stationer's Company. John Wolfe was a notorious pirate who argued in defence of piracy that "it was lawfull for all men to print all lawfull bookes what commandement soever her Majestie gave to the contrary".[43] Following spells in prison and the seizure of pirate copies, Wolfe was appointed beadle of the Stationer's Company, having been offered nearly twice the regular wage.[44] Loewenstein argues that Wolfe "abandoned" his poor printing associates given a lucrative opportunity to police the company on behalf of the powerful.

---

[40] "Democratic Franchise and the Electronic Frontier," in Ziauddin Sardar & Jerome R. Ravetz, *Cyberfutures* (Pluto Press, London, 1996), p. 85.

[41] Virtual reality is not necessarily an internet technology, nevertheless Sobchack's analysis of it is also of relevance to a discussion of MUDS and MOOs. This issue is taken up further below. See "Responsible Relationships".

[42] Dominique Jackson, "Hack a Mac", *Australian Personal Computer*, Oct. 1997, p. 24.

[43] Joseph Loewenstein, "For A History of Literary Property: John Wolfe's Reformation", (1988) 18 *English Literary Renaissance* 401.

[44] *ibid* at p. 404.

The co-option of technology "rebels" suggests that it is wrong to presume a firmly held commitment to lofty ideals in everyone who justifies their actions in the name of the excluded. Objections to regulation of either print or internet technology, may be grounded in sincerely held Enlightenment and/or democratic ethics, which leads to protest action against the creation of monopolies in cultural goods. But it cannot be denied that rebels may also be motivated by quite instrumental reasons. As Oguibe says, we cannot rely upon the esotericism of such discourses, no matter how much we might want to believe in a right of democratic access to internet technologies.

Access to Information

Educom Review: I'm sure you've heard the currently popular slogan, "Information wants to be free". What do you make of that slogan?
Bruce Lehman: I don't know what it means. That information should be free? I'd say: freely accessible, yes; free of charge, no.[45]

The *"information wants to be free"* slogan is most often associated with John Perry Barlow and his discussion of what your rights should be on the "electronic frontier".[46] His concern for access to information assumes a broader right of access to internet technologies. However whilst the former is seen as an exciting and volatile issue, the latter is barely raised. If the free flow of information on the Net is so important, surely the right to access internet technologies must also be equally vital? The neglect of the latter issue is what informs the critique of writers like Oguibe.

It is not surprising that Barlow fails to dwell on the issue of access to technology. He is not against the market as a distributive mechanism. His well-known disagreement with Lehman[47] concerns, rather, the definition of what the internet market involves. Barlow sees the internet as *a market for information services*, whereas Lehman sees it as *a market for information content*.

Barlow objects to the operation of intellectual property rights in cyberspace because he considers that these laws solidify the fluid character of internet relations and destroy the life inherent in the online medium and media. In his view, intellectual property laws were designed for a different time and space:

"Copyright worked well because, Gutenberg notwithstanding, it was hard to make a book. Furthermore, books froze their contents into a condition that was as challenging to alter as it was to reproduce".[48]

---

[45] "Royalties, Fair Use and Copyright in the Electronic Age", 30(6) *Educom Review*, Nov./Dec. 1995, republished at http://www.educom.edu/web/pubs/review/review Articles/30630.html
[46] See "The Economy of Ideas: A Framework for Rethinking Patents and Copyright in the Digital Age" *Wired*, March 1994, at p. 84; recently republished as "Selling Wine Without Bottles" in Ludlow, above n. 35 at p. 9.
[47] Lehman, who chairs the Working Group on Intellectual Property Rights within the Information Policy Committee on the Information Infrastructure Task Force, is Assistant Secretary of Commerce and Commissioner of Patents and Trademarks in the USA.
[48] Above n. 46, p. 11.

Intellectual property laws protected distribution rights in tangible goods in order to reward "the ability to deliver (ideas) into reality. For all practical purposes, the value was in the conveyance and not the thought conveyed."[49]

Prior to digital technology it made sense to attribute works to a particular person:

"Cultural production, literary or otherwise, has traditionally been a slow, labour-intensive process. . . . The time lapse between production and distribution can seem unbearably long . . . Before electronic technology became dominant, cultural perspectives developed in a manner that more clearly defined texts as individual works. Cultural fragments appeared in their own right as discrete units, since their influence moved slowly enough to allow the orderly evolution of an argument or aesthetic. Boundaries could be maintained between disciplines and schools of thought. Knowledge was considered finite, and was therefore easier to control."[50]

However:

"Environments like the Net tend to grow organically. They expand not according to any one person's conscious design, but because the Net is by nature a collection of individuals all making contributions to it. The growth is at an exponential rate, though not as much in terms of size as in terms of features and feature sets . . . Today's Web will be unrecognizable in five years . . .

One of the biggest misperceptions about content is that it's an asset that endures, that has value, like catalogs, libraries, film records, music records, or written archives. However, as Esther Dyson points out, the time value of information on the Net is extremely short."[51]

On the electronic frontier the positions of author, reader and subject merge. This disrupts the spatial and temporal presumptions that have traditionally delineated and separated the legal rights and roles of original author, text, publisher, distributor and consumer.

The internet involves individuals and corporations who, in embracing the potential of these new technologies, have created new communities, relationships, identities, activities, lifestyles and markets. To the *information wants to be free* camp it is unethical to inflict laws designed for a different technological age upon these people: a different technological age deserves a different legal and ethical culture. The fear is that without appreciation of this, "life" online will be extinguished and emerging technical and cultural developments will be thwarted. Intellectual

[49] *ibid.*
[50] Critical Art Ensemble, "Utopian Plagiarism, Hypertextuality, and Electronic Cultural Production", in *The Electronic Disturbance*, (Autonomedia, New York, 1996), at p. 89.
[51] "The Thinker: Doug Carlston", in Brockman, above n. 22, p. 41.

property laws do not "belong" in cyberspace and in order to enforce them a new world-wide administration of regulation and control has to be developed, which will interfere with the natural "disorder" of the internet and corrupt the freedoms on offer to those with access to them.

It is difficult to define the ethic behind this position more positively. Ethics here appear in the guise of an attitude shared toward the internet and online activity, rather than as principles that guide or instruct action. Critics such as Lehman draw attention to this, and infer from it that the *information wants to be free* position is of little practical guiding force in "the real world". However, this dismissive attitude is unwarranted. The real situation is more complicated.

The organic metaphors[52] used to describe the internet and its possibilities suggest that underlying the chaotic connection of humans and machines there is order, stability and progress. No one individual or organisation can speak for the Net, or is able to control it. In such circumstances there is no sense in positing universal cyberethics. What should constitute cyberethics will depend upon the time, space, people and circumstance. Faith in human-centred technological progress and inhuman capacity to develop appropriate ethics, underpins these organic analyses.

Despite a dilution of power on the Net, individuals and organisations still feel that they can influence the internet's development. For many such influence is their reason for being. However, interventions tend to coalesce around particular issues, cases and events considered detrimental to the growth of online life. Ethics are made visible in the context of a reaction to a specific problem, and in the context of the slogan used to publicise the issue. Regarding the *information wants to be free* position, it makes no sense to try and abstract ethics from the particularity of Web politics at any one time.

So what does the *internet as a market for services* look like? Barlow's economy of cyberspace takes for granted that consumption is not a passive process, capable of being contrasted with, say, an active mode of production. Consumption is not understood as a way of servicing needs, nor is production the process of manufacturing goods. Rather consumption is understood as an activity "consisting of the systematic manipulation of signs."[53]

An object, such as a book, may be useful for what it says but as an object of consumption it is neither the book nor the ideas in it that are consumed. What is consumed are the relationships suggested by the book's marketing, packaging and promotion. As a commodity the value of the book is not its content or, in legal terms, the expression ©. Hence Howard Rheingold's claim:

---

[52] Despite Haraway's description of cyberculture as encompassing a movement from an organic, industrial society to a polymorphous, information system (above, n. 2), organic metaphors are still prevalent, *e.g.* Web.

[53] Jean Baudrillard, "Conclusion: Toward a Definition of Consumption", in *The System of Objects*, James Benedict (trans.), (London, Verso 1996), p. 200.

"The concept of 'content' is so poorly defined. One, there's the myth that content is king . . . content is not what drives a business. It's the story. It's the emotion. It's the way that the information is packaged and programmed.

. . . Magazine publishers and newspaper publishers looked at the internet as being an ancillary revenue stream. They would repackage their content and make it available on CD-ROM, then put it on the Web or America Online. That's proven not to work, because this medium demands more. Content is not the end-product. Content is the activator of the conversation and the community."[54]

The wonder of cyberspace is the opportunity it offers for sponsoring new relationships. That this is taken for granted is reflected in the view that:

"The successful internet sites are not repurposing data from other sources. They are new breeds of services. The Yahoos!, the directories on the Internet, are a completely new kind of content. These areas are ones that are really going to grow. How long will text be the dominant form of information on the Internet? I would say it is not the dominant form now. Most people are not using the Internet and the Web for what they were designed for, which was the hypertext linking of documents to documents. They're using it as an interface toolkit for doing actual services, for interacting with customer service, finding things, doing searches. This shows that the interactive nature is really what's important to the Internet . . ."[55]

The value that lies in "the manipulation of signs" is also appreciated by those who claim that instead of authors receiving payment via copyright, they can receive payment for the performance of their works. Whilst appearing on the public speaking circuit, Barlow noted that "audiences will still want to have authors express themselves in person and universities, corporations, and other sponsors will still pay authors to be creative thinkers. Under this system, we would return to the old-time notion of patronage of the arts, sciences and humanities."[56]

Contrary to what is often supposed, the *information wants to be free* versus the *right of intellectual property owners* debate is not really a pro-commercialised versus anti-commercialised cyber-future. Both sides of the debate recognise that many individuals will contribute online with no expectation of financial gain, but some, will want financial return. The difference then comes down to a disagreement about who should get paid, for what, and by whom.

Where the internet is characterised as *a market for services* "content providers" get paid as "media personalities".[57] Payment is not for what

---

[54] "The Marketer: Ted Leonsis", in Brockman, n. 22, p. 240.

[55] "The Searcher: Brewster Kahle", *ibid*, at p. 148.

[56] David B. Resnic, "Conference Report: Ethics in Cybersociety", (1996) 26(4) *Computers and Society* 23.

[57] It is interesting to note that Barlow is nearly always credited as a "retired cattle rancher and Grateful Dead lyricist". What do these personas lend to his message?

they say, but who they are and our ability to "get close" to them. Payment is also due to internet service providers, and conference holders, and indeed to all those who make some form of "relationship" with celebrity possible. In this sense the departure from copyright actually involves a concentration of the "author function". Whilst the author has no right of ownership to their text in cyberspace, the ability to make a living as a writer is in fact dependent upon recognition of the author "unplugged" as the original source of an important message. Why else would anyone pay to see and hear them? In order for celebrities to stand out on the internet they need to be already famous in another medium, or they need to market themselves effectively across the media spectrum so that the online merging of roles as author, reader and subject doesn't erase their identification or too quickly move them from "wired" to "tired".

The *information wants to be free position* places confidence in the power of publicity to generate returns, whereas the *right of intellectual property owner's* position is concerned with controlling cyberspace as a new medium for "distribution" of works. The fear is that conventional media forms, particularly magazines and seminars will be put out of business by the internet.[58] In order to make the transition from the traditional economy for works to this new one, the current information owners need as much control as possible over their investment in communications technologies. For Lehman, the facts that the internet has expanded profitable ventures for traditional media publishers by the development of new newspaper sections, walls of magazines and books and endless seminars explaining the internet, is no compensation for the real loss of control entailed by conflation of the roles of author, producer and distributor in the absence of strong intellectual property protection on the internet.

Other media technologies have also disrupted established habits of communication and transformed economies. The typewriter, for instance, radically affected oral cultures and, consequentially, the connection between speech and writing. Marshall McLuhan argues that the typewriter "carried the Gutenberg technology into every nook and cranny of our culture and economy".[59] It changed writing patterns, styles and methods of composition; brought writing, speech and publication into closer association leading to standardised spellings and grammar; developed new social roles such as the professional "lady typist"; and in conjunction with the telephone, changed commercial culture by the ability to send memos to confirm phone conversations.[60] Whilst oral culture had little protection by way of copyright rules, intellectual

---

[58] Bruce Lehman as quoted above n. 45.
[59] "The Typewriter: Into the Age of the Iron Whim", in *Understanding Media* (First Sphere Books London, 1967), p. 279.
[60] *ibid.*, pp. 275–282.

property rights in cultural accretions such as business communications were largely ignored.[61]

Personal computers and desktop publishing capabilities had a similar impact to that of the typewriter in affecting writing and visual styles, presentation and distribution of texts. The P.C. and laserprinter opened up avenues for self-publishing and distribution. Resources and energy permitting, graphic artist/writer/publishers could publish and mass reproduce works without oversight of traditional media enterprises, placing them in shops and selling by mail order. Publications such as *The Face*, *Mondo 2000* and *Wired* magazine are examples of "fringe" publications that have achieved mainstream distribution. Whilst these magazines may not have overtly threatened the intellectual property rights of multinational media players, they are purveyors of a new "do it yourself" ethic where copyright was represented through graphic styles and editorial contributions as inconvenient, rather than as a benefit.

As noted above with respect to Barlow, identification of the author of a work is still imperative in digital culture. However, writing contributions are closely integrated with the other creative inputs in these enterprises. Appreciation of the written work depends upon all stylistic aspects of the production of the issue being "cutting edge":

"In the decision-making and 'make happen' aspect of the work operation, the telephone and other such speed-ups of information have ended the divisions of delegated authority in favour of the 'authority of knowledge'."[62]

This "authority of knowledge" is not derived from co-ordinating and consolidating rights to "content", and/or rights to the separate kinds of works that copyright individually recognises. Rather, it is based in compressing and unifying the various aspects of production, such as graphic design, writing, publishing, promotion and to a lesser extent, advertising. Integrating the technology with the content, creating a culture of and for the new technologies, is what has given these enterprises a new and dangerous authority.

Some of these "innovative" enterprises have now achieved a scale that has caused them to re-adopt many of the old divisions of labour. In terms of organisation and style, they now mimic their adversaries who have (at least superficially) adopted some similar stylistic motifs. This leads to a challenging of the legitimacy of the "innovators" to deliver a counter-cultural message. Nevertheless this hallmark of success only brings home how effectively their message has been delivered, and

---

[61] Lehman actually acknowledges this: "As a practical matter, a lot of letters are photocopied, and in fact, it's an extremely common business practice to photocopy letters that you get and send them around to scores of people. It happens every day. I suppose that technically, if you are doing that without having gotten permission from somebody, you may be violating the copyright of the author of the letter. But I know of no lawsuits that have ever been brought in that area". See above n. 45

[62] McLuhan, above n. 59, p. 281.

signals more grounds for concern at how the foundations of the older cultural enterprises, based upon ideals such as copyright, have been undermined.

The *right of intellectual property owners* position is more than an argument against "piracy" although it is also certainly that. It involves a cultural intervention designed to slow the acceptance of the internet, coupled with select legal actions and proposals for specific legislative reform, so time temporarily "freezes", disrupting the establishment of the new hegemony. A slower pace is not only more familiar; it is conducive to a fuller consideration of developments so that strategies allowing for profitable participation in the internet can be implemented.

Strategies for slowing the pace of Net developments include Lehman's proposals for legislative reform presented in the Clinton "White Paper" on the National Information Infrastructure (NII).[63] Suggestions include:

- redefining access to information using an electronic medium (such as reading a copy of a text on a computer) as involving a "reproduction" of a work for which permission, and theoretically a licence, is needed.
- redefining electronic transmission of a work as a "distribution" of it, to which a license could be applied.
- attaching "copyright management information" to electronic copies of works. This is:

"a kind of license plate for work on the information superhighway. Under the proposed amendment, copyright management information is defined as the name and other identifying information of the author of a work, the name and other identifying information of the copyright owner, terms and conditions for uses of the work, and such other information as the Register of Copyrights may prescribe by regulation."[64]

It is proposed that these initiatives would be supported by encryption technology and legislation making tampering with the "tracking" of information in digital form a civil and criminal offence. The point is to enable the "owner" of information to more easily identify who accesses a work, and how often.

The technology required to support these proposals is not available. It is not easy to account for all the possible ways in which a computer can interact with a work. For example, by configuring networks and

---

[63] Information Infrastructure Task Force, *Intellectual Property and the National Information Infrastructure: The Report of the Working Group on Intellectual Property Rights*, September 5, 1995. (The NII "White Paper").

[64] Bruce A. Lehman, Statement to *Subcommittee on Courts and Intellectual Property Committee on the Judiciary*, United States House of Representatives and the Committee on the Judiciary United States Senate, November 15, 1995. S. 1284 & H.R. 2441. http://www.uspto.gov/web/offices/com/doc/ipnii/

machines, many workstations can access only one copy; or a single workstation can be set up so that it stores many copies or parts of a copy in the process of generating what appears as the "one copy" seen on the screen. In these circumstances, managing "copyright management information" would be an undertaking of such difficulty that it would probably not be worth while. Reform proposals like these, therefore, amount merely to an ambit claim designed to redirect the development of the culture of technology.

Such proposals try to slow interactions with digital media by reintroducing the cost of accessing information into the culture. Lehman takes the loss of temporality that occurs in the electronic media and turns it into an advantage to traditional content owners. If implemented, his proposals would allow for greater extraction of profit for accessing works in digital form than would apply were the same work circulated as a hard copy, such as a magazine or book. After the initial purchase of a book, a reader can return to it as often as they choose, and share the one copy amongst any number of people without infringing copyright. Copyright does not prevent the one work being viewed at various times and locations. Lehman's "White Paper" proposes to limit access to an electronic copy of a work to a particular point in time and space, and every access at a different time or space can be separately monitored and costed. These proposals do more than extend copyright onto electronic frontier: they take advantage of the technology to create altogether new opportunities to (theoretically) profit from works.

Lehman argues that these proposals work in the public interest:

"Creators and other owners of intellectual property rights will not be willing to put their interests at risk if appropriate systems—both in the U.S. and internationally—are not in place to permit them to set and enforce the terms and conditions under which their works are made available in the NII environment. Likewise, the public will not use the services available in the NII and generate the market necessary for its success unless a wide variety of works are available under equitable and reasonable terms and conditions, and the integrity of those works is assured. All the computers, telephones, fax machines, scanners, cameras, keyboards, televisions, monitors, printers, switches, routers, wires, cables, networks and satellites in the world will not create a successful NII, if there is no content. What will drive the NII is the content moving through it."[65]

This appraisal fails to consider the huge amount of material already made available online from which no profit is directly derived and where "integrity" cannot be guaranteed. It also fails to consider that many poorly funded institutions, including many publicly-funded schools and libraries, would probably have to refuse access to sites where users had to pay to view the content.[66]

---

[65]*ibid.*

[66] For a longer critique of the White Paper see Pamela Samuelson, "The Copyright Grab", (1996) *Wired.*, Vol 4.01., p. 134.

Case law examples that attempt to insert mechanisms of control into cyberspace include actions to prohibit hypertextual linking without permission.[67] The point of such mechanisms has not been to profit from the link itself, although where a party might pay for the privilege, this can create a new revenue stream. Generally the point has been to create a legal situation that allows for the maximisation of profit from web advertising, by forcing all those that access a site to browse particular advertising spaces, for example, on the front page. If there is no control over how you can link to a page, links can be designed to bypass front page advertising by linking directly deeper into the site. Another possibility is that rather than a link seeming to transfer you to another site, a party can design its web site so that somebody else's web page can appear like a smaller movie within the site. The linked page is not only reduced in size, but the new framing can feature more prominent advertising, reducing the impact of the ads on the linked page. There are technological means of preventing someone linking to your page without permission. In these circumstances, the motives behind attempts trying to reinvent copyright law to prevent unauthorised linking needs to be questioned.[68] Threats of copyright and trademark actions[69] are attempts to stifle the development of a culture of unregulated access, to slow the velocity of the internet message.

The *right of intellectual property owners* position draws upon ethical arguments in a number of ways. First, the language of "theft" and "property rights" draws upon an investment in traditional arguments for private property: notions of desert, entitlement and freedom of contract. These notions are powerful because they are generally understood and broadly accepted in their traditional context. The conceptual leaps involved in first, applying notions that arose in the traditional circumstance of real property to that of intangible property, and then reapplying these concepts, the case of intangible property in cyberspace is ignored. Such reapplications abuse the traditional ethical arguments for private property in an attempt to make emotional connections with audiences.

Second, there is an appeal to an ethic of authorship. The suggestion is that authors only make their creative works available because of state-sponsored financial returns that encourage mass distribution: as a society, if we want to access the great works, we need to protect copyright, regardless of the medium of delivery. This position ignores the multiplicity of motivations behind creative work, and the reality that far more than "creative" works are protected by copyright. It thus

---

[67] See *Shetland Times v. Dr Jonathon Wills and Zetnews Ltd* [1997] F.S.R. 604; "The Shetland Times' case", at http://www.shetland-news.co.uk/appeal.html; Michelle Boccia, "Look Before You Link", at http://www.updateit.com/ifiwereyou/msticket.htm; and PaulAndrews, "Microsoft lawsuits tests Web linking practices", *Seattle Times*, Business News, 29 April, 1997.
[68] It should be noted that all the cases refered to in the above articles are either undecided or are in early stages of appeal hearings.
[69] Threats of actions against "The Simpsons", and "Star Trek" fan sites are regularly reported on the Net. see http://www.ozemail.com.au/~copy/cright

appeals to a particular cultural value—respect for authors of "great" (undefined) works—and generalises from that circumstance to the case of all authors, for all kinds of works. It also ignores the reality that commercial imperatives can make distribution of a "great work" unviable, for instance where it is judged too *avant garde* for popular reception.

Third, an appeal to an ethic of copyright, can be seen in both the positions above. Copyright is presented as naturally evolving, adapting to technological change, without losing its "natural" direction:

> "Intellectual property is a subtle and esoteric area of the law that evolves in response to technological change. Advances in technology particularly affect the operation and effectiveness of copyright law. Changes in technology generate new industries and new methods for reproduction and dissemination of works of authorship, which may present new opportunities for authors, but also create additional challenges. Copyright law has had to respond to those challenges, from Gutenberg's moveable type printing press to digital audio recorders and everything in between—photocopiers, radio, television, videocassette recorders, cable television and satellites."[70]

Copyright law had to respond to the challenge of the press? In this formulation, copyright is abstracted and reified. It appears as a good in itself. Further, it's evolution is represented as vulnerable to technological innovation and inadequate legal drafting, factors that may/can affect the efficacy of copyright, but not its sanctified status.

What is the "natural" direction of copyright? Lehman does not provide illumination on this key point. To suggest copyright actually predates the press reveals his deep reluctance to acknowledge that copyright is a product of history, that it is based upon contested philosophical foundations and, that it has encompassed diverse legislative interests.

The most likely foundation for Lehman's notion of copyright implied by Lehman is an abstract, timeless, appeal to a "natural right" of authors. An enormous number of the theoretical analyses of copyright discuss the case of authors in light of the natural rights implicit in Locke's labour theory of property and/or personality theories of Hegel or Kant. However, the purpose of such analyses is generally to point the reasons for the law's failure to live up to a commitment to philosophical principles of desert and entitlement.[71]

The literature also reveals numerous analyses of British late eighteenth century literary property debates.[72] A large part of this writing traces the cultural currency of the "right of authors" and the influence of romantic

---

[70] Lehman, above n. 64.
[71] See for example, Linda Lacey, "Of Bread and Roses and Copyright" (1989) *Duke Law Journal* 1532; Margaret Radin, "Property and Personhood", (1982) 34 *Stanford Law Review* 957.
[72] The most influential piece is still probably by Mark Rose, "The Author as Proprietor: Donaldson v. Becket and the Genealogy of Modern Authorship", (1988) 23 *Representations* p. 51.

theory on case law and nineteenth century legislative reform. However here, too, can be found universal acknowledgment that "Anglo"-derived copyright is ultimately a creature of positive law.[73] Respect for the "natural rights of authors" may have influenced the law, particularly in the late-eighteenth to mid-nineteenth centuries, but this notion has never been the undisputed cause of copyright. Further, in analyses where author's rights are of concern, it is rarely claimed that the author's interest naturally coincides with that of publishers and distributors. In these writings "respect for the author" is often criticised as a notion abused by publishers and distributors who have engaged it for their own advantage, often to the neglect of or at the expense of the author.

Pamela Samuelson concludes her critique of the "White Paper":

"During the first centuries after the invention of the printing press, publishers had considerably stronger monopolies than modern copyright laws grant them. They used these broader rights to charge excessive prices and censor dissenting views. When the English Parliament passed the first modern copyright law, in 1710, it did so in part to stop publishers from oppressing authors, potential competitors, and the public."[74]

From the start, the copyright legislation was controversial because it altered terms of the trade that established London publishers had understood and profited from. However it should also be remembered that:

". . . at the beginning of the eighteenth century it was clear that England and Scotland were to unite, which happened in 1707, be it noted.
    The Act of Union of 1707 created a 'common market' of Great Britain, and threw the lucrative English book trade open to the canny entrepreneurs from across the Tweed. These publishers of Edinburgh and Glasgow . . . were not subject to the London printing trade.
    . . . The real motive behind the first Copyright Act seems to have been an attempt to export copyright control to a region of Great Britain where the Stationers' Company writ did not run."[75]

Whilst London Stationers lost opportunities for profit because the Statute limited their "perpetual copyrights" to a term of 14 or 28 years, new opportunities were also provided: the statute extended trade monopolies to an entirely new domain.

This earlier copyright debate heard an equivalent cry to *Information wants to be free*. In *Donaldson v. Beckett*[76] Lord Camden claimed:

---

[73] The strongest proponent of this view is David Saunders, "Dropping the Subject: An Argument for a Positive History of Authorship and the Law of Copyright", in Brad Sherman & Alain Strowel, (eds), *Of Authors and Origins: Essays on Copyright Law* (Clarendon Press, Oxford, 1994), pp. 93–110.
[74] Above n. 66, at 191.
[75] Peter Prescott, "The Origins of Copyright: A Debunking View", [1989] 12 E.I.P.R. 453 at 454–45.
[76] 4 Burr. 2408, 98 Eng. Rep. 257.

"Most certainly every Man who thinks, has a right to his thoughts, while they continue to be HIS; but here the question again returns; when does he part with them? When do they become *public juris*? While they are in his brain no one indeed can purloin them; but what if he speaks, and lets them fly out in private or public discourse? Will he claim the breath, the air, the words in which his thoughts are cloathed? Where does this fanciful property begin, or end, or continue?"[77]

That generated the response that "Authors have ever had a property in their Works, founded upon the same fundamental maxims by which Property was originally settled." It was further argued that "The Invention of Printing did not destroy this Property of Authors, nor alter it in any Respect, but by rendering it more easy to be invaded."[78] It can be seen that arguments in the electronic age over the right to access information are far from new. The reality that ethics are tethered to political causes and used and abused in attempts to win public sympathy also has long precedence.

The issue of access to information is primarily an issue about the construction of the marketplace for knowledge: how is the market to be legally defined?; what rights will be allocated over what and to whom? The role law plays is not all that different in this instance from the role played by law in settling conditions for the right to access technologies. However the rhetoric evoked in each case is different. Historically, the claims of copyright emerged under the banner of private property, even though the law did not wholeheartedly embrace that categorisation. By contrast, once a given technology had been characterised in terms of services, rather than in property terms (*i.e.* as goods), claims of infrastructure were commonly argued in terms of public policy. Legal language makes a powerful contribution to the culture of a new technology. Influencing the direction of that culture also involves reinventing the language of law.

Responsible Relationships?

"They say he raped them that night. They say he did it with a cunning little doll, fashioned in their image and imbued with the power to make them do whatever he desired. They say that by manipulating the doll he forced them to have sex with him, and with each other, and to do horrible, brutal things to their own bodies. And though I wasn't there that night, I think I can assure you that what they say is true, because it all happened right in the living room—right there amid the well-stocked bookcases and the sofas and the fireplaces—of a house I've come to think of as my second home."[79]

---

[77] "The Pleadings of the Counsel before the House of Lords in the Great Cause concerning Literary Property . . .", in *The Literary Property Debate: Six Tracts 1764–1774*. (ed.) Stephen Parks (Garland Publishing, New York, 1975), p. F32.
[78] *The Case of Authors and Proprietors of Books*, as quoted in Rose, above n. 72, p. 57.
[79] Julian Dibbell, "A Rape in Cyberspace; or How an Evil Clown, a Haitian Trickster Spirit, Two Wizards, and a Cast of Dozens turned a Database into a Society", in Ludlow, above n. 35, p. 375.

The above is an account of a virtual rape that took place in "LambdaMOO" MUD (Multi User Domain). In a MUD the way a player "looks" and "behaves" depends upon the textual information forwarded by the creator of the identity. Biological and cultural constructions of the body (gender, race, class, age) can be manipulated in an atmosphere of privacy and anonymity, allowing a great deal of freedom and playfulness with respect to identity formation. In the LambdaMOO case, the perpetrator, "Mr Bungle", wrote a subprogram (the voodoo doll). This allowed him to write the actions of other people's characters, making them behave as he wished. "Mr Bungle" was a student from New York University. Eventually he was stopped from interfering with other characters in the MUD when a more experienced player, Zippy, created another program that allowed him to detain Mr Bungle in a cage and stopped his ability to exercise power over other characters. The crisis that ensued was about how to deal with Mr Bungle. Had he committed any wrong? And if so, what should be done about it?

To those who see MUDS as fantasy realms, Mr Bungle's transgressions may seem no more heinous than discovering a cheat in the middle of a game of *Scrabble*. However, to the "victims" in this case, the offence was not so much in the placing of unauthorised texts, but in the way text/action was used:

> "while the *facts* attached to any event born of a MUD's strange, ethereal universe may march in straight tandem lines separated neatly into the virtual and the real, its meaning lies always in that gap. You learn this axiom early in your life as a player, and it's of no small relevance to the Bungle case that you usually learn it between the sheets, so to speak . . ."[80]

Debate about what to do with Mr Bungle took place inside and outside of LambdaMOO, with many public postings appearing on internet fora. Discussion did not focus on the "corruption" of a game but engaged with the nature of sexual assault and harassment, models of governance, policing and ethical conduct. Whilst many of the aspects of the Mr Bungle case are peculiar to LambdaMOO, the reaction to the case also encompassed a broader debate over the legitimacy of privacy, remailing and anonymity on the internet, responsibility for moderating MUDS, internet-relay chat (IRC), news groups, list serves, bulletin boards, overseeing email, censoring messages and web pages, and cancelling a "trouble-maker's" accounts.

The "gap" Dibbell sees as connecting real and virtual worlds is mediated by language, (mostly, English), enhanced by a large array of signs and symbols specifically developed to convey feelings via typed internet communications.[81] Quoting Lyotard, Michael Beuabien argues that:

---

[80] *ibid*, p. 381.
[81] See Elizabeth Reid, "Communication and Community on Internet Relay Chat: Creating Communities", in Peter Ludlow, above n. 35, p. 397 *et seq*.

"meaning is created socially through participating in language games, in which the rules defining a game are 'agreed on by its present players and subject to eventual cancellation'."[82]

Beuabien suggests that the trouble at LambdaMOO reflects uncertainty as to the language rules that apply in cyberspace, where technology mediates all communications.

For those who saw language as constitutive of identity, and those who invested a great deal of energy and thought into developing an online persona(s), a "virtual" assault could cause real distress. The harm was not only borne by the character, but also its author. However, the ensuing discussion was not conducted in terms of the "ownership" rights to a character, akin to a moral rights argument in copyright where the author is vested with the authority to protect the integrity of his [sic] creative work. Rather the discussion viewed the problem as the merging of identities of author, reader and subject, leading to a shared sense of injury amongst many of the inhabitants of LambdaMOO. Damage was not understood in terms of an abuse of property rights, but in terms of the infliction of psychic harm upon the collective. Dibbell notes that discussion of sexual assault often addresses victim damage as both physical and psychic.[83] Participants in the debate distinguished between the respective gravity of what happened in LambdaMOO and a sexual assault or harassment offline; however many participants, including some nominated as survivors of sexual assaults, felt that appropriate mechanisms were needed to redress virtual sexual offences that harm virtual communities and can distress participants.

Throughout the discussion there was little interest in considering the use of law because of the "virtual" nature of the incidents and implications for online free speech. In any case, criminal assault posed problems in establishing language as a cause of criminal injury[84] as well as connecting any such crime with a real (as opposed to a virtual) victim. In other cases legal intervention in the form of a tort action for nervous shock, defamation or legislation prohibiting the making of obscene "phone calls" have been suggested as possible remedies for inappropriate online conduct.[85] In this example, however, the issue was generally characterised as one of establishing appropriate ethics for the LambdaMOO community—developing standards of civility, rather than enforcing criminal or civil laws.

To discuss the possibility of community-based sanctions and specifically the "toading" of Mr Bungle,[86] a meeting was called in

[82] "Multi-User Dungeons and Social Interaction in Cyberspace", in (eds.) Lance Strate, Ron Jacobson & Stephanie Gibson, *Communication and Cyberspace* (Hampton Press, New Jersey, 1996), p. 185.
[83] Dibbell, above n. 79, p. 381.
[84] This concept is not unknown to criminal law but generally it relates to specific, controversial pieces of legislation that proscribe free speech such as racial vilification laws.
[85] See Cotton Ward, "Sympathy for the Devil", *.net*, Issue 35, August 1997, p. 53.
[86] Whereby the "wizards" who adminster the MUD turn Mr Bungle into a toad, effectively erasing the online identity.

LambdaMOO. At this point the "real" nature of virtual communities became apparent. To enforce decisions about the future of Mr Bungle, the LambdaMOO community would need assistance from a "wizard", a programmer of the MOO. Prior to the Mr Bungle incident, Pavel Curtis, the chief architect of LambdaMOO, had decided that wizards should not become involved in disagreements between players over the use of the domain. His "New Direction" document, left in the living room of the MOO for all participants to see, stated that wizards were only technicians who would implement decisions as reached by the whole community.

What did the community think?:

"Parliamentarian legalist types argued that unfortunately Bungle could not legitimately be toaded at all, since there were no explicit MOO rules against rape, or against just about anything else—and the sooner such rules were established, they added, and maybe even a full-blown judiciary system complete with elected officials and prisons to enforce those rules, the better. Others, with a royalist streak in them, seemed to feel that Bungle's as-yet- unpunished outrage only proved this New Direction silliness had gone on long enough, and that it was high time the wizardocracy returned to the position of swift and decisive leadership their player class was born to.

And then there were what I'll call the technolibertarians. For them, MUD rapists were of course assholes, but the presence of assholes on the system was a technical inevitability, like noise on a phone line, and best dealt with not through repressive social disciplinary mechanisms but through the timely deployment of defensive software tools. Some asshole blasting violent, graphic language at you? Don't whine to the authorities about it—hit the @gag command and the asshole's statements will be blocked from your screen (and only yours). It's simple, it's effective, and it censors no one."[87]

Dibbell notes that blocking out what happens to your character does not really work when offences take place, as these did, in full view of all the other players.

Perhaps such a diversity of views should be expected, given the newness of the medium, the fluid nature of MOO culture and the ability of participants to hide their real identities. Also if the MUD is interpreted as primarily a reading culture, then perhaps the opinion diversity is a standard characteristic. In contrasting the culture of the printed book with that oral culture, Elizabeth Eisenstein notes that:

"By its very nature, a reading public was not only dispersed; it was also more atomistic and individualised than a hearing one. To catch the contrast, Walter Ong suggests that we imagine a speaker address-ing an audience equipped with texts and stopping at one point with a

---

[87] Dibbell, above n. 79, p. 384.

request that a textual passage be read silently. When the readers look up again, the fragmented audience has to be reassembled into a collectivity . . . To be sure, bookshops, coffeehouses, reading rooms provided new kinds of communal gathering places. Yet subscription lists and corresponding societies represented relatively impersonal group formations, while the reception of printed messages in any place still required temporary isolation—just as it does in a library now."[88]

In the bookshops and coffeehouses,[89] whether the focus was serious political discourse or fun and entertainment, works were read aloud, debated and discussed. There, texts recovered some of their fluidity and textual meaning was constructed by many voices. In some ways the more informal interactions in these clubs is analogous to that in today's online communities.[90]

MUDs can be seen as both connecting and disconnecting participants: "readers" can also be "writers", if they choose; the meaning of the text continues as long as anyone remains interested. Some cyber-theorists suggest that the keyboard is simply a mechanical extension of the cyborg body.[91] Given these possibilities, it is perhaps not surprising that an amnesiac attitude can develop so that players forget that individuals participate from various locations, and that their experiences are mediated by a machine and its sensory limitations. These mediating and sensory qualities are said to transcend the notions of individuality that inhere in more traditional text based media.

Nevertheless not all participants have equal typing dexterity. Interactions suffer from time delays and, partly because of that, conversations can have multiple, disjointed threads. Whilst the analogy with conversation is well recognised, Pavel Curtis notes that coherence is affected by constant interruptions. He argues however, that these interruptions are simply less significant on MUDs than they are in real life.[92]

The diverse culture of participants and the perceived nature of the medium affected the outcome of the LambdaMOO meeting. Despite nearly all participants voicing strong disapproval about Mr Bungle's

---

[88] Elizabeth Eisenstein, *The Printing Revolution in Early Modern Europe* (Cambridge University Press, Cambridge, 1993), p. 95.
[89] Habermas notes the significant political and social role reading societies and coffeehouses played in the 17th to the 19th centuries. Jurgen Habermas, *The Structural Transformation of the Public Sphere* (MIT Press, Massachusetts, 1992).
[90] Such as in the gentleman's club called *The Sublime Society of Beef Steaks*. The motto was "liberty and beef". As Boswell puts it, the purpose of the society was to enjoy wine and punch in plenty and freedom, accompanied by a number of songs. See James V. Schall, "Duty and Sacrifice", *An Address to the Fifth Annual Symposium on Public Monuments on "The Firefighters' Legacy"*. *The Public Monuments Conservancy* by James V. Schall, S. J., Professor, Department of Government, Georgetown University, at Time-Life Building, Rockefeller Center, New York City, republished at http://www.georgetown.edu/schall/wsjvs6a.htm#1
[91] Elizabeth Reid, "Text-based Virtual Realities: Identity and the Cyborg Body", in Ludlow, above n. 35, p. 328.
[92] See "MUDding: Social Phenomena in Text-based Virtual Realities", in *ibid.* p. 362.

conduct, there was no resolution: "The perspectives were just too varied, the meme-scape just too slippery . . . People started drifting away".[93] One of the wizards acted on his own initiative and quietly erased Mr Bungle. Since then, the archwizard has built into the database a system of petitions and ballots so anyone can seek a popular vote on social schemes that require wizards to implement them.

In this fantasy realm where "real world" laws are seen as inapplicable, engagement with the ethical implications of virtual relationships has led to the creation of a system that mimics a familiar political and legal forum: a virtual public sphere where ethical responses can be debated and decisions formally executed, as the need arises. Such a solution reveals a sensitivity to the interest of diversity within these communities as well as to the power of those members with privileged technological access.

Perhaps more commonly "wizards" (or the system equivalents) simply resort to "kill" commands in respect of identities they find troubling, or "censor" disturbing discussion by "archiving" the topic.[94] These interventions can be interpreted as a refusal to engage in an ethical discourse about the best interests of the online community and the rights of those who share internet access. Operators can also avoid ethical discourse by taking a passive stance, leaving those who claim to be suffering harassment or abuse to their own devices, refusing to offer technical help or other mechanisms for resolving disputes. Passivity can often be justified by an indiscriminate appeal to the "free speech" or the "privacy" rights of users. Whilst it is open to users to relocate to more friendly service providers and/or internet communities, some harassers make a point of tracking quarry to their new homes. Where the ethics of such situations are not dealt with on site, it is important to consider the role played by more traditional, powerful regulators, such as federal policing agencies. Generally such organisations become involved on a selective basis, as in the Church of Scientology cases.[95] For all the rhetoric about the democracy of the internet, there are no "real" rights for citizens of cyberspace, apart from those granted by and to members of virtual communities with an interest in enabling ethical conduct.

Conclusion: Ethics and Laws

"The Three Laws of Robotics
I. A robot may not injure a human being or through inaction allow a human being to come to harm;
2. A robot must obey the orders given it by human beings except when such orders would conflict with the First Law;

---

[93] Dibbell, above n. 79, p. 388.
[94] For a discussion of the use of this tactic on WELL, a renowned haven for democratic discourse, see humdog, "pandora's vox: on community in cyberspace", in Ludlow, above n. 35, p. 440.
[95] See http://www.eff.org/pub/legal/Cases/Scientology_cases/

3. A robot must protect its own existence as long as such protection does not conflict with the First or Second Law."[96]

Asimov's three laws imbue technology with human-centred ethics, however in essence his "robot stories" problematise the ability to predict the complexity of interactions between humans and their technologies. His tales convey a tension between desire for "good" behaviour and the unanticipated results that follow the application of ethics as rules.

It is not true, however, to say that all rules are unworkable in cyberspace. Despite questions of jurisdiction and conflict of laws,[97] there is ongoing pressure to "harmonise" laws that impact on global trade. In reinventing the markets for and in cyberspace, acceptance that there are major problems in refashioning laws is uneven:

> "our insertion into an increasingly electronic and digitised life-world occurs in modalities that are *both* technologically "transparent" (that is, the technology is effortlessly and unproblematically "incorporated" into our very being) and "hermeneutic" (that is, the technology is seen as something other than ourselves and thus in need of interpretation).[98]

The possibilities for law reform have to be considered in light of the specific cultures of the internet technologies concerned, and in the context of the history of the development of the various legal categories involved. Some laws can incorporate the changing temporality, spatiality, embodiment and subjectivities of cyberspace technologies better than others.

But, in the absence of workable rules and appropriate rule-makers for cyberspace, ethics take on a more intense importance. Their significance derives from their status as outcomes of an evolving, contextual process of community formation, not from their position as positivist law, abstract rules of correct behaviour. This is ultimately the point underpinning the three laws of robotics, and whilst they were envisioned for a different technological future, the message and the metaphors still resonate.

---

[96] These laws first published in 1941 featured in numerous short stories about artificial intelligence. See Isaac Asimov, *I, Robot* (Harper Collins, London, 1968), p. 8.
[97] See David Post, "Anarchy, State and the Internet: An Essay on Law-Making in Cyberspace", (1995) *Journal of Online Law*, Art. 3.
[98] Sobchack, above n. 40, p. 80.

2. No Other Law? Author–ity, Property and Aboriginal Art

Anne Barron

London School of Economics

BCL (University College Dublin), LL.M. (Harvard), Lecturer in Law, London School of Economics and Political Science. She has published articles on various aspects of post-structuralist theory and its implications for the analysis of law and legal institutions. Her current research interests focus on copyright in its technological, economic, political and cultural contexts, and her book on copyright law will be published by Butterworths for the *Law in Context* series in 1999.

No Other Law? Author–ity, Property and Aboriginal Art

Authorship, in Western culture, designates a legal status, a mode of aesthetic production, a form of moral subjectivity, a figure of political citizenship/sovereignty, and a representation of paternity. Much scholarly attention has been devoted of late to the apparent contiguity of these forms of personhood,[1] and in particular to the relationship between the category of the author in copyright law and the various philosophical elaborations of aesthetic personality yielded by the Kantian and Hegelian traditions, notably Romanticism and German Idealism. A concern to expose the Romantic ideal of authorship—and with it, the legal structures which are said to institutionalise it—to a particular kind of 'ethical' interrogation motivates a great deal of this research. Given that, in terms of the Romantic aesthetic, the author is an exceptional individual, inspired from within by a unique and original genius and expressing this 'soul' in works of the imagination,[2] the ethical question is generally assumed to ask how this personage has established its claim to universal author-ity as *the* mode of creative being, and indeed a model of individuality to which all should aspire. What, this literature asks, is excluded or negated in the process by which the status of the individual genius as a transhistorical and transcultural category is created and sustained? This characteristically postmodern orientation to what might be termed 'the ethics of aesthetics' is particularly evident in a recent reflection on "the ethical reaches of authorship":

> With its emphasis on originality and self-declaring creative genius, this [Romantic] notion of authorship has functioned to marginalize or deny the work of many creative people: women, non-Europeans, artists working in traditional forms and genres, and individuals engaged in group or collaborative projects, to name but a few.[3]

To the extent that copyright law gives juridical form and force to the Romantic conception of authorship, it too is open to the same kind of ethical challenge:

---

[1] See, *e.g.*, M. Woodmansee, "The Genius and Copyright: economic and legal conditions of the emergence of the 'Author'" (1984) 17 *Eighteenth Century Studies* 425; M. Rose "The Author as Proprietor: *Donaldson v. Beckett* and the genealogy of modern authorship" (1988) 23 *Representations* 51; *Authors and Owners: the invention of copyright* (Harvard UP, Cambridge, 1993), pp. 38 to 40; and "Mothers and Authors: *Johnson v. Calvert* and the New Children of Our Imaginations" (1996) Vol. 22(4) *Critical Inquiry* 613 to 633; J. Boyle, "The Search for an Author: Shakespeare and the Framers" (1988) 37 *Am.U.L.Rev.* 625; P. Jaszi, "Towards a theory of copyright: the metamorphosis of 'authorship'" (1991) *Duke L. Jnl.* 445.
[2] Osborne, *Aesthetics and Art Theory* (Longmans, London, 1968), pp. 131 to 154.
[3] P. Jaszi and M. Woodmansee, "The Ethical Reaches of Authorship" (1996) 95:4 *South Atlantic Quarterly* 947 to 977 at 948.

[I]t should not surprise us to learn that this body of law tends to reward certain producers and their creative products while devaluing others: no copyright can exist in a work produced as a true collective enterprise (rather than by one or more identifiable or anonymous "authors"); a work cannot be copyrighted unless it is "fixed" (which excludes a wide range of improvised works and works of oral tradition); copyright does not extend to works that are not "original" (which rules out protection for folkloric productions that are valued for their fidelity to tradition rather than their deviations from it); and copyright does not protect "basic" components of cultural productions (which bars protection of, say, the rhythms that are most characteristic of both traditional musical forms and certain contemporary forms such as rap and hip hop).[4]

The strategy of uncovering copyright's negations and denials is explicable philosophically in terms of Emmanuel Levinas's 'ethics of alterity', an ethics which is not the measurement of actions or institutions against a set of moral norms so much as the experience of a relation with an absolute otherness, that 'exteriority' which eludes reduction to the 'Same': for Levinas, ethics is the putting into question of the Same—here the aesthetic/legal personality of the author, complete with its pretensions to universality—by this Other.[5] "Ethics, for Levinas, is critique; it is the critical *mise en question* of the liberty, spontaneity and cognitive emprise of the ego that seeks to reduce all otherness to itself."[6] This perspective is undeniably compelling, and to a considerable extent informs this paper, but there is another approach to ethics—perhaps more historical/anthropological than philosophical in orientation—which is no less 'critical' for being even more obviously distinct from the traditional concerns of moral philosophy. Michel Foucault's 'historical ontology'[7] is a mode of reflection upon the available forms of human subjectivity in which the critique of these personae is at the same time the historical analysis of the limits that they impose and an experiment with the possibility of going beyond them.[8]

Criticism indeed consists of analyzing and reflecting upon limits . . . [but] the critical question today has to be turned back into a positive one: in what is given to us as universal, necessary, obligatory, what

---

[4] *ibid.*
[5] This posing of the question of ethics in terms of an encounter with what is irreducible to the given forms of subjectivity is also present in the work of Jacques Lacan, Michel Foucault and Jacques Derrida: see, *e.g.* J. Rajchman, *Truth and Eros: Foucault, Lacan, and the Question of Ethics* (Routledge, London, 1991); S. Critchley, *The Ethics of Deconstruction: Derrida and Levinas* (Blackwell, Oxford, 1992). For a Lacanian analysis of the negations on which authorship as citizenship is founded, see A. Barron, "The Illusions of the 'I': Citizenship and the Politics of Identity" in A. Norrie (ed.) *Closure or Critique? New Directions in Legal Theory* (Edinburgh University Press, Edinburgh, 1993) pp. 80–100.
[6] Critchley, *ibid.* p. 5.
[7] M. Foucault, "What is Enlightenment?" in P. Rabinow (ed.) *The Foucault Reader* (Penguin, Harmondsworth, 1984), pp. 32–50, 45.
[8] *ibid.* p. 50.

place is occupied by whatever is singular, contingent, and the product of arbitrary constraints? The point, in brief, is to transform the critique conducted in the form of necessary limitation into a practical critique that takes the form of a possible transgression.[9]

'Practical' critique requires, not a search for "formal structures with universal value",[10] but an *historical* investigation of the actual practices through which individuals form themselves as subjects in relation to the models of personality that are available to them. As far as the authorial personality is concerned, it involves an analysis of how the subjectivities which are indeed accommodated by the name 'author' are actually internalised and lived: the rituals and forms of training through which individuals equip themselves with the capacities appropriate to them; the techniques for embedding and refining these capacities; the individual comportments and modes of action which result. Foucault, following Weber in part, has characterised these as 'ethical' practices, a characterisation which links the ethical more with the quotidien activity of cultivating an *ethos* than with the theoretical concerns of moral philosophy. And although his own most sustained genealogy of ethical activity did indeed focus on its relationship with moral codes, and in particular with codes regulating sexual behaviour,[11] Foucault's approach to ethics can be and has been adapted to analyse practices of self-formation elaborated in relation to legal rules[12] and aesthetic doctrines.[13] So conceived, ethics connotes not a set of moral principles so much as a mode of internalising a form of conduct by intensely practical and technical means.

Foucault's linking of ethical activity with the formation of *ethos* connects in turn with Pierre Bourdieu's usage of the concept of the *habitus*. Here again, an antique term for those learned behavioural responses that characterise a way of life is deployed as a category of social theory, developed specifically to overcome the antinomies between structure and agency in the explanation of social behaviour. Bourdieu's habitus is a practical sense, a set of dispositions which orients the subject's actions and reactions without completely determining them: it has been aptly characterised as "the capacity for structured improvisation".[14] Although experienced as 'naturally' embedded within the subject's innate character rather than as a system of conscious influences and

---

[9] *ibid.*
[10] *ibid.* p. 46.
[11] M. Foucault, *The Use of Pleasure: The History of Sexuality, Volume Two*, (trans. R. Hurley) (Penguin, Harmondsworth, 1985), especially pp. 25–32; "On the Genealogy of Ethics" in R. Dreyfus and P. Rabinow, *Michel Foucault: Beyond Structuralism and Hermeneutics* (Chicago University Press, Chicago, 1983), pp. 229–252.
[12] A. Barron, "The Governance of Schooling: Genealogies of Control and Empowerment in the Reform of Public Education" (1996) Vol. 15 *Studies in Law, Politics and Society* 167–204.
[13] I. Hunter, "Aesthetics and Cultural Studies" in L. Grossberg *et al.* (eds) *Cultural Studies* (Routledge, London, 1992), pp. 347–372.
[14] M. Postone *et al.*, "Introduction: Bourdieu and Social Theory" in C. Calhoun *et al.* (eds) *Bourdieu: Critical Perspectives* (Polity, Cambridge, 1993), pp. 1–13, 4.

constraints, the habitus is a social artefact, the effect of a process of inculcation that is successful precisely to the extent that its genesis in processes of cultural transmission and training—its artificiality—is repressed. A great deal of Bourdieu's work has involved an exploration of the habitus characteristic of producers of art, and consequently provides something of an antidote to Romantic and other idealist conceptions of artistic production as the pure expression of the individual artist's creative interiority. For Bourdieu, the pure aesthetic experience,

> with all the aspects of singularity that it appears to possess . . . is itself an institution which is the product of historical invention and whose *raison d'etre* can be reassessed only through an analysis which is itself properly historical. Such an analysis is the only one capable of accounting simultaneously for the nature of the experience and for the appearance of universality which it procures for those who live it, naively, beginning with the philosophers who subject it to their reflections unaware of its *social conditions of possibility*.[15]

Although the similarities between Bourdieu's account of the operations of the habitus and Foucault's account of ethical activity could be overstated, each exemplifies this impulse to historicise and contextualise the processes by which the social arrangements constitutive of the present, including the available forms of human agency, take shape: to unwrap the layers of mystification which obscure their conditions of possibility and represent them instead as natural and universal.[16] The notion of "practice" encapsulates these commonalities. For Bourdieu, practices are those unquestioned representations, crystallised in the taken-for-granted ways of living that socialisation engenders, through which individuals experience the world. In Foucault's work, practices are "places where what is said and what is done, rules imposed and reasons given, the planned and the taken for granted meet and interconnect,"[17] "places" being, not physical locations, but relatively durable and embodied routines, behaviours and understandings. Genealogy is the description of these contingent intersections, a description which aims to capture the singularity of practices—including those which may seem mundane or insignificant—and avoid attributing them to some fundamental determining instance. In this sense it breaks with traditional historical method. "The way they [historians] work is by ascribing the object they analyse to the most unitary, necessary, inevitable and (ultimately) extra-historical

---

[15] P. Bourdieu, "The Historical Genesis of a Pure Aesthetic" in *The Field of Cultural Production* (Polity, Cambridge, 1993), pp. 254–266, 255–256 emphasis in original.
[16] Ian Hunter's Foucault-inspired project of "describ[ing] the aesthetic ethic as an historical invention; a device for living, made up of autonomous components, self-supporting, and entering into relationships with other spheres of existence of the most contingent and unpredictable kind" (above n. 13, p. 359) is not too distant, to say the least, from Bourdieu's exploration of "the historical genesis of the pure aesthetic."
[17] M. Foucault, "Questions of Method" in G. Burchell *et al.* (eds.) *The Foucault Effect* (Harvester, London, 1991), pp. 73–86, 75.

mechanism or structure available",[18] so making the contingent appear self-evident and indispensable. Yet genealogy is something other than a kind of hyper-positivism, consisting only in the relentless recording of discontinuous particularities: "[the] further one breaks down the processes under analysis, the more one is enabled and indeed obliged to construct their external relations of intelligibility."[19] This approach to history, then, is simultaneously oriented towards undoing the received explanations for existing practices, and towards building up new grids of analysis for them which can enable their intelligibility to be appreciated differently.

What is to be gained from an historicisation of authorship[20] along these lines? As David Saunders has indicated, it may offer a way out of the impasse that appears to have deadlocked the contemporary debate on the relationship between copyright law and its aesthetic 'context'. The contours of this debate are by now familiar. On the one hand it is argued that the copyright author is but a reflection of the artistic genius of Romantic theory; on the other that there is no connection whatsoever between legal and aesthetic constructions of authorship. From one perspective copyright doctrine is composed of nothing more than a series of empty conceptual vessels, standing ready to be filled with whatever meanings of authorship happen to be dominant within the cultural field as a whole;[21] from the other, copyright doctrine is robustly independent of the aesthetic domain. As Saunders points out, in what at times appears as a declaration of unqualified support for the latter view,[22] the denial of copyright's autonomy is achieved only by negativing the author-in-law's status as a "historical positivity", a form of personhood "sufficiently particular and independent to merit description on its own terms, rather than in terms of some supposedly more fundamental reality."[23] Saunders' own position is considerably more than a restatement of 'black letter' orthodoxy, however: as has been noted above, there is a difference between attempting a genealogy of a historical positivity and writing the positivist history of a (legal) concept. Genealogy uncovers a legal conception of authorship which, far from being a mere receptacle

---

[18] *ibid.* p. 78.

[19] *ibid.* p. 77.

[20] D. Saunders and I. Hunter, "Lessons from the 'Literary': How to Historicise Authorship" (1991) 17(3) *Critical Inquiry* 479.

[21] Cf. Jaszi, above n. 1 at 471: "The 'authorship' construct, although still incomplete when introduced into English law in 1710, was a charged receptacle, prepared to collect content over the next century. Although the concept of 'authorship' was introduced into English law for the functional purpose of protecting the interests of booksellers (and continued to do so throughout the eighteenth century and beyond), the term took on a life of its own as individualistic notions of creativity, originality, and inspiration were poured into it."

[22] David Saunders, *Authorship and Copyright* (Routledge, London, 1992).

[23] *ibid.* p. 18.

for whatever philosophical notions might be "poured into it"[24] from time to time, is a specifically legal construct, the contours of which have been crucially shaped by the forms, practices and procedures of the legal institution and by the purposes which this institution has been called upon to serve. To resist determinisms of whatever variety—aesthetic, economic, or other—is in no way to deny that there may be linkages between the legal and other domains: affinities can undoubtedly be identified between the conceptual structures of copyright law and those which underpin the cultural field, not least in relation to that most contested of categories, 'authorship'. But these resemblances are better understood as signs of overlap and intersection than as evidence of a single dynamic driving legal and aesthetic development alike. As Saunders recommends, copyright's connections with the aesthetic domain can be reconceived in terms of the "grids of relations"[25] that it forms with other systems of practices in other spheres, including the aesthetic.

The process of excavating these 'grids' is at once diagnostic *and* critical, for to attend to the singularity of practices is at the same time to expose their historical contingency, to show that things could have been, and could yet be, otherwise. It is this critical dimension to genealogy that connects it with Levinas's ethics of alterity. To identify that which is contingent in law's construction of authorship is the very *mise en question* that Levinasian ethics also is, since it undermines this construct's claim to a necessary authority. Indeed even to concede its positivity is already to have raised the ethical stakes, for now the specificity of the law's resistance to alterity has to be confronted: copyright can no longer be explained as merely an institutionalisation of aesthetic doctrine's own exclusionary logic. Genealogy, then, at the same time as it disqualifies the assumption that the legal personality of the author is reducible to the aesthetic personality of the artist-genius—and is *therefore* vulnerable to a kind of one-size-fits-all attack—multiplies the possibilities for critique.

What will be attempted here is a genealogy of the legal construction of authorship which presupposes an openness to alterity. In particular, the project of this paper is to excavate the 'grid' formed when the practices associated with the legal and aesthetic constructions of the author meet and intersect. It will ask, not so much what ideal forms of personhood these constructions express, as how and to what specific ends they have emerged; what their limits are; and what possibilities all this reveals of their being transgressed and re-imagined. The site chosen for this excavation is *Yumbulul v. Reserve Bank of Australia*,[26] a case decided by the Federal Court of Australia in 1991.

---

[24] Jaszi, supra n. 21.
[25] Saunders, above n. 22, p. 32.
[26] (1991) 21 IPR 481.

I Art, Ethos and an Aboriginal 'Way of Life'

"In a world that is the reflection of an order . . . in which all things are representation, endowed with meaning and transparent to the language that describes them, artistic "creation" proposes only to describe. The appearance of things has the keys to the city, being itself the signature of an order that is given there to be recognised and not to be analysed. The oeuvre wishes to be the perpetual commentary of a given text, and all copies that take their inspiration from it are justified as the multiplied reflection of an order whose original is in any case transcendant. In other words, the question of authenticity does not arise, and *the work of art is not menaced by its double*. . . . *The Forgery does not exist*. Nor is the signature there in order to turn the oeuvre into a pure object, which has surged with emotional power from the act of painting. Even if he signs it . . . the artist does not attest to its truth: he is never more than the one who gives."[27]

In 1988 the Reserve Bank of Australia released a 10 dollar banknote to mark the bicentenary of the first European settlement of the country. The note incorporated elements of a number of Aboriginal artworks including a reproduction of a "wooden [pole] . . . decorated with painted designs, feathers and string"[28] made in 1986 by Terry Yumbulul, an Aboriginal artist. The reproduction was made under a sub-licence of the copyright in the work granted to the bank by the Aboriginal Artists Agency Ltd; the latter, a collecting society administering reproduction rights in works of Aboriginal art, had in turn been granted an exclusive licence of the copyright by Yumbulul in return for the sum of 850 Australian dollars, 85 per cent of the fee paid to the agency by the bank. Yumbulul brought an action claiming that the licence to the agency (and therefore the sub-licence to the Bank) was invalid, first, because the agency had misrepresented its nature and effect to him; second, because even if there had been no misrepresentation, the licence was an unconscionable contract since, to the agency's knowledge, the artist did not understand it and the agency had done nothing to ensure that it was properly explained to him; and third, because the consideration paid for the licence was inadequate. The trial judge found that there had been no misrepresentation, and was "satisfied on the evidence that Yumbulul understood the general nature of the licence he was signing."[29] Nor was there any basis for concluding that the consideration was inadequate. The action was dismissed. As the author of what was admitted to be an original artistic work, and the owner of copyright in it, Yumbulul was, in law, the person solely entitled to authorise its reproduction, and this he had validly done.

Terry Yumbulul, however, was "an individual of several persons",[30] a number of which, in addition to his legal status as author of the work in issue, are alluded to by the trial judge. One marks him out as "an . . .

---

[27] J. Baudrillard, *For a Critique of the Political Economy of the Sign* (Telos Press, St Louis, 1981) pp. 103–104 (emphasis in original).
[28] *Yumbulul*, above 26 at 482.
[29] *ibid*. at 490.
[30] Saunders and Hunter, above n. 20, p. 485.

artist of considerable skill and reputation",[31] some of whose works had been shown in private galleries throughout Australia; others recommended for acquisition by the Australian Museum on the basis that they were "excellent . . . examples of the output of a young artist who is rapidly becoming famous."[32] The work in question was acknowledged to have been made by Yumbulul "without the assistance of any other person and [with] . . . considerable care and attention on his part": it is described variously as "delicate", "intricate", "complex" and "unique to him".[33] The second presents him as an honoured citizen of Australia, a local hero whose art had been "purchased by the Northern Territory Government as official gifts for visiting foreign dignitaries"[34] and was now to adorn the currency at the proud moment of Australia's two hundredth birthday—as a white nation. The third pictures him as a successful entrepreneur of his artistic output who had been exploiting his skills commercially for 10 years prior to the trial of the action by selling paintings and other works, and had taken the opportunity to deal with the copyright in one of these by licencing it to the defendant Agency in return for the standard fee. The fourth representation, however, somewhat problematises the other three. For Terry Yumbulul is also an *Aboriginal* person, whose commercial dealings with the work in issue constituted a desecration of one of the most sacred ritual objects in the spiritual life of the Yolngu people of Northeast Arnhem Land: the Morning Star Pole.

Central to Yumbulul's argument before the court was his plea that the proposed action of the Bank in reproducing images of the Pole—albeit that it affirmed his identity as artist, as hero and as proprietor of the copyright in his artistic product—violated the ethos of the Yolngu people and his identity as a member of a Yolngu clan. The elements of this identity have been documented in a corpus of anthropological literature which in general counsels caution in "imposing on other cultures a Western concern about 'self' and 'selfhood' with its belief in the irreducible reality of the individual".[35] Within Aboriginal societies, identity is not in the first instance an attribute of individuals, but attached to an individual's kin, 'country' and, especially, spirit ancestors: individuals acquire identity to the extent that they come to recognise and enact their relatedness to particular others, places, objects and ancestral beings. Fred Myers' account of the 'Pintupi self', for example, emphasises how even the emotional repertoire of individuals—so often assumed to be transcultural and transhistorical—is shaped by the priority given in the practical activities and interactions of this Western Desert people to these forms of relatedness. The structures of social order are continuous

---

[31] *Yumbulul v. Reserve Bank*, above n. 26, at 482.

[32] *ibid*. at 484.

[33] *ibid*.

[34] *ibid*. at 482.

[35] F. Myers, *Pintupi Country, Pintupi Self* (Smithsonian Institution, Washington, 1986), p. 105.

with and rely upon these emotional orientations: the Law is an objectification, in the form of a transcendental, externally imposed code, of the lived and felt imperative to sustain these bonds. But since it is external to any human initiative, whether individual or collective, "Law—legitimate authority—does not stem from the self"[36]: in marked contrast to Kant's conception of the mature subject of Enlightenment,[37] true maturity for the Pintupi is the condition in which individual will, far from giving itself its own law, is subordinated to the law of an impersonal authority. Moral personality is an achievement of initiation and other rituals in which knowledge of this law is progressively acquired.

For all Australian Aboriginal peoples, the Law is a dimension of what is referred to in English as The Dreaming,[38] the origin of all things and the very ground of being itself. The Dreaming is "an ontologically prior set of events,"[39] a mythical past that conditions and participates in every aspect of the present, in which the ancestors of everything that now exists performed the actions that created the world. Geographical features, animate species, the norms that organise human relations and the order of the world itself owe their existence to the events of the Dreaming: an outcrop of rock may mark the spot at which an ancestor 'went into the ground,' or a track the line of its movement across the landscape. Individuals are believed to be conceived from the ancestors (which may be human, animal, vegetable, or combine elements of each) through spirit conception, and every individual's spiritual home is the place from which his or her ancestor comes. Clans—ostensibly groups of individuals linked by a common patriline—are in terms of The Dreaming united by a more fundamental spiritual essence: its members are descended from the same ancestral being and the same set of mythological events. The clan, then, and each of its members, is an incarnation of the ancestral being, and the actions of the spirit ancestors will often be described in the first person. More specifically, the clan is an incarnation of the geographical features made by the ancestral being: the clan is identified with the spirit ancestor through an identification with what the ancestor did at particular locations in space. Thus the events of the Dreamtime constitute the identities of places and persons alike, establishing meanings for what exists that have always been, and will always be, the same. It is the duty of the clan and each of its members to discover and reaffirm these meanings and the law that they reveal in rituals of repetition and re-enactment of Dreaming events, rituals which, in renewing ancestral connections, 'cathect' their human participants to the person of the ancestor and the moral imperatives that it embodies.

---

[36] *ibid.* p. 126.

[37] Foucault, "What is Enlightenment?", above n. 7, and see generally, D. Owen, *Maturity and Modernity: Nietzsche, Weber, Foucault and the Ambivalence of Reason* (Routledge, London, 1994).

[38] Eric Michaels elaborates on the significance of The Dreaming as Law for the Warlpiri of Central Australia in *For a Cultural Future* (Artspace, Melbourne, 1987), pp. 28–34.

[39] Myers, above n. 35, p. 54.

47

Because of the significance of place as a sign of ancestral power, land is a central focus of ceremonial life: sites are more or less sacred depending on the degree to which spiritual potency resides there, and in ceremony the clan's ancestral track—the territory marked out by the narrative of what the clan's ancestors did in the Dreamtime—is mapped out and its sacred associations are revealed. Ownership is what attaches to the spiritual identification of clan with place: a clan is said to own the land in which its Dreaming story is encoded, its 'country'. Stories are therefore charters of 'title' to land and ritual is oriented towards the repetition of stories and so towards assertions of identification. The production of images, objects, songs and dances is a ritual activity in this sense, simultaneously recounting the stories of what the ancestors did and representing the clan's territory: Aboriginal paintings function as highly detailed maps of topographical features. But further, like the land itself, they are manifestations of, and therefore contain, ancestral power: far from being merely human creations, they are left or bestowed by The Dreaming and inscribe its law. Therefore they too are the clan's property[40]: as one Aboriginal artist has explained, "[a] painting is the visual expression of the story of our ancestors and spiritbeings, and the right to depict it has been handed down through the ages from the original Dreamtime people."[41]

The ontological, epistemological and moral status of the Dreaming yields a concept of property which is, however, wholly devoid of the subject-object antinomy characteristic of Western legality. Whereas the latter assumes the owning subject to be absolutely prior to and distinct from the owned object, and conceives of that object merely as a material resource available for use and exploitation, the former sees (ancestral) subjectivity—and therefore *spiritual* potency—as residing *in* objects ('country' and sacred relics).[42] Since this subjectivity is constitutive of the clan's identity, the objects in which it is externalised are "integral to the very existence of the clan."[43] Hence references to 'our country', 'our story' or 'our paintings' are statements about identity as much as assertions of entitlement. Further, since The Dreaming story is also the unique source of truth and moral authority for the clan, these objects embody an imperative reality which is already given and which human beings can only discover and acknowledge. It follows that to 'hold' land,

[40] H. Morphy, *Ancestral Connections* (University of Chicago Press, Chicago, 1991), pp. 48–49.
[41] Wanjuk Marika, quoted in Vivien Johnson, "A Whiter Shade of Paleolithic", in S. Cramer (ed.) *Postmodernism: a Consideration of the Appropriation of Aboriginal Imagery* (Institute of Modern Art, Brisbane, 1989), p. 15.
[42] Morphy, above n. 40, at 102: "Paintings and ancestral designs do not simply represent the ancestral beings by encoding stories of events which took place in the ancestral past. As far as the Yolngu are concerned, the designs are an integral part of the ancestral beings themselves. . . . [T]he designs themselves possess or contain the power of the ancestral being." See also S. Harrison, "Ritual and Intellectual Property", (1992) 27(2) *Man* (N.S.), at 225–244.
[43] *ibid.* p. 57.

ceremonial forms, ritual artefacts—anything, in short, which depicts The Dreaming—is to have burdens or obligations as well as rights. 'Keeping the law strong' by recognising and caring for the sacred evidence of The Dreaming is a matter, firstly, of *knowing* it[44]: the primary obligation attaching to ownership of these objects is to acquire understanding of the law they express, and having acquired it, to pass it on to related others. To know the law left behind by the spirit ancestors is to observe it: to observe it is to have the basis for rights in that which the ancestors have bestowed.

How, then, does one obtain knowledge of the law? First, one has to have a spiritual identification with the ancestor who has produced it: amongst all Aboriginal peoples, this is a basis for an entitlement to be instructed in the law. Membership of a clan through patrilineal descent is one way of establishing a connection with that clan's spirit ancestors, and amongst the Yolngu the most important way. Knowledge can be acquired primarily through the teachings of a senior clan member and through participation in ceremonies where knowledge is revealed, but in all cases the acquisition of knowledge is a gradual and cumulative process, and depends on a variety of factors such as gender, age, seniority relative to siblings, willingness and ability to learn, and trustworthiness in the eyes of other members of the clan.[45] Knowledge of the law expressed in artefacts, like other forms of ritual property, brings with it rights in respect of those artefacts, and again the acquisition of rights is a progressive achievement. Having the status of an initiated male, while generally amongst the Yolngu a pre-requisite of access to restricted knowledge,[46] is no guarantee that one will enjoy the full panoply of rights: the initiate may by right produce his clan's paintings, but then only those paintings which are 'public' in nature (*i.e.* not secret or sacred). However, at the same time that they begin to produce public paintings by themselves, young men may start assisting their fathers or elder brothers in the production of sacred paintings, although they do not as yet paint them on their own. Amongst the Yolngu, the right to produce paintings that represent the designs on *rangga* (sacred objects) remains restricted to the most senior male members of a clan.

The effect of the operation of the principles of primogeniture and deference to elders is to produce a stratification of rights within the clan—in respect of land as well as paintings, for rights in both are distributed in the same way.[47] Because the acquisition of rights is bound up with the acquisition of knowledge, and because that in turn is a cumulative process, the extent and nature of clan members' rights will vary widely. Further, not only are rights fragmented within clans, but also between clans: entitlements are therefore widely dispersed among

---

[44] *ibid.* pp. 75–99; Myers, supra n. 35, pp. 149–151.
[45] *Ancestral Connections* p. 61; *Pintupi Country*, pp. 127–158.
[46] *Ancestral Connections*, pp. 60–61.
[47] *ibid.* pp. 57–74.

those who claim identification with the relevant Dreaming stories. An initiated and sufficiently knowledgeable man will have the right to produce the paintings of his mother's clan and to be consulted by members of that clan before they use the paintings in ceremonial contexts; he may also have rights in the paintings of his mother's mother's clan and of clans which own different parts of the same ancestral 'track'. In ascending order of importance, the kinds of rights which may be claimed are rights to produce paintings, to understand their meanings, to divulge those meanings to others, and to authorise or restrict production by others. Yet within each of these categories of right, there is a further series of stratifications, arising out of the fact that there are gradations of paintings—and within each painting, gradations of meaning—from the more to the less secret/sacred. Morphy suggests[48] that two representational systems, the figurative and the geometric, are employed in Yolngu art. Figurative representations, being iconic in form, are more easily interpreted than the more abstract geometric elements, and are therefore generally less secret/sacred than the latter. The sacred ritual property of Yolngu clans includes a determinate set of geometric elements which are deemed to be direct manifestations of the clan's spirit ancestors: these 'clan designs' are the crucial visual inscriptions of the relationship between people, place and the ancestral past, and are at once maps of the clan's land, 'title deeds' to that land, signatures of the clan, and, most importantly, codes of ancestrally authorised law. Each design, however, is deemed in turn to possess layers of meaning ranging from the 'outside' or publicly known to the 'inside' or most restricted meanings,[49] and a painter's 'career' is a process of gaining access to ever deeper (*i.e.* more secret/sacred) layers of meaning. When a man can paint, understand, and authorise others to paint and understand the most sacred designs of his clan, he achieves a full identification with the spirit ancestors and becomes a developed personality, a complete adult. Thus the oldest and most knowledgeable men of the clan are themselves said to be sacred.[50]

Within this framework of understanding, then, the value of a product of human artistry is measured by reference neither to its economic nor its aesthetic worth but to the degree of spiritual power inscribed within it. This power is not seen as resulting from an investment of individual personality in the work, but from the work's capacity to reveal that which precedes the individual: the spirit ancestors and the law that they inaugurated. It follows that to misappropriate the value contained in the work is neither to steal nor to plagiarise it but to *desecrate* it: to use it indiscriminately without an understanding of its meaning and power.[51] It was just such an act of desecration that Terry Yumbulul's copyright licence had authorised the Federal Reserve Bank to carry out. The

---

[48] *ibid.* pp. 142–180.
[49] *ibid.* pp. 75–99.
[50] *ibid.* pp. 103–105.
[51] *Yumbulul*, above n. 26, at 483.

Morning Star Pole has a central role in Yolngu ceremonies commemorating the death of important persons within a clan. While the commemoration ceremony is in public, the making of the Pole only takes place in the presence of suitably initiated men; this is in keeping with the system of regulated access to knowledge, for it enables the details of the design, manufacture and meaning of the object—details, that is, of the way in which it encodes ancestral power—to be kept from those not yet ready to receive such knowledge. Yumbulul, being a senior member of his clan who had "passed through various levels of initiation and revelatory ceremonies in which he [had] gradually learned the designs and their meanings",[52] had authority within his mother's clan, as well as his own, to produce its most sacred objects, amongst which was the Morning Star Pole, and to paint the sacred clan designs which appeared upon them. It was also acceptable for him to make such objects for sale to museums: museums are regarded as appropriate places for sacred artefacts, since their display in a suitably reverential context can help to educate whites about Aboriginal culture without at the same time divulging secret meanings. It was not acceptable, however, for Yumbulul to authorise the production or reproduction of the Morning Star Pole, least of all for use on banknotes. His doing so constituted an offence against—and the act of the Bank an assault upon—the ancestral inheritance of the clan, or in other words, its law, its property, and its very identity.

II Property, Legality and Identity

Insofar as this kind of injury could be expressed in the idiom of Anglo-Australian legal discourse, it could only have been represented as the infringement of some right vested in the clan—a 'community claim'—in respect of the copyright work. Predictably, French J. felt unable to acknowledge that such a claim was capable of recognition under Australia's copyright law. What the plaintiff encountered here was not a hostile judge, French J.—expressed himself to be personally sympathetic to Yumbulul's predicament—but rather an incommensurability between two ways of thinking about objects and the possible forms of relationship subjects may have with them, and the intractability of positive law as the instituted structure of authority in the modern nations of the West. In particular, the case presents us with a conflict between two understandings of property. Within the Western legal imaginary generally, property signifies that set of rules governing access to "resources" (or, to use a more revealing Marxian term, productive forces), and private property signifies a mode of allocation which is underpinned by the "organising idea" that "resources are on the whole separate objects each assigned and therefore belonging to some particular individual"[53]—an owner—exclusively. By 1991, when Yumbulul's case came before the Federal

---

[52] *ibid.* at 482.
[53] J. Waldron, *The Right to Private Property* (Clarendon, Oxford, 1988), p. 38.

Court of Australia, the Supreme Court of the Northern Territory had already been confronted with the question of whether this logic could accommodate an Aboriginal conception of property which presumed a wholly other set of understandings concerning the function and organisation of ownership. *Milirrpum v. Nabalco Property Ltd. and the Commonwealth of Australia*[54] involved a land claim by representatives of two Aboriginal clans from the Gove Penninsula in Northern Australia against a mining company which had been granted a lease to mine bauxite in the region and the Australian Government, which had granted the lease. The plaintiffs claimed that under Aboriginal law, the clans owned the land in question, and that the common law itself ought to recognise and respect the rights claimed by the clan under the doctrine of native title. To succeed in this contention, however, they first had to show that the Aboriginal 'title' was capable of recognition by the common law. Blackburn J. interpreted this issue as requiring that the following matters be addressed: first, the identity of the community claiming the land according to Aboriginal law and custom; second, the limits of the land claimed; third, whether the interest claimed was proprietary; and fourth, the incidents of that interest.

In addressing these issues, Blackburn J. relied heavily on the evidence of anthropologists who had appeared before him as expert witnesses. In order to ascertain the identity of the community claiming the land, he invoked a distinction, common within anthropological accounts of Aboriginal territorial organisation, between groups organised on the basis of common descent, and groups organised on the basis of co-residence, here reduced to a further distinction between 'clans' and 'bands'. Where clans have a ritual or spiritual relationship to land, bands have an economic relationship to it, and these different relationships are defined by means of yet another opposition between 'estate' (land as ritual property) and 'range' (land as a site of economic, *i.e.* hunting and gathering, activity).[55] The evidence presented to the court reflected the consensus which had emerged within the anthropological literature by the early 1970's, that, at least according to the ideology by which Aboriginal communities sustain themselves, clans own land, whereas bands use it. Although he was careful to distinguish anthropological from legal usages of the word 'ownership', preferring to describe the clan as the group to which land could be 'attributed', Blackburn J. did accept the priority, as far as Aboriginal law was concerned, of the clan's relationship with its estate over that of the band with its range. The expert witnesses were less clear about whether there was any connection between these two relationships. The witnesses suggested, tentatively, that they were probably

---

[54] [1971] 17 F.L.R. 141.
[55] "The estate was the traditionally recognised locus ('country', 'ground', 'dreaming place') of some kind of patrilineal descent group . . . The range was the tract or orbit over which the group . . . ordinarily hunted and foraged to maintain life. . ." W.E.H. Stanner, "Aboriginal Territorial Organisation: estate, range, domain and regime" (1965) 36 *Oceania* 2. Stanner was one of the anthropologists who gave evidence before Blackburn J. as to forms of Aboriginal social organisation.

co-extensive: most of a given band's members would be members of one particular clan, and that band would tend to stay mainly upon land to which that clan laid claim. On the evidence, Blackburn J. disagreed. "My finding is that the clan system, with its principles of kinship and of spiritual linkage to territory, was one thing, and that the band system which was the principal feature of the daily life of the people and the modus of their social and economic activity, was quite another."[56] In terms both of membership and territory, clans and bands were different entities. Thus the band could not in any sense be seen as the "economic arm of the clan."[57]

Blackburn J. was not prepared to "withhold from a clan's relationship to a piece of land the description 'proprietary' because the boundary of the land is less precisely definable than those to which we are accustomed",[58] but his characterisation of that relationship as 'spiritual' rather than 'economic' was of considerable importance to the third and fourth issues that he had elected to consider: whether, as such, it was a proprietary relationship, and what its incidents were. The proper approach to this issue, in the judge's view, was "to bear in mind the concept of 'property' in our law, and in . . . other systems which have the concept . . . and look at the aboriginal system to find what there corresponds to or resembles 'property'."[59] Property, he went on, "generally imples the right to use or enjoy, the right to exclude others, and the right to alienate".[60] The relationship of the clan to the land had none of these incidents. Firstly, the clan, as such, could not be said to have the right to use and enjoy the land with which it was associated. "Its members have a right, and so do members of other clans, to use and enjoy the land of their own clan and other land also".[61] But this was a right which could be relied on by a person as a member of a band, a grouping of people whose connection with land was economic in nature. The rights of band members could not be interpreted as rights of persons in their capacity as clan members, because, as the judge had already found, there was no connection between the band, an economic unit, and the clan, a spiritual unit. The clan as such could not be said to have a significant economic relationship with the land. *Qua* clan, its right to use and enjoy clan territory consisted only in the right to tend it by performing ritual ceremonies upon it, and this, as far as Blackburn J. was

---

[56] *ibid.* p. 171.
[57] *ibid.*
[58] *ibid.* p. 271. "A boundary need only be as precise as the users of the land require it for the uses to which they put the land" (*ibid.* p. 176). Since the uses here involved "hunting animals, obtaining vegetable food, getting materials for clothing and ritual observances and moving about from area to area as the economic exigencies required" (p. 168), as opposed to cultivating the soil, "the question, 'where exactly does one area end and the other begin' would be a useless or meaningless question." (p. 177).
[59] *ibid.* p. 270.
[60] *ibid.* p. 272.
[61] *ibid.*

concerned, did not constitute a right of property. Secondly, the clan seemed to have no right to exclude others from any part of its territory. It was customary, the judge found, to inform a senior member of a clan before approaching any of the sacred sites on that clan's territory, but it was not necessary to obtain permission to do so. And finally, there was clearly no right to alienate clan territory. The judge concluded that "there is so little resemblance between property, as our law, *or what I know of any other law*, understands that term, and the claims of the plaintiffs for their clans, that . . . these claims are not in the nature of proprietary interests".[62] Aboriginal law, it seems, was simply too 'other' to be capable of recognition as a source of rights 'in the nature of' property. Blackburn J. accepted that the anthropological evidence he had heard pointed unequivocally to the existence of an aboriginal system of law, "a subtle and elaborate system highly adapted to the country in which the people led their lives"[63]: the absence of an identifiable sovereign authority with the capacity to enforce the system did not undermine this conclusion. Nonetheless, he dismissed evidence of the Aboriginal witnesses, which showed that they thought of the land as belonging to the plaintiff's clan, as lacking in weight. "To ask what they 'think' begs the question: the problem at present before the court is to characterise what the aboriginal relationship [to the land] *is* . . .",[64] and he went on to characterise that relationship in terms of the concept of property recognised by the common law. Nor could an argument from 'mythology' establish that the right claimed was proprietary: in response to the argument that "the aborigines [sic] regard rights in land as given to the clans by their spirit ancestors", Blackburn J. professed indifference,[65] devoting only one paragraph of his long judgment to this issue. He concluded with the following observation: "It is dangerous to attempt to express a matter so subtle and difficult by a mere aphorism, but it seems easier, on the evidence, to say that the clan belongs to the land than that the land belongs to the clan".[66]

It was this cluster of limits on what property is for, what relationships between persons and things it presupposes, and what kinds of persons and things can be its subjects and objects, that Terry Yumbulul's clan encountered in seeking to phrase their claim to the Morning Star Pole as a right justiciable against the Federal Reserve Bank of Australia. Australian law clearly identifies copyright as a species of private property: the 1968 Copyright Act makes it clear that copyright will usually be vested in a private legal person, who, as owner of the copyright in a

---

[62] *ibid.* p. 273, (emphasis added).
[63] *ibid.* p. 267.
[64] *ibid.* p. 268 (emphasis added).
[65] "I hesitate to venture into this field, and I do not think it is necessary" (*ibid.* p. 270).
[66] *ibid.* pp. 270–271.

work[67] has certain exclusive rights in relation to it.[68] Although copyright ownership attracts relatively few of the standard incidents of chattel or land ownership, it crucially includes the right to use the work, to exclude others from carrying out certain acts in relation to the work without authorisation, to receive the income derived from granting authorisation, and to realise the capital value of the copyright by selling it: all of the rights, in short, comprised in Blackburn J.'s definition of property. In both its function and its form, copyright is clearly congruent with the institution of property generally: it is oriented towards the economic end of ensuring that informational 'resources' are put to their most productive use, and is organised according to a logic which posits a determinate person as the owner of a definable thing. One of the features of this logic, as *Milirrpum* makes abundantly clear, is that it relies upon an antinomy between objects and subjects of ownership and insists upon the irreducibility of each pole of this antinomy to the other: subjectivity cannot reside in objects, as such, nor objectivity in subjects, as such. Thus in law there can be no 'copyright work' without some author who can be said to originate it: an entity must be capable of being conceived of as the result of some human intervention in the 'real', whether or not this intervention is mediated by mechanical or other technical means.[69] But further, both persons and things must be legally cognisable: a work must be both identifiable with certainty and attributable to some determinate person if it is to be susceptible to the kinds of actions and transactions that private property contemplates.

These limiting conditions on what kinds of subject-object relationships can count within the realm of copyright law are, it should be noted, *internal* to the institution of copyright itself, not given to it by some determining instance located elsewhere. In particular, rules such as those requiring an identifiable author, fixation of the work in a material form, originality, and the exclusion of "basic components of cultural production" from protection[70] are not explicable by reference to "a thoroughly Romantic conception of authorship"[71] that supposedly constitutes the "linchpin"[72] around which copyright law turns. Copyright law exists to regulate the commercial exploitation of certain intangible entities, and to this end, it must both define these entities as objects in which rights can coherently be said to subsist and provide a means of identifying a legal actor in whom those rights can coherently be said to be vested. To be

---

[67] Australian copyright law distinguishes between (literary, dramatic, musical and artistic) "works" and "subject matter other than works" (films, television and sound broadcasts, and published editions of works). Since the subject matter in issue in *Yumbulul* qualified as an artistic work, the following discussion will be confined to the law relating to "works".

[68] The exclusive rights of the copyright owner under Australian law are enumerated in s. 31(1) of the Copyright Act 1968 (hereinafter "CA") with respect to literary, dramatic, musical and artistic works.

[69] "The real must become the production of the subject in order to be protected by the law" (B. Edelman, *Ownership of the Image* (Routledge, London, 1979), p. 43).

[70] See text accompanying n. 4, above.

[71] Jaszi and Woodmansee, above n. 3, p. 948.

[72] *ibid.*

sure, the words used to designate the quality in a work which will
guarantee its protection by copyright law—original expression—conjure
up the Romantic aesthetic. But in law, originality is simply the description of a causal relationship between a person and a thing: to say that a
work is original in law is to say nothing more than that it originates from
[can be attributed to] its creator. Further, the expression which is
protected need not be of any particular nature or quality: indeed,
expression in copyright law designates nothing more than the form taken
by the work, as opposed to the ideas underlying it.[73] If ideas are
excluded, it is because they, unlike the expressive forms which clothe
them, are perceived as unbounded and lacking finitude.[74] If the "basic
components of cultural production" are excluded, it is because they seem
incapable of assuming a shape for which some determinate individual
can be deemed responsible, and so cannot be conceptualised as products
of an identifiable person, clearly separable both from the property of
others, and from that which is in the public domain. And if fixation is
required,[75] it is because this circumscribes the intangible object: it
supplies stability, certainty and permanence to the work, thus turning it
into an object which can be incorporated in a commodity and subjected
to the process of exchange. Copyright law, in short, is more concerned
with technical questions oriented towards delimiting property rights—
who can claim rights in a work? how is the thing in which rights subsist
to be defined?—than it is with abstruse debates within art theory.

To say this is in no way to deny that copyright has operated to exclude
certain kinds of cultural product and producer from its ambit. On the
contrary, it is to render that exclusion all the more visible by revealing its
specificity, and to open up more fruitful paths to its critique than those
made available by importing a post-structuralist 'anti-aesthetic'[76] wholesale from the domain of the arts. If copyright law's conception of the
author-work relation is indeed a product of its own logic, then it is
highly unlikely to disappear just because post-structuralist theory has
declared the death of the author[77] and the dissolution of the work within
the 'intertext' of language.[78] By analysing it as a singular construction
with discrete conditions of existence, overlapping with but not determined by other equally singular and historically specific constructions in

---

[73] *Plix Products Limited v. Frank M Winstone (Merchants) and Others* (High Court of New Zealand)
[1986] F.S.R. 63.
[74] Yates J.'s objection in *Millar v. Taylor* to the proposition that there could be property in ideas
expresses an anxiety that remains current in the modern law: "the property here claimed is all ideal;
a set of ideas which have no bounds or marks whatever, nothing that is capable of visible
possession, nothing that can sustain any of the qualities or incidents of property." [1774] 4 Burr.
2303, 2361.
[75] "[I]t is . . . an essential feature of every copyright action that the plaintiff should start with a work
in permanent form" per Hirst J., *Fraser v. Thames TV* [1983] 2 All E.R. 101, 117; s. 22(1) of the CA.
[76] H. Foster (ed.) *The Anti-Aesthetic: Essays on Postmodern Culture* (Bay Press, Port Townsend,
Washington, 1983).
[77] R. Barthes, "The Death of the Author" in *Image Music Text*, (trans. S. Heath), (Fontana, London,
1977), pp. 142–148.
[78] R. Barthes, "From Work to Text" in *Image Music Text, ibid.*, pp. 155–164.

other spheres, the contingencies within it can be exposed *as* mere contingencies: only then can it be imagined otherwise than as it is. With this in mind, the next two sections analyse the limits and potentialities revealed by the encounter between Aboriginal art and the rules, both written and unwritten, that cross-cut the Western art mileu.

III Authorship in Law and Aesthetics—from culture to Culture

Terry Yumbulul was not the first Aboriginal artist whose work was used to adorn an Australian banknote. In 1966, the Federal Reserve Bank issued a new one dollar note incorporating a bark painting by David Malangi, a living artist who, like Yumbulul, came from Northeast Arnhem Land.[79] No effort was made at that time either to trace Malangi or negotiate a licence of his copyright. The same could not have been said of the Bank's treatment of Terry Yumbulul two decades later, and in other respects too, Malangi's situation at the time contrasted markedly with that of Yumbulul in 1987. Malangi was not recognised as an Australian citizen—Aborigines were not granted full Australian citizenship until 1967—much less a celebrated one. He resided, probably in considerable poverty, at one of a number of government sponsored "mission stations" established in Arnhem Land before the Second World War; Yumbulul, by contrast, was a participant in the outstation movement—"an option created by Yolngu (and Aborigines elsewhere in Australia) which enables them to live a life relatively free from outside intrusion"[80]—that by the early 1970s had begun to initiate a trend towards the return of clan-based groups to traditional territories and away from large government-controlled population centres. Though Malangi's work was striking enough to have been noticed by the Paris-based collector Karel Kupka—who, it appears, purchased it at the mission station where Malangi resided—he would not, in 1963, have been identified in white Australia either as an 'artist' or as one who regularly sold his paintings for significant sums of money in the fine art market, much less dealt with the copyright in them. The production of bark paintings was at that time generally still regarded as 'mission work', no different from farm or other manual labour; it was paid for at piecework rates and sold, as 'handicraft', in mission shops.[81] It is in this context that the Governor of the Reserve Bank explained its failure to deal with or pay Malangi as due to the assumption that the painting was "the work of some traditional Aboriginal artist [who was] long dead".[82]

---

[79] D. Bennett, "Malangi: the man who was forgotten before he was remembered" (1980) 4(1) *Aboriginal History* 43–47.

[80] Morphy, above n. 40, p. 42.

[81] "Craftwork for wages was seen as a good place to begin to instill the European values that would eventually lead to a complete integration within the Australian economic system. The manufacture of handicrafts was an initial small step that would eventually be replaced by other productive activities. It was not seen as something that would eventually lead to the creation of Aboriginal fine art." (*ibid.* p. 29)

[82] H.C. Coombs, quoted in Bennett, above n. 79, p. 44.

Twenty years on, the Bank had doubtless become rather less complacent: the issuance of the bicentennial note was preceded by an elaborate correspondence with the large bureaucracy which by then administered copyrights in Aboriginal art works, and ultimately a licence from this agency to use Yumbulul's work in the manner proposed. And the Bank's readiness to acknowledge Yumbulul's copyright was mirrored in French J.'s comment, when the case came to trial in 1991, that "in the sense relevant to the Copyright Act 1968, there is *no doubt* that the pole was an original artistic work, and that he [Yumbulul] was its author, in whom copyright subsisted."[83] What accounts for this dramatic shift in the perception of the Aboriginal artist's status, from tradition-bound non-entity to full-fledged proprietor? French J. hints at an explanation: "[t]he reproduction was . . . a mark of the high respect that has all too slowly developed in Australian society for the beauty and richness of Aboriginal culture."[84]

There is, though, a certain ambivalence in the way in which the term "culture" is invoked throughout the judge's text. In the passage just quoted, it is the sign of a "great, if threatened, human potentiality"[85]: an aesthetic sensibility. Yet by this point in the judgement, Yumbulul's responsibilties in relation to the Morning Star Pole under Aboriginal law have already been reduced to the status of merely "cultural"[86] obligations, recognised by members of his community only amongst themselves—and not cognisable within the Australian courts. Further, Yumbulul's betrayal of his 'culture' is deemed morally irreproachable *because* he had produced an acknowledged work of art: it is for this reason that "it would be most unfortunate if Mr Yumbulul were to be the subject of continued criticism within the Aboriginal community for allowing the reproduction of the Morning Star Pole design on the commemorative banknote."[87] In this second usage, 'culture' signifies in its relativising anthropological sense of "the 'whole way of life' of a distinct people"[88]: local, particular, and as such incapable of withstanding the force either of Australia's copyright law or of the 'universal' imperative, valid for the entire species even as it is incompletely realised in fact, to appreciate beautiful artefacts. For reasons which will be explained below, French J. is not to be taken as suggesting that

---

[83] *Yumbulul*, above n. 26, at 484 (emphasis added).
[84] *ibid.* at 492.
[85] P. Fuller, *Aesthetics after Modernism* (Writers and Readers, London, 1983), p. 12.
[86] *Yumbulul* above n. 26, at 490.
[87] *ibid.* at 492.
[88] R. Williams, *Culture* (Fontana, London, 1981), p. 10; J. Clifford, *The Predicament of Culture* (Harvard University Press, Cambridge, Mass, 1988). Rosemary Coombe draws on the work of James Clifford in noting the distinction between "'Culture' with a capital C—representing the height of human development, the most elevated of human expression as epitomised in European art and literature" and "plural 'cultures' with a small c—imagined as coherent, authentic ways of life characterised by . . . wholeness, continuity and essence . . ." (R.J. Coombe, "The Properties of Culture and the Politics of Possessing Identity: Native Claims in the Cultural Appropriation Controversy" (1993) 4(2) *Canadian Jnl. Of Law and Jurisprudence* 249–285, 256).

Yumbulul's status as an author-in-law is *derived* from his status as a respected creator of fine art. Nonetheless, the position Yumbulul occupies within the judge's text—poised precariously at a point where the anthropological and the aesthetic modes of discourse intersect—places him within the law's field of vision in a way that David Malangi, in 1966,[89] was not. To understand how the Aboriginal artist emerged into this field, then, it is necessary to investigate the forces that have constructed Aborigines by turns as a people without culture (*i.e.* without a discernible form of social organisation; without law or religion; barely human), a culture ('way of life') without art, and a cultivated civilisation producing works of aesthetic value.

It was the perceived paucity of 'material culture' within Aboriginal societies which persuaded early European observers that Aborigines were "the miserablest People in the World".[90] By the mid-nineteenth century, the first collections of tools, weapons and other 'artefacts' had been amassed-mainly on an *ad hoc* basis, and often as 'trophies', by individual explorers, missionaries, government officials and landowners—and with the establishment of public museums in Australian cities, such material gradually became the object of investigation by ethnographers and the first anthropologists. Museum collections became more systematic and comprehensive as the century progressed, but the prevailing view throughout this period, exemplified in the preponderance of utilitarian objects on display, was that Aborigines were preoccupied with the mundane business of survival rather than with ceremonial or artistic life.[91] The first substantial museum collection of bark paintings did not take shape until the early part of this century, but even then, as Aboriginal art began for the first time to be seriously investigated by professional scholars, it attracted attention chiefly for its ethnographic significance—for the light it could throw on the nature and meaning of Aboriginal religious beliefs and ceremonial practices—rather than for the beauty of its visual forms. Even the emergence, during the first decade of the century, of an international trend towards the appreciation of the formal aesthetic qualities of 'primitive' art did not immediately affect the perception of Aboriginal art: the attention of Picasso, Braque, and other members of the artistic avant-garde was

---

[89] Malangi's own personal trajectory reproduced the movement from producer of cultural artefacts to certified artist, at the same time as it evidenced the deployment of art by Aborigines as a form of resistance to the "whitewashing" of European-Australia's history of violence towards the Aboriginal population. In 1985, the National Gallery of Australia purchased Karel Kupka's collection, including the painting reproduced on the one dollar note. That institution is also home to *The Aboriginal Memorial* (1988), a work in the form of two hundred painted hollow-log coffins, one to mark each year of white presence in Australia. This, a memorial to the thousands of Aborigines killed as a result of European settlement, was produced by forty three Arnhem Land artists, one of whom was David Malangi (W. Caruana, *Aboriginal Art* (Thames and Hudson, London, 1993) p.205–7).
[90] W. Dampier (1697), quoted in C. Symes and B Lingard, "From the Ethnographic to the Aesthetic" in P. Foss (ed.), *Island in the Stream: Myths of Place in Australian Culture* (Pluto Press, London, 1988), pp. 188–232, 191.
[91] P. Jones, "Perceptions of Aboriginal Art: a History" in P. Sutton (ed.), *Dreamings: the Art of Aboriginal Australia* (Viking, London, 1989), pp. 143–179, 155.

primarily directed towards Africa, and later, Polynesia. "Before the first major exhibition of Aboriginal art in Melbourne in 1929, this art was widely regarded as being so far removed from the sophistication of Western culture that it was hardly discussed as art at all."[92] That exhibition, entitled *Primitive Art*, signalled that the re-evaluation of the primitive was finally being extended to Aboriginal material, a trend which gathered momentum in 1930s Australia in the form of an urge— exemplified particularly in the work of Margaret Preston—to find or create a national artistic style that would put Australia on the inter- national art world's map and at the same time inspire and motivate local artists. Preston's commentary on the works of Aboriginal art included in a 1941 collection, *Art of Australia* 1788–1941, accompanied this exhibition on its tour of North America: the first presentation of Aboriginal material outside Australia as 'art'.

The new perception was inseparable from the shift in curatorial practices that accompanied it. From the 1940s onwards, Aboriginal material began to move from the natural history museum to the art gallery, a change of spatial setting that itself enables a new way of seeing the exhibited object. Assessments formed in these hushed, uncluttered, judiciously illuminated spaces will tend to focus on the object not as an ethnographic artefact, incomprehensible outside of its cultural context, but as pure visual form, susceptible to aesthetic appreciation. Under the informed gaze of the connoisseur, the object becomes available for analysis by reference to the body of doctrine yielded by fine art scholarship, and judgments of its value are in turn institutionalised in the unstable form—part brochure, part academic treatise—of the gallery catalogue. Thus, when in 1960–1961 the state art galleries of Australia mounted a large exhibition of Aboriginal 'art', art critic/historian Tony Tuckson's catalogue entry 'sees' culture purely as visual style, spirit as a property of imagery, and the work (now, of art) as something to be appreciated in relation to other works:

[W]orks of art exhibited in an art gallery (*i.e.* rather than in an anthropology or natural history museum) can be contemplated in some form of isolation. They can be compared with other works of their period, and furthermore, differences between productions of various cultures can be quite easily observed, yet there is a unifying quality over and above the different styles. There is the question not only of visual sense of balance and proportion, but of the underlying spirit of their imagery. These two factors make it possible for us to appreciate visual art without any knowledge of its particular meaning and original purpose.[93]

---

[92] *ibid.* p. 165.
[93] T. A. Tuckson in R.M. Berndt (ed.), *Australian Aboriginal Art* (Collier and Macmillan, London, 1964), p. 63, quoted in A. Marrie, "Killing Me Softly: Aboriginal Art and Western Critics" (1985) Vol. 14 *Art Network* 17–21, 17.

The 'we' referred to here is the community of art connoisseurs and critics, for whom the availability of objects in particular authorised spaces is, it seems, both a prerequisite and a guarantee of their being subjected to serious critical attention.[94] Aesthetics, as Howard Becker has shown, is an activity as much as a body of doctrine,[95] a set of techniques for (literally) framing objects in physical and perceptual space, naming the artists responsible for them, and evaluating them in terms of their relationships with other objects already certified as art.

The sheer contingency of the art object's status upon the applicability of these techniques is nowhere more evident than in relation to Aboriginal material, which in its traditional practice eludes them. As Morphy summarises in his study of the Yolngu,

> Painting is a ritual act surrounded by rules and restrictions on who can paint which design in what context and who can see which design where. Paintings are usually destroyed within hours of being produced or at least made invisible, either by rubbing out the designs, as with body paintings, or by burying the objects with the paintings on them. If the paintings survive for longer it is not to be admired or preserved but, as is the case with hollow log coffins and memorial posts, to be left to undergo a natural process of decay. The individual artist is almost absent from the process of painting: paintings are frequently done by a number of people, usually men, working together. Although one man may sketch out the initial design, the painting is not thought of as an individual's work, nor is it referred to as "his" painting. The paintings are done for religious purposes, sometimes with a hint of political intent . . . [and] the significance of a painting depends on the specific features of its context (and contexts are multiple).[96]

In order to become objects amenable to curatorial administration, technical changes in the means by which Aboriginal paintings were produced were required. Initially, however, these changes were instituted as a response to the demands, not of the art world and its rules, but of the craft market opened up by the mission station network, a market which simply required tangible items that were portable, cheap, durable but still recognisably 'Aboriginal'. Bark was already an important traditional medium in Arnhem Land, but as the demands of the market made themselves felt, natural binding agents were gradually replaced or supplemented by synthetic glues—"[t]he durable properties

---

[94] Bourdieu draws attention to Marcel Duchamp's knowing participation in the "game" by which the object is miraculously transubstantiated by its emergence into the field of art: "he produces objects whose production as works of art presupposes the production of the producer as artist: he invents the *ready made*, that manufactured object promoted to the dignity of an art object by the artist's symbolic stroke [the signature]". *The Rules of Art* (Polity, Cambridge, 1996), pp. 246–247.

[95] H. Becker, *Art Worlds* (University of California Press, Berkeley, 1982), p. 131.

[96] Morphy, above n. 40, pp. 21–22.

of commercial binders made them suitable for the production of art intended for the outside world"[97]—as were twigs and other instruments by artists' brushes. In Central Australia, the transformations wrought by the shift in the means of artistic production were even more dramatic. From the early 1970s, traditional surfaces of bodies, rocks and sand were giving way to canvas; ochres and other natural pigments were being replaced by acrylic paints. The crucial agents of these changes, there and to a lesser extent in the Northern Territory, have been the art advisors appointed by the Australian Government as part of the bureaucratisation of the burgeoning Aboriginal arts and crafts industry from the early 1970s.[98] Since at least the 1930s, white intermediaries have intervened to significant effect in the processes by which Aboriginal creative practices have been translated for reception by white audiences, and in particular white buyers.[99] Their interpretation of the market's demands has influenced not simply the paint and materials used, but often also the substance of what is painted—colour, composition and design details. Be that as it may, the success of these intermediaries in marketing Aboriginal works was in some measure responsible for the expansion in sales towards the end of the 1960s: the production of bark paintings for sale to the general public increased fivefold between 1968 and 1969,[1] and the revenues yielded by the industry rose accordingly. Production appears primarily to have been motivated by financial considerations, coupled with a concern to inform European-Australians of the complexity and value of Aboriginal culture and thereby to advance Aboriginal political claims, including claims to land.[2] As Morphy points out, it was the motivation of the purchaser, rather than that of the producer, which constituted the product as art rather than souvenir or ethnographic curiosity: "on the whole the purchasers . . . were all purchasing the same kind of thing."[3]

Here curatorial expectations met the rules of art enunciated in fine art scholarship: those who looked for fine art in Aboriginal material did so

---

[97] W. Caruana, *Aboriginal Art* (Thames and Hudson, London, 1993) p. 25.

[98] Aboriginal Arts and Crafts Ltd (AACL) was set up by the Government in 1971. This body ran retail outlets in the major cities and a wholesale business selling crafts to tourist shops until its functions were taken over by Inada Property Holdings Ltd. in 1984: it also funded art advisors. The subsequent history of Inada is recounted by French J. in *Yumbulul* (n. 26 above, p. 485). The Aboriginal Arts Board of the Australian Council for the Arts was formed in 1973 after a National Seminar on Aboriginal Arts in Australia. The Board, as well as providing funding for the promotion of Aboriginal art by various bodies, including AACL, set up the Aboriginal Artists Agency Ltd in 1976 with the objectives of taking action against copyright infringers and authorising copyright clearances. The Agency was one of the defendants in *Yumbulul*. A 1988 Report, *The Aboriginal Arts and Crafts Industry* (Department of Aboriginal Affairs, Canberra, 1989) documents the vast web of public and private institutions that has taken shape around Aboriginal art produced for the market in the years since 1970.

[99] Albert Namitjirra, an Aboriginal landscape painter who became well known in the 1930s and 1940s, painted in the European style, with watercolours, having been introduced to both by a white artist teaching at the mission where he was based.

[1] H. Morphy, "Audiences for Art" in A. Curthoys *et al.* (eds), *Australians from 1939* (Fairfax, Syme and Weldon, Sydney, 1987), p. 171. For a contemporary assessment of the market for Aboriginal art, see T. Ingram, "Black Market" (1997) 35(1) *Art and Australia* 126–127.

[2] See G. Yunupingu, "Indigenous Art in the Olympic Age" (1997) 35(1) *Art and Australia* 64–67.

[3] See, above n. 40, p. 23.

with a particular kind of eye, an eye trained to see those visual forms which at that historical moment were characteristically 'arty.' Thus, for Margaret Preston, writing in the 1920s, the representational systems of Arnhem Land art were "equivalents to the cylinder, sphere and cone"[4] the signature motifs of Cubism. More generally, the recurrence of geometric elements within this work, the two-dimensionality of the representational elements, the symmetry of the pictorial composition and the choice of bark as the painting medium converged with those aspects of modernist art theory that stressed "flatness and the delimitation of flatness" as "the irreducible essence of pictorial art".[5] By the 1980s, too, critics could see in the brightly coloured acrylic-on-canvas dot paintings of the Western Desert the 'look' of then contemporary modern art movements: "it is the similarity between Aboriginal acrylics and familiar forms of Western painting that has allowed their entry into the art world. The Western Desert acrylic movement has been likened to, among others, Surrealism, Abstract Expressionism, Minimalism and Conceptualism."[6] A contemporary figure frequently alluded to in these comparisons was Jackson Pollock, the exemplar of Abstract Expressionism's romantic ideology. Both Tuckson and Kupka noted the affinities between the processual characteristics of Aboriginal painting—the fact that "the process of making art was often more important than the finished product"[7]—and Pollock's supposed recovery of unconscious immediacy in his muscular, emotionally charged painting style. Yet here again, coincidence was the condition that made this analogy possible:

Not unlike Pollock, some Aboriginal acrylic painters work their canvases flat on the ground. . . . Yet, in other respects, the thoughtful patience of a group of Aboriginal painters—sitting on or around a canvas while they work—could not be more different from the now mythic image of the lone creative genius attributed to Pollock in his "action painting", where he is seen hovering over the canvas at his feet making gestures of theatrical intensity.[8]

What should be clear from this brief history is that the Romantic ideal of the aesthetic personality neither dictated nor denied the admission of Aboriginal material into the privileged canon of works of art. Rather, it

---

[4] M. Preston, quoted in Symes and Lingard, above at p. 59, n. 90, p. 201.
[5] C. Greenberg, "After Abstract Expressionism" in J. O Brian (ed.), *Clement Greenberg: The Collected Essays and Criticism Volume 4* (University of Chicago Press, Chicago, 1993), pp. 121–134 at 131.
[6] N. Baume, "The Interpretation of Dreamings: The Australian Aboriginal Acrylic Movement" (1989) 33 *Art & Text* 110–120, 112. Baume rightly points out that the acrylics of the Western Desert are more easily assimilable to the Western aesthetic than the bark works of the Northern Territory: "For us, the look or aesthetic quality of ochre on bark is dominated by an aura of 'authenticity,' retaining a ritual, almost mythic potential, whether in terms of their own material production (the 'natural' extraction of ochres from the earth, the curing of freshly cut bark, etc.) or in the trace of their identity as ceremonial objects." Thus the acceptability of bark paintings in terms of contemporary art in part "depends on the breakthroughs made by acrylics" (*ibid.* pp. 118–119).
[7] Caruana, above n. 97, p. 25.
[8] Baume, above n. 6, p. 113.

was when it became commensurable with the formal language, conditions, materials, institutions and spaces in which, at a particular historical moment, Western art was produced, distributed, viewed and evaluated that this material began to be perceived as susceptible to aesthetic attention. If this is so, then the appearance of the Aboriginal artist within the frame of copyright law cannot be explained, either, as the working out of the Romantic ideal within legal doctrine. Instead, the logic of this transformation must equally be sought in the limiting conditions that are internal to the institution. Just as a given product of human action must be constituted as amenable to aesthetic evaluation in all the practical ways mentioned above, so it must be constituted as something which is susceptible to the protection afforded by copyright law. In both instances, this is primarily a technical matter. It depends, for example, upon the available techniques of reasoning about the object and its producer, mechanisms for the enforcement of judgements, and so forth. To be sure, the limiting conditions to which the objects of aesthetics and copyright respectively must adhere may well be similar—similar 'jumping-off points', that is, for the very different operations that each institution performs upon them. But these conditions are not given by a single philosophical ideal: they are separately elaborated for the separate and different purposes which these institutions serve.

The emergence of the Aboriginal artist as an acknowledged proprietor of the copyright in his or her works, then, has its own specific trajectory, a path which crosses but does not follow that which led to his or her construction as an 'artist.' The issue of whether copyright subsisted in Aboriginal works was first raised in 1973, at a National Seminar on Aboriginal Arts in Australia, in a context of widespread unauthorised reproduction of Aboriginal imagery on such items as place mats and tea towels. The Seminar led to the establishment of the Aboriginal Arts Board of the Australian Council for the Arts, which immediately launched a campaign to control unauthorised reproductions. The Board's priorities were, first, to assist Aboriginal copyright owners to enforce their rights against infringers, and, second, to consider whether new forms of legal protection were needed where copyright was unavailable. The latter task was subsequently (in 1975) devolved by the Australian Government to a Working Party comprising officers representing the Attorney-General's Department, the Australia Council, the Australian Copyright Council and the Departments of Aboriginal Affairs, Home Affairs and the Environment, and the Prime Minister and Cabinet. The setting up of the Working Party, and the range of governmental concerns represented by its membership, gives an indication of the political significance of the Aboriginal arts industry at this time. If the period from the end of the Second World War to the early 1970s was marked by a policy of assimilating the Aboriginal population into the mainstream of Australian life, then it was to be replaced, with the election of a Labour Government in 1972, by one of 'self-determination' thereafter. The theme of self-determination, though initially finding expression in movements of Aboriginal resistance to political and cultural oppression—especially the struggle over land rights—was subsequently taken up as the official response to the 'Aboriginal problem'.[9] It manifested itself in, amongst other aspects of social policy, government support both for the outstation movement and for the development of the art industry, and in general in a new awareness of the potential of the industry to bring a measure of economic independence to the newly empowered outstation communities (by reducing reliance on welfare) and to promote respect for the accomplishments of Aboriginal culture.

It was in this commercial and political context that the Working Party conducted its deliberations. When its report was finally completed, in 1981,[10] questions were indeed raised about whether Aboriginal art was adequately protected under Australian copyright law. One issue was whether Aboriginal artistic works would satisfy the criterion of originality contained in section 32 of the Copyright Act 1968. Because the correct transmission of Dreaming stories is the paramount obligation of the Aboriginal artist, and because designs and images embody these stories, a premium is placed on their accurate reproduction, and the capacity for individual creativity is carefully controlled. Although the authors of the report acknowledged that "the degree of tolerance of variation in transmission of these themes varies from one area of Aboriginal Australia to another and from one medium to another"[11] the concern that at least some works might fail the 'not copied' test were felt to be particularly justified in relation to the art of Northeast Arnhem Land. Unlike the dot paintings of Central Australia, Northeast Arnhem Land bark paintings tend to adhere strictly to a determinate set of conventions of representation, and to reproduce a given repertoire of graphic elements: it is therefore easy for the untutored eye to see each work as a more or less exact copy of pre-existing designs. Those designs would in turn be excluded from protection, however, because of the operation of section 33 of the Act, which measures the term of copyright from the death of the author of the work. The duration of this term—50 years in the case of an artistic work—was therefore a second important limitation of the copyright legislation from the perspective of the Aboriginal artist, for it was not calculated to ensure that protection would be afforded to ancient designs whose authors were long dead: these would be in the public domain. A third limitation derived from the way in which ownership of copyright was defined in the Act. Under section 35(2) the author of a work is the first owner of any copyright in it, and the author of a work will be the person who originates it.[12] This structure, in the view of the Working Party, could not do justice to the systems of rights prevailing in Aboriginal communities:

---

[9] T. Rowse, "Assimilation and After" in A. Curthoys *et al.* (eds.) *Australians from 1939* (Fairfax, Syme and Weldon, Sydney, 1987), pp. 133–149.

[10] *The Protection of Aboriginal Folklore: Report of the Working Party* (Department for Home Affairs and Environment, Canberra, 1983).

[11] *ibid.* para. 505.

[12] *Sands & McDougall Pty Ltd. v. Robinson* (1917) 23 C.L.R. 49.

To give the individual artist full copyright protection would be to give rights which the person does not have under traditional law. A right given without the limitations of tribal [sic] custom, and without debt to any body of tradition which might otherwise encumber it, would enable the individual artist to give or refuse permission to the reproduction of the work beyond that which the person would be entitled to give under traditional law. Such non-exclusive rights are a particular feature of Aboriginal law and are not readily compatible with the exclusive rights of copyright.[13]

This comment directly anticipated the situation that arose in *Yumbulul*, but the first test of whether the Working Party's concerns were justifiable happened earlier, in the context of a dispute between an individual Aboriginal artist and a commercial T-shirt manufacturer in which it was the originality of the artist's work that was primarily in issue. In 1989, an Arnhem Land artist, Johnny Bulun Bulun, "took the apparently unprecedented step of bringing an action for breach of copyright"[14] arising out of the unauthorised reproduction of two of his paintings on T-shirts. The case was settled after the defendants undertook to cease manufacturing and selling the shirts, and so did not receive extended judicial consideration, but the outcome was greeted as a "'landmark' . . . of vital importance to Aboriginal artists and artistry."[15] It showed, according to Colin Golvan, who acted as counsel for the plaintiff, that "no blanket view ought to be adopted in relation to the application of the concept of 'originality' to Aboriginal artworks".[16] Bulun Bulun himself deposed that although he had been trained to paint the Dreaming stories of his clan by his father, the latter "painted such scenes in his own way. I do not have any of his works, and have never tried to copy any of them."[17] Thus while many bark paintings represent traditional designs in an ancient genre which is "regulated by tribal customs,"[18] it ought to be possible, Golvan maintained, to show by evidence that particular artists—as in this case—have their own distinctive way of expressing those designs, and do so through the application of considerable skill and labour.

To what extent was this recognition of Bulun Bulun as a producer of original works protected by copyright driven by a Romantic aesthetic embedded in the law? Not at all. To interpret originality, as Golvan does, as requiring distinctiveness—which in the context of works based on pre-existing sources is the correct interpretation[19]—is to assert that copyright law demands, not that the author manifest genius in her work, but

---

[13] *Report of the Working Party*, para. 1006.
[14] C. Golvan, "Aboriginal Art and Copyright: the Case for Johnny Bulun Bulun" [1989] 10 E.I.P.R. 346, 347. This action, like Yumbulul's, was initiated in the Federal Court in Darwin, Northern Territory.
[15] *ibid.*
[16] *ibid.* p. 349.
[17] *ibid.* p. 348.
[18] *ibid.* p. 351.
[19] See *Interlego v. Tyco* [1988] 3 All E.R. 949.

simply that it be recognisably hers, clearly attributable to her and no-one else. In this sense, originality is simply the mechanism by which attributability is demonstrated for the purposes of the law: arguably, at least in the Anglo-Australian context, it imposes no further requirement of creativity.[20] Bulun Bulun's case was indeed a landmark to the extent that it demonstrated how Aboriginal art practices could be assimilated to the model of origination assumed by the Copyright Act, but it in no sense took this conclusion from the Romantic aesthetic. Nor did Bulun Bulun's ability to meet the other requirements for copyright protection derive from the recognition of any particular aesthetic theory. As the sole originator of the paintings in issue—he alone had wielded the paintbrush—he was the person who had created the works, and was therefore their author and the owner of the copyright in them. The paintings themselves were clearly "paintings" within the meaning of section 10(1) of the 1968 Act: they were expressed in durable form on a "surface" (bark) and the complexity of the visual images took them well beyond the *de minimis* threshhold.[21] The artistic quality of the paintings was irrelevant to the question of whether they fell within section 10(1): the section expressly provides that a painting is an artistic work "whether [it] is of artistic quality or not." The Working Party's concerns notwithstanding, it could no longer be doubted after Bulun Bulun's case that the Aboriginal artist could also be, as far as copyright law was concerned, an author. Thus when Terry Yumbulul's case came to trial two years later, the subsistence of his copyright was acknowledged without question, but French J.'s certitude on the matter is born out of his assessment of the status of the sculpture under the Copyright Act—not out of his recognition of its status as a work of art.

Johnny Bulun Bulun was a pioneer in more than one respect. As well as being the first Aboriginal person to assert his copyright before the Australian courts, he was also the first Aboriginal artist to be honoured with a commercial exhibition devoted solely to his *oeuvre*.[22] His own career, then, expresses a history in which Aboriginal persons emerged first as artists and subsequently as proprietors of copyright in the products of their creativity. What this section has aimed to show is that the emergence of the Aboriginal *artist* has followed a separate path from that of his or her emergence within the sphere of copyright law, and that each of these emergences is better seen as a singular "event"[23] constituted by a muliplicity of historical processes than as the sign of a single determination. The next section explores both the points at which the paths of these histories have intersected, and the limits they impose.

---

[20] *Football League Ltd. v. Littlewoods Pools Ltd.* [1959] Ch. 637; *Ladbroke (Football) Ltd. v. William Hill (Football) Ltd.* [1964] 1 W.L.R. 273; *Kalamazoo (Australia) Pty Ltd. v. Compact Business Systems Pty Ltd.* (1985) 5 I.P.R. 213.

[21] *Merchandising Corporation of America Inc v. Harpbond Ltd* [1983] F.S.R. 32.

[22] The exhibition took place at the Hogarth Gallery in Sydney in 1981: Morphy, "Audiences for Art", above n. 1, p. 175.

[23] Foucault, "Questions of Method", above n. 17, pp. 76–78.

What will be suggested is that the success of Aboriginal people in the domains of copyright and the arts has been equivocal, for the forms of recognition bestowed respectively by the courts and the art world have been accompanied by a series of negations of the unique character of Aboriginal conceptions of ownership and artistic production. In what follows I identify five limits to legal protection—the requirement of originality, the exclusion of narrative from the scope of the law's protection of artistic works, the exclusion of ideas from copyright protection, the requirement of a 'surface' for artistic works, and the limitation of the status of 'author' to those who inscribe that surface—and investigate the ways in which these intersect with the conditions imposed by the art world on the recognition of Aboriginal material as "art".

IV Limits

Copyright doctrine is replete with judicial pronouncements emphasising the breadth and generosity of the concept of originality. In the now classic words of Peterson J. in *University of London Press v. University Tutorial Press*, "[t]he word does not mean that the work must be the expression of original or inventive thought [but that] the expression must originate from the author, the result of his/her own efforts, and not copied from another work."[24] Originality is established in this sense when the author shows that the work came into being as a result of his or her own effort, and the amount of effort expended may well be slight. But where a work has indeed been copied from another work, effort expended in the process of copying, no matter how considerable, will not count towards the assessment of the product's originality. As Lord Oliver has said, in the context of a case in which a drawing was produced from a pre-existing drawing with very minor visual alterations:

> Skill, labour or judgment merely in the process of copying cannot confer originality . . . There must in addition be some element of material alteration or embellishment which suffices to make the totality of the work an original work. Of course, even a relatively small alteration or addition quantitatively may, if material, suffice to convert that which is substantially copied from an earlier work into an original work. Whether it does so or not is a question of degree having regard to the quality rather than the quantity of the addition. But copying, *per se*, however much skill or labour may be devoted to the process, cannot make an original work.[25]

Thus the criterion of originality, though not a bar to the protectibility of a new *composition* of pre-existing graphic elements, will operate to exclude

---

[24] Peterson J. in *University of London Press Ltd. v. University Tutorial Press Ltd.* [1916] 2 Ch. 601, at 608–609; *Sands & McDougall Pty Ltd v. Robinson* (above n. 12 of page 65).
[25] *per* Lord Oliver, *Interlego AG v. Tyco Industries Inc.* above at p. 66, n. 19 at 971–972.

individual elements within the composition to the extent that these have been copied. The effect of this exclusion is to eliminate protection for the clan designs which, amongst the Yolngu, are the most sacred manifestations of the clan's ancestral past[26] for it is in relation to these geometric patterns that the cultural imperative of accurate reproduction is most urgent. Whatever creative initiative is permitted to the artist in depicting the (less sacred) figurative elements of a painting,[27] or in putting these together with geometric elements, deviation from the ancestrally authorised pattern manifested in clan designs is frowned upon. Thus the very aspects of a painting that constitute its value and significance in Aboriginal terms are likely to be dismissed as lacking originality in terms of copyright law. The implications of this exclusion are serious, for it is clear from the case law on copyright infringement that a part of a work which by itself has no originality will not normally count as a 'substantial part' of the work such that its reproduction would constitute an infringement.[28] Thus whereas the Morning Star Pole produced by Terry Yumbulul could not, as an original sculpture or work of artistic craftsmanship, be reproduced in its entirety without his permission, the sacred clan designs appearing on the Pole, assuming that they were accurately depicted, would presumably have been regarded as available for general use.

Also available for general use as a matter of copyright law are the themes and scenes—the sacred 'stories'—depicted in works of Aboriginal art. This is in part an effect of the law's refusal to accommodate ideas or concepts as protectible components of a work, but it also manifests the rigid distinctions that the law maintains between the expressive modalities that are deemed to be characteristic of the works that it protects. The category 'artistic work' contemplates material which is "visually significant"[29]: an artistic work is something which can be appreciated by the eye; its essence consists in the fact that it can be seen, not read. The category 'literary work', on the other hand, deals with material which is meaningful: a literary work "contains information and can be read by somebody."[30] This categorical separation of the visual from the meaningful extends to the rules on infringement of artistic and literary copyright: neither expressing visual material in verbal form nor giving the form of a visual representation to written matter amounts to a taking of the work which can be enjoined by the copyright owner.

[A] written verbal description of an artistic work, however precise and explicit, is not an infringement of any copyright subsisting in that work. That, of course, is because the two media are so completely different that one can never, in a real sense, be a medium in which it is

---

[26] See text accompanying, nn. 48 and 49, above.
[27] Morphy, supra n. 40, pp. 153–154.
[28] s.14(1)(a) of the CA; *Warwick Film Productions Ltd v. Eisinger* (1969) 1 Ch. 508.
[29] *Interlego v. Tyco*, above at p. 66, n. 19, at 974.
[30] *Anacon Corporation Ltd v. Environmental Research Technology Ltd* [1994] F.S.R. 659.

possible to reproduce the other—just as a painting cannot be played on a gramophone record.[31]

Protection of the meanings encoded by Aboriginal iconography is therefore only possible insofar as the status of the graphic work as 'artistic' is denied. But even then, the likelihood of their being protected bears an inverse relationship to their importance within the Aboriginal system of knowledge. Morphy characterises 'inside' (secret/sacred) knowledge as "concerned with the more general, with the more true, with the underlying properties of things, with the generation of surface events."[32] A painting's most restricted and most sacred meaning, therefore, is its 'deepest', most general meaning, but a meaning located at a "layer of abstraction"[33] within the work which is likely, as far as copyright is concerned, to lie beyond the boundary separating protectible expression from unprotectible idea. Lawton J.'s dictum in *Merchandising Corporation of American Inc v. Harpbond Ltd*[34] that "a painting is not an idea: it is an object"[35] conveys what is at stake here—the urge to reduce the intangible to the (legally) manageable—even as it displays a certain confusion as to the conceptual distinction between works and physical objects, or between the requirement of expressive form and the requirement of fixation. In *Harbond* itself, paint applied to a human face was held not to constitute an artistic work because "paint without a surface is not a painting":[36] if this is so, then the category of the artistic work in turn excludes characteristically Aboriginal practices such as body art, sand painting, and possibly also rock art.[37]

The denial of protection to clan designs and Dreaming stories demonstrates the limits of the legal construct of the original work in the face of conventions which constitute 'the painting' otherwise than as a visual form owing its source to the individual who inscribes its surface. Difficulties of a similar order attend the interpretation of the concept of authorship in law. Aboriginal ideology subscribes to a notion of authorship which encompasses both human and spiritual entities, and indeed refers the agency of the former to the power of the latter: "[c]lan designs", as Morphy points out, "were created through ancestral action."[38] It hardly needs to be stated that the author contemplated by the Copyright Act is a human person: Dreaming ancestors, it seems safe

---

[31] *Plix Products Limited v. Frank M Winstone* [1986] F.S.R. 63, 90, *per* Prichard J., *Catnic Components Ltd v. Hill & Smith Ltd.* [1982] R.P.C. 183.
[32] Morphy, above n. 40, p. 83.
[33] *Nichols v. Universal Pictures* (1930) 45 F. 2d 119.
[34] above n. 21.
[35] *Merchandising Corporation of America Inc v. Harpbond Ltd*, above n. 21, at 46.
[36] *ibid.*
[37] It is not clear whether Lawton J.'s objection to the face as an appropriate surface for a painting was based on the fact that facial make-up is not designed to be permanent—"if the marks are taken off the face there cannot be a painting" (*ibid.* at 46)—or on his perception that the make-up took its form in part from a pre-existing natural surface—"if there were a painting, it must be the marks plus Mr Goddard's face" (*ibid.*).
[38] Morphy, above n. 40, p. 179.

to say, would not be regarded as loci of creative potency in the sense relevant to the Copyright Act 1968,[39] and ancient graphic patterns would be attributed in the eyes of the law to some human originator, whose work, given that s/he is indeed "long dead" would now be in the public domain. Authorship, and the prerogatives deriving from it, proceed for copyright purposes from the act of originating the expressive form of the work.[40] Aboriginal norms, on the other hand, attribute the work to the person who has initiated the *recreation* of a Dreaming event in the form of a work: the key issue in determining attribution is not whether that person has originated the expressive form,[41] but whether he or she could claim an appropriate spiritual link with what it depicts. For copyright law, the right of the human author to produce works and to accede to a proprietary interest in them is taken as given by her capacity for originality and nothing more: the birth of the modern copyright system as a regime of property as opposed to a regime of regulation[42] is marked by its separation both from a system of censorship of works and from guild practices that made proprietorship of works dependent upon status. Within Aboriginal communities, by contrast, status (one's 'country'—which in turn depends on place of conception, birth and residence—clan membership, gender, age) determines both *who* can produce and *what* can be produced by those so privileged. The capacity for authorship is not given by the presumed autonomy of the individual, but is an effect of spiritual affinities and social relations; the author's body of work is an inheritance, the content of which is pre-determined and which it is the author's right and obligation to reveal.

The webs of kinship with place, persons and spirit ancestors which position and structure authorial capacities in turn generate complex systems of entitlement which are not remotely analogous to the scheme of rights recognised by copyright law. The law's single concession to the notion that authorship might be a collective rather than an individual achievement is the concept of joint authorship, but this is recognised only where two or more persons have actively collaborated[43] in the production of the expressive form of a specific work.[44] Although works of

---

[39] In *Cummins v. Bond* [1927] 1 Ch. 167, Eve J. rejected the proposition that writings produced by a medium while under the alleged influence of an external psychic agent could not be the work of the plaintiff medium since she was "the mere conduit pipe by which it has been conveyed to this world" (*ibid.* at 175). "I can only look upon the matter as a terrestrial one, of the earth earthy, and . . . [i]n my opinion the plaintiff has made out her case" (*ibid.*).

[40] *cf. Cala Homes (South) Ltd. v. Alfred McAlpine Homes East Ltd* [1995] F.S.R. 818, where Laddie J. dismissed the suggestion that authorship is reducible to mere penmanship but agreed that it does at least connote a contribution to the expressive form assumed by the work.

[41] "People who initiate the choice of Dreaming event to be depicted will always present themselves as the painter even if they have been assisted by other people and, occasionally, even if they have done none of the actual painting themselves." C. Anderson and F. Dussart, "Dreamings in Acrylic: Western Desert Art" in P. Sutton (ed.) *Dreamings*, above n. 91, pp. 103–5.

[42] Rose, *Authors and Owners*, above n. 1, p. 15.

[43] "What the claimant to joint authorship of a work must establish is that he has made a significant and original contribution to the creation of the work and that he has done so pursuant to a common design" (*per* Blackburne J. in *Godfrey v. Lees* [1995] E.M.L.R. 307, 325).

[44] s.10(1) CA; *Cala Homes*, above n. 40.

Aboriginal art are often produced by groups of individuals, such groups do not necessarily coincide with clan membership, but since authorship is closely linked with proprietorship in copyright law, joint authors will jointly own the copyright in the resulting work. Under Aboriginal law on the other hand, clans own their Dreaming stories and any depictions of them. Joint ownership apart, it is difficult to imagine circumstances in which copyright ownership could be mapped onto the Aboriginal concept of clan ownership of sacred images and designs, but even if it could, the unification of copyright ownership in a single entity, albeit a collective one, would not mirror the distribution of rights among individual members of the clan. According to a leading anthropologist of Yolngu art, rights in paintings and other sacred artefacts under Yolngu customary law must be distinguished from ownership of paintings.[45] The particular rights that Yolngu law recognises as existing in relation to sacred things—rights to produce paintings and to divulge their meanings, for example—are distributed widely among clan members: some individuals have rights of one kind, others rights of another kind, and some have no rights at all, and it makes no sense to speak of the clan as having these rights, despite the fact that it owns that in which they subsist. The 'community', then, is a thoroughly inapt representation of the locus of entitlements under Yolngu law, convenient though it may be as a unified site of attribution which Anglo-Australian copyright law can recognise.

How does this cluster of legal exclusions and limitations connect with those effected by the unwritten rules of art? For Jaszi and Woodmansee, the link is clearly and unambiguously to be found in Romantic aesthetics:

> With its emphasis on originality and self-declaring genius, [the Romantic] notion of authorship has functioned to marginalise or deny the work of . . . artists working in traditional forms and genres . . . Our intellectual property law has evolved alongside of and to a surprising degree in conformity with Romantic literary theory. At the center—indeed, the linchpin—of Anglo-American copyright as well as of Continental "authors' rights" is a thoroughly Romantic conception of authorship.

For Rosemary Coombe, too, the connections between the exclusionary logics of copyright and Romanticism are undeniable: copyright, she argues, "developed to protect the expressive works of authors and artists—increasingly perceived in Romantic terms of individual genius and transcendant creativity . . ."[46] and now supports and sustains the Western art system—"'Culture' with a capital C".[47] Despite the apparent plausibility of these explanations—for the legal formula identifying the

---

[45] Morphy, above at p. 48, n. 40, p. 57.
[46] R. Coombe, "The Properties of Culture", above n. 88, p. 258.
[47] *ibid.* p. 256.

quality in a work which will guarantee its protection by copyright law, original expression, certainly calls to mind the Romantic aesthetic—they are not adequate to the task of grasping either the encounter between Aboriginal creative practices and the rules of art, or the connections between those rules and the norms of copyright. Romanticism, it will be argued, has actually been irrelevant to the assessment of the aesthetic value of Aboriginal works: it is Modernism, and art critical movements forged in relation to Modernism, that have figured these works in the artistic domain. Further, while there are certain resemblances between the doctrinal categories of copyright and those of Abstractionist-Modernism, these cannot be regarded as effects of the determining influence of aesthetics upon law.

A belief in originality is one of a cluster of ideas which from the latter part of the eighteenth century produced "a new attitude towards art with new concepts of its functions and new standards of assessment."[48] As well as the exaltation of originality, Osborne has identified as the characteristic ideas of Romanticism "the elevation of the artist, the new value set on experience as such with a special emphasis on the affective and emotional aspects of experience, and the new importance attached to fiction and invention."[49] Within the Romantic aesthetic, the artist is no longer (as within the Classical tradition) a 'seer', acting through art as a channel for a divine message: now he or she is a 'genius' equipped with an exceptional intellectual and spiritual endowment, which manifests itself in breaking rules, departing from traditions, effecting break-throughs, that is in originality. Fine art, Kant argued, "is only possible as a product of genius", and "originality must be its primary property".[50] There is a "complete opposition between genius and the spirit of imitation",[51] as there also is between genius and mere craft or technique. The wellspring of original creative endeavour, inspiration, ceases to be seen as the effect of a (divine) force acting upon the artist from outside, and is conceived of as having its source in the unconscious part of his or her own being[52]: thus the real subject of every work of art is the artist, and the compulsion to express oneself comes to mark out the artistic sensibility. "By expressing his superior nature, embodying his superior endowment in his art, it was held that the artist-genius could enable less fortunate men through the medium of the art work to make contact with him and benefit from the communion with the artist's personality."[53] It followed that it was acceptable to appraise the work of art by reference to the quality of the artist's personality or the quality of the emotions communicated: "Art should communicate shades and colours of feelings

---

[48] H. Osborne, *Aesthetics and Art Theory* above n. 2, p. 132.
[49] *ibid.*
[50] I. Kant, *The Critique of Judgement*, quoted in Osborne, above n. 2, p. 133.
[51] *ibid.*
[52] *ibid.* p. 139.
[53] *ibid.* p. 134.

not otherwise accessible or enable the observer to experience standard emotions with fresh insight or vividness, thus adding an increment to the sum total of human experience."[54] Indeed it becomes incumbent on the artist to extend his or her actual experience by sympathetic imagination through the invention of fictitious situations or identities.[55]

There is, admittedly, the faintest echo of Romanticism's rejection of 'the spirit of imitation' in the legal requirement that a work be not copied in order to qualify for copyright protection. But as has been shown, the legal criterion of originality excludes only slavish copies, copies which exemplify no 'material alteration or embellishment' of the work of another. The criterion of originality, then, is no bar to the protection of a work which incorporates pre-existing material and is, to that extent, imitative. Nor must the material addition be the outcome of imaginative endeavour: the claimant must simply demonstrate the expenditure of his or her own skill, labour, judgment or capital (the formulation varies) in its production. It is therefore very difficult to see in the legal concept of originality the clear reflection of Romantic aesthetics that Jaszi and Woodmansee *et aliter* claim to find. But in any case, the admission of Aboriginal works to the artistic canon has never depended on their fulfilling the criteria established by Romantic theory. Morphy notes that the fine art market, if not the theorisations that support its operation, appears to be able to sustain a variety of often contradictory criteria for the evaluation of Arnhem Land art: these include both 'craft' values and criteria derived from indigenous modes of valorisation (*i.e* criteria which judge its 'authenticity', whether it is significant within the Aboriginal frame),[56] neither of which, clearly, are compatible with the rules of Romantic aesthetic doctrine. Further, to the extent that Aboriginal works have been subjected to art critical analysis, they have been valorised in relation to the norms of modernist aesthetics, which are characterised by a fundamental *break* with Romanticism. Modernist criticism conceives of the work as a self-contained, autonomous object, possessed of an intrinsic nature which is independent of the personality or intentions of the artist who created it. In literary theory, this reification of the work has manifested itself in an exclusive concern with the 'words on the page': with the work as "existing for its own sake"[57]—regardless of its meaning for the author or its effect on the reader—as an organic artefact with its own integrity and coherence. Writing in 1946, two prominent New Critics, W.K. Wimsatt and Monroe Beardsley, denounced "intentionalism" as a romantic "fallacy",[58] Wimsatt subsequently defining the proper domain of literary criticism as "the verbal object and its analysis",[59] and

[54] *ibid.* p. 135.
[55] *ibid.* p. 136.
[56] Morphy, above at p. 48, n. 40 pp. 22–23; P. Anderson, "Aboriginal Imagery: Influence, Appropriation or Theft?" (1990) 12 *Eyeline* 8–11.
[57] J.C. Ransom, "Criticism Inc." (1937), reprinted in D. Lodge (ed.), *Twentieth Century Literary Criticism* (Longman, London, 1972), pp. 228–239, 236.
[58] "The Intentional Fallacy", reprinted in W.K. Wimsatt, *The Verbal Icon* (Lexington University of Kentucky Press, 1967).
[59] "The Domain of Criticism", *ibid.* pp. 221–232, 232.

railing against the "injustices" perpetrated against the verbal medium by "three centuries of insistent parallel between the arts and the furious melange of media which ushered in the . . . era of general aesthetics."[60] This resistance to any mode of evaluating the aesthetic object—such as by reference to the mind of an artist—which ignores the specificity of its medium and its form is also evident within modernist art theory. Clement Greenberg's critical method is informed by the conviction that art finds in its own 'purity' (that which is unique and irreducible not only in art in general but in each particular art, such as painting or sculpture) "the guarantee of its standards of quality as well as of its independence."[61] Thus "visual art should confine itself exclusively to what is given in visual experience, and make no reference to anything given in any other order of experience".[62] More particularly, "[t]he essential norms or conventions of painting [particularly flatness, two-dimensionality] are at the same time the limiting conditions with which a picture must comply in order to be experienced as a picture."[63] The measure of a painting's quality, then, is to be found in the standards of achievement—as realised within the painting of the past—peculiar to that medium.

Arguably (and notwithstanding the comparisons with Pollock), it was in relation to standards such as these, and not the artist-centric norms of Romanticism, that Aboriginal works came to be valorised as art in the 1970s and 1980s. 'In relation to', because these works emerged as objects of aesthetic consideration at a moment of contestation in the history of modern art: they were perceived simultaneously as consistent with the Abstractionist-Modernism of Greenberg and his followers, and as cap-able of being enlisted in the attack on Greenbergian judgements of quality and relevance that was gathering steam from the late 1960s onwards. Thus on the one hand they could be viewed as abstract forms, obeying the purely visual logic of that emblematic modernist figure, the 'grid'.[64] The grid is a pure, evacuated surface: it is "an absolute beginning . . . [a] fresh start, a ground zero,"[65] and it is in the finding of this ground "by peeling back layer after layer of representation",[66] rather than in the individual feeling which animates it, that the artist's act of originality is to be located. Within this aesthetic, too, inspiration is theorised as a purely visual conception rather than as an unconscious force: "The *exact* choices of colour, medium, size, shape, proportion—including the size or

[60] ibid., p. 225.
[61] C. Greenberg, "Modernist Painting" in Clement Greenberg: The Collected Essays and Criticism Volume 4, above n. 85–93, p. 86.
[62] ibid. p. 91.
[63] ibid., p. 89.
[64] For an explanation of the significance of the grid for the artistic avant garde, see R. Krauss, The Originality of the Avant Garde and Other Modernist Myths (MIT, Cambridge, Mass., 1985), pp. 151–170. For a survey of attempts to explain Western Desert paintings in terms of a grid structure, see N. Baume, "The Interpretation of Dreamings", above at p. 63, n. 6, pp. 114–116.
[65] Krauss, ibid. p. 158.
[66] ibid.

shape of the support—are what alone determines the quality of the result, and these choices depend . . . on inspiration or conception."[67]

The modalities of exclusion within this version of modernism are quite specific to the discourse. Greenberg characterises the visual art of the avant garde as the child but also the negation of Romanticism,[68] and identifies as "the first and most important item upon its agenda . . . the necessity of an escape from ideas, which were infecting the arts with the ideological struggles of society. Ideas came to mean subject matter in general. . . . This meant a new and greater emphasis upon form . . ."[69] It also involved, concomitantly, an assertion of the absolute autonomy of the separate arts, and in particular, an insistence on the entitlement of painting and sculpture—the central forms of visual art—"to respect for their own sakes, and not merely as vessels of communication".[70] Thus, as well as a separation of form from ideas, Greenberg's avant-garde observes a further distinction between art and text, the field of the former being radically delimited from that of the latter. Referring with approval to the passing of art's subservience to literature after the 17th century, Greenberg writes that "[t]he arts lie safe now, each within its own 'legitimate' boundaries. . . Purity in art consists in the acceptance, the willing acceptance, of the limitations of the medium of the specific art."[71] For painting, this 'surrender' necessitates a rejection of any attempt to create an illusion of three-dimensional space: painting must therefore resist the sculptural, since three dimensionality is the province of sculpture. "Flatness alone [is] unique and exclusive to pictorial art",[72] and even a stretched canvas already exists as a picture, albeit not necessarily as a successful one.[73] But not all marks upon the canvas are truly painterly:

> Painting abandons chiaroscuro and shaded modelling. Brush strokes are often defined for their own sake. . . Primary colors, the "instinctive", easy color, replace tones and tonality. Line, which is one of the most abstract elements in painting since it is never found in nature as the definition of contour, returns to oil painting as the third color between two other color areas. Under the influence of the square shape of the canvas, forms tend to become geometrical—and sim-plified, because simplification is also a part of the instinctive accomodation to the medium. But most important of all, the picture plane itself grows shallower and shallower, flattening out and pressing together the fictive planes of depth until they meet as one upon the real and material plane which is the actual surface of the canvas . . .[74]

---

[67] C. Greenberg, "After Abstract Expressionism" in *Clement Greenberg: The Collected Essays and Criticism Volume 4*, above n. 5 (emphasis in original) p. 132.
[68] C. Greenburg, "Towards a Newer Laocoon" in J. O'Brian (ed.) *Clement Greenberg: The Collected Essays and Criticism Volume 1* (University of Chicago Press, Chicago 1986).
[69] *ibid.*
[70] *ibid.*
[71] *ibid.*, p. 32.
[72] C. Greenburg, "Modernist Painting", above n. 61, p. 87.
[73] C. Greenburg, "After Abstract Expressionism", above n. 5, pp. 131–132.
[74] C. Greenberg, "Towards a Newer Laocoon", above n. 68, pp. 34–35.

Sculpture, meanwhile, is required to display its constructed-ness. It is the juxtaposition of the elements comprised in the work—their discontinuity—rather than the coherent object that they compose, that gives it 'abstractness' and so enables it to escape "the illusion of organic substance or texture".[75]

Aboriginal art, even as "primitive" art, could be accommodated within these norms: "Oriental, primitive and children's art", Greenburg was prepared to acknowledge, could be pointed to "as instances of the universality and naturalness and objectivity of [the] ideal of purity"[76]—proof, for him, that this ideal was no mere "bias in taste".[77] Thus, the apparently abstract, geometric flatness of the Aboriginal painting, and particularly the brightly coloured dot canvases of the Western Desert, would have readily appealed to this Modernist sensibility. But the grid could be as reductive as it was inclusive: Baume, for example, draws attention to "the limiting, conservative nature of this desire for systematisation" of Western Desert painting and argues that "[t]he flat, geometrical, ordered, mechanical, "scientific" grid is inadequate to characterise either the surface or structure of Aboriginal acrylics."[78] Further, the idea/form and art/text dichotomies operated to dismiss, as irrelevant to their appreciation as art, the narrative content of Aboriginal works, just as the notion of purity and autonomy ruled out any consideration of the context of their making in ceremonial practices, much less their significance as part of a strategy of political resistance. And in the following telling passage, having identified the norms that constitute the medium of painting (the flat surface, the shape of the support, and the properties of pigment: finish; paint texture; value and colour contrast), Greenberg clarifies the limits of his aesthetic's capacity to incorporate characteristically 'primitive' surfaces which ignore these technical conventions:

> The making of pictures has been controlled, since it first began, by all the norms I have mentioned. The Palaeolithic painter or engraver could disregard the norm of the frame and treat the surface in a literally sculptural way only because he made images rather than pictures, and worked on a support—a rock wall, a bone, a horn, or a stone—whose limits and surface were arbitrarily given by nature. But the making of pictures means, among other things, the deliberate creating or choosing of a flat surface, and the deliberate circumscribing and limiting of it. This deliberateness is precisely what Modernist painting harps on: the fact, that is, that the limiting conditions of art are altogether human conditions. . . .[79]

It was precisely the arrogance of this claim to the universal validity of Greenberg's 'limiting conditions' that provoked a series of challenges to

---

[75] C. Greenberg, "Sculpture in Our Time" in *Clement Greenberg: The Collected Essays and Criticism Volume 4*, above n. 5, pp. 55–61, 59.
[76] "Towards a Newer Laocoon", above n. 68, p. 32.
[77] *ibid.*
[78] N. Baume, above n. 6, p. 115.
[79] "Modernist Painting", above n. 6, p. 92.

his formalism from the late 1960s onwards. One of these counter-tendencies found expression in Conceptual Art, which problematised the assumption that art is purely and primordially visual. "In conceptual art the idea or concept is the most important aspect of the work."[80] Further, "[t]he idea itself, even if not made visual, is as much a work of art as any finished product. . . . Conceptual art is made to engage the mind of the viewer rather than his eye or emotions."[81] Thus the form of this art is unimportant: ideas may be stated not merely in two–and three–dimensional images, but with "numbers, photographs, or words or in any way the artist chooses."[82] For Baume, it was Conceptual Art which, more than any other contemporary art form, paved the way for the reception of Aboriginal acrylics, despite the lack of visual similarity between the two genres. "[It is the *idea* rather than the *touch* which may confer authorship in Aboriginal art. So too is the case with LeWitt, whose wall drawings, for example, "exist" whether drawn or not. . . . In a neo-Conceptualist age, the lingering desire to look beyond the painted surface to its conceptual basis is gratified by Aboriginal art."[83] Here again, however, the analogy contains its own limits, for the 'concepts' revealed by Aboriginal works resist translation into the lexicon of secular Western understanding: "we are more impressed by the fact of signifi-cance than the content so signified."[84]

It has been argued that Modernism, rather than Romanticism, must be the crucial reference point in any history of the construction of Abori-ginal creative practices as art. What then of the aesthetic determination thesis? Could it be argued that, as the influence of Romanticism on the practice and evaluation of the arts has waned in the twentieth century, so copyright has absorbed and codified the characteristic tenets of this more recent paradigm of aesthetic evaluation? For the American copyright scholar, Robert Rotstein, there is indeed a clear and direct link between modernist criticism and copyright's concept of the work: "copyright has generally embraced the New Critical idea of the 'work' as an object with fixed characteristics existing independently of context and audience."[85] Rotstein therefore argues that the modernist work, rather than the Romantic author, is now "the central focus" in the determination of originality (as well as other key issues in copyright disputes) under US copyright law[86]: he attempts to illustrate "the evolution of the notion of originality from a standard requiring a Romantic level of originality to a standard that focuses merely on the existence of variations between works."[87] Viewed from this perspective, he argues,

---

[80] S. LeWitt "Paragraphs on Conceptual Art" (1967) in C. Harrison and P. Wood (eds.) *Art in Theory* (Blackwell, Oxford, 1992) pp. 834–837, 834.

[81] *ibid.* p. 836.

[82] *ibid.* p. 837.

[83] Baume, above at p. 63, n. 6, pp. 117–118.

[84] *ibid.* p. 116.

[85] R. Rotstein, "Beyond Metaphor: Copyright Infringement and the Fiction of the Work" (1993) 68 *Chicago-Kent Law Review* 725, 741.

[86] *ibid.* 742.

[87] *ibid.* 743.

[T]he level of creativity necessary to support "copyrightability" has little to do with author and everything to do with difference. A work of "authorship" is original if it is different from other works, no matter how slight the difference and no matter how the difference arises. For copyright, it is the attempt to draw boundaries between works that becomes important in deciding whether a work may receive protection. . . .[88]

Considered in relation to the Romantic-determination thesis outlined above, this is certainly a more plausible attempt to root the legal concept of originality in aesthetic theory, not least because it explains the law's (surprising, from a Romantic perspective) generosity towards works based on pre-existing sources. And although Rotstein's analysis is chiefly focused on copyright's connections with literary New Criticism, one could, without too much difficulty, equally identify how its categories and distinctions mirror those enforced by Modernist art theory. The idea/expression dichotomy recalls Greenberg's separation of idea from form. The definition of the 'artistic work' in terms of what is visually significant, and the strict demarcation of the artistic from the literary (as well as the dramatic and the musical), calls to mind Greenberg's insistence that "visual art should confine itself exclusively to what is given in visual experience, and make no reference to anything given in any other order of experience. . . . Modernist painting asks that a literary theme be translated into strictly optical two-dimensional terms before becoming the subject of pictorial art—which means its being translated in such a way that it entirely loses its literary character."[89] The legal requirement that a 'painting' must, if nothing else, have a 'surface'—preferably a flat surface—is uncannily similar to Greenberg's identification of the flat surface as the key limiting condition of painting as an art form. And so on.

Interesting though these convergences are, they are, however, simply that: convergences. Johnny Bulun Bulun's case itself provides a striking instance of the radical *singularity* of the law's categories and procedures, at the same time as it shows how these can form any number of contingent *connections* with the equally singular constructions and methods of judgment prevailing in other domains. Here, gallery curators, art advisors and dealers in fine art were called upon to offer their assessments of Bulun Bulun's works. Some of these assessments focused on the look of the works themselves, but the criteria invoked were varied, combining 'craft' values with an analysis of their visual and conceptual density. The works were said to display a considerable amount of skill in their execution: the lines were fine, detailed and precise; the paintings as a whole were "very decorative, very busy and very nicely composed";[90] their style was distinctive to the artist; and they

---

[88] *ibid.* 746.
[89] Greenburg, "Modernist Painting", above at p. 75, n. 61, p. 86.
[90] M. West, quoted in Golvan, above n. 14, p. 350.

had "strong story content."[91] One deponent invoked the notion of rarity: "[h]is work is . . . not readily available."[92] These judgments were mixed together with other, non-aesthetic, modes of evaluation. Emphasis was placed on the physical labour involved in producing the works: "people who produce this kind of work often complain of backache from sitting over a painting, as well as eyestrain."[93] Reference was made to the high prices the works were able to command in the market—"[h]is work sells for between $600 and $5000. There are few living Aboriginal bark painters who can command fees of over $5000 for their work"[94]—as well as to the fact of the plaintiff's standing within the institutions of high art: he had an "established exhibition record and artistic reputation"[95] and his works had been acquired by a number of major galleries. Finally, evaluations of the works were offered which hinted at their meaning and significance for Bulun Bulun's clan: Bulun Bulun's "detailed personal knowledge of the country of his tribe, through his hunting and cere- monial experiences . . . guides [him] in his attention to detail, for which his works are much sought after. He is amongst a small group of artists . . . entitled by tribal custom to depict designs in very precise detail, with this entitlement following from the skill he has demonstrated in under- standing the dreaming stories of his tribe and by virtue of his particular gifts as an artist."[96]

As well as confirming that, as a practical matter, the criteria for admission of the Aboriginal work to the category of fine art are varied and even contradictory—is it visual form, signed object, art gallery exhibit, commodity, craft, ritual artefact?—this case also casts doubt on any attempt to reduce the legal decision to a single external logic. In the event, the originality of Bulun Bulun's works was never subjected to formal judicial analysis—because, as with so many copyright disputes, the procedural machinery of the interlocutory injunction, strategically deployed by counsel, deterred the defendant from proceeding to trial. In this practical manner, the legal issues were resolved and Bulun Bulun's paintings institutionally affirmed as copyright works, just as they had already acquired the separate positive status of works of art. Even if their originality or his authorship had been tested at trial, the legal assessment of these matters would have depended upon the application of doctrinal criteria which are internal to the legal institution. Any attempt to assimilate the development of copyright doctrine to that of aesthetic discourse therefore misreads as the necessary effect of an external determination what is better seen as a series of fortuitous intersections. What these intersections yield, nonetheless, is a discursive *apparatus* (Saunders' "grid") which constructs as aesthetically and legally signifi-

[91] K. Steinberg, *ibid.*
[92] *ibid.*
[93] P. Cooke, *ibid.*
[94] *ibid.*
[95] W. Caruana, *ibid.*
[96] C. Godjuwa, *ibid.*

cant (though in different ways and for different reasons) an object whose identity is constituted by what it negates: an autonomous (not dependent on context or audience) form (not the ideas underlying it), pure in its visuality (to be appreciated by the eye, not read), and materialised in a particular kind of thing (though not just any thing), for which some human hand (an individual, not collective, intentionality) is responsible.[97] An object, in short, by and for a subject.

V Transgressions

By 1991, when Terry Yumbulul's action came to trial, Aboriginal painting and sculpture had become acknowledged both as art forms and as 'works' in which copyright could subsist. This paper has attempted a history of these developments with a view to thinking their relatedness in ways that avoid reducing the one to the force exerted by the other. It is a history which makes no claim to be complete, for the lines of connection linking the aesthetic and legal with the economic, political, and social meanings— and the associated practical logics—of Aboriginal cultural production are in principle endless. Amidst the fortuitousness and contingency of these connections, however, is to be found a certain intelligibility: the encounter between the Aboriginal work and the order of Western art and law has been marked by a movement of incorporation and reduction—of the other into the same. Modernist art criticism redeemed the Aboriginal 'cultural artefact' as art only by subjecting it to a de-contextualisation and a radical abstraction that permitted the critic's norms of visuality to be projected onto the surface of the work: it discovered 'affinities' in what were nothing more than morphological coincidences.[98] In consequence, not surprisingly, it found a universality of form in place of "different orders of the socius and of the subject, of the economy of the object and of the place of the artist."[99] Difference has been (literally) seen as visual innovation under-pinned by a more fundamental formal continuity, and thereby misrecog-nised as sameness. As a result, Aboriginal motifs have now become available for use by Western artists as part of a common iconographic heritage, a universal language of imagery.[1]

For copyright law, likewise, accomodation has been accompanied by a series of reductions: of the spiritual to the economic, the inalienable to the saleable, the ritual process to the commodifiable thing, the situated, already-obligated self to the originary and originating author-proprietor.

---

[97] "The painting is a signed object as much as it is a painted surface." (J. Baudrillard, *For a Critique of the Political Economy of the Sign*, above n. 27, p. 102.

[98] See the reviews of the Museum of Modern Art's 1984 exhibition, "'Primitivism' in the Twentieth Century: Affinity of the Tribal and the Modern" in Clifford, *The Predicament of Culture* (above n. 88) pp. 189–214 and H. Foster, *Recodings: Art, Spectacle, Cultural Politics* (Bay Press, Seattle, Wash., 1985), pp. 181–194. See further T. Fry and A. Willis, "Aboriginal Art: Symptom of Success?" (1989) *Art in America*, pp. 108–116, 159–163.

[99] Foster, *ibid.* p. 186.

[1] See the essays in S. Cramer (ed.), *Postmodernism: a Consideration of the Appropriation of Aboriginal Imagery* (Institute of Modern Art, Brisbane, 1989).

However much these dual recodings of Aboriginal objects as cultural and economic 'currency' may be represented as effects of progress and enlightenment, they are achieved, as Hal Foster has noted, precisely through the denial of their "colonialist condition of possibility."[2] The dynamics of this repression can be seen very clearly in *Yumbulul* itself. Here the Aboriginal image is literally appropriated as, and for, currency: the banknote requires the Morning Star Pole to signal (and celebrate) the moment of Australia's colonisation by the forbears of its white inhabitants, notwithstanding that the very foundation of 'Australia' had been premised upon the negation of the Aboriginal. As Brennan J. observed in *Mabo v. Queensland*,[3] "[the] dispossession [of the Aborigines] underwrote the development of the nation."[4] As the internationalisation of Australia's economic links and demographic structure has diminished the Crown's resonance as the definitive sign of Australian nationhood, Aboriginal imagery has emerged as a mine of symbolic resources with which to forge a new identity founded on a romance of the mysterious bush and its indigenous inhabitants. This 'ethnocide' "does not massacre and imprison and institutionalise a subservient people, but more gently . . . absorbs the values of the peripheral culture into the larger system of the dominant one."[5] Absorption, however, is represented as reward: hence French J. in *Yumbulul* can admonish the plaintiff's clan elders for their resistance to the reproduction of the Morning Star Pole on the ground that it "was, and should be seen, as a mark of the high respect that has all too slowly developed in Australian society for the beauty and richness of Aboriginal culture." The problem is not simply that the reward—the Pole's elevation to the status of art/copyright work—is inadequate compensation for the injustice which founds it: the ripping of the object from its context—and the constraints that control its use in that context—and the evacuation of its ritual significance. It is also "a repression of the fact that a breakthrough in our art, indeed a regeneration in our culture, is based in part on the breakup and decay of other societies."[6]

What is emphatically blocked in these movements of accomodation is the possibility that the encounter with the Aboriginal could result in the transgression or disruption of the categories that sustain Western art and law. Two antithetical views have emerged as to what form such a 'counterpractice' might take. The first sees in Aboriginal creative practices a prefiguration of postmodern 'intertextuality', an aesthetic of reproduction that refuses the notions of originality and authorial sovereignty: here, the repressed alterity of Aboriginal art re-emerges in

---

[2] Foster, *Recodings*, above n. 98, p. 191; Fry and Willis, "Aboriginal Art: Symptom or Success?", above n. 98.

[3] (1992) 66 A.L.J.R. 408.

[4] *ibid*. at 434.

[5] K. Coutts-Smith, "Australian Aboriginal Art", (1982) 7 *Art Network* 53, 55 (quoted in Marrie, "Killing me Softly", above n. 93, p. 17); Fry and Willis, "Aboriginal Art: Symptom or Success?", above n. 98.

[6] Foster, *Recodings*, above n. 98, pp. 198–9.

contemporary 'appropriation art' as a kind of deracinated 'aboriginality' (the work of Imants Tillers springs to mind here). The second, however, argues that the easy equation of the Aboriginal with the postmodern is itself the effect of a negation: "the sacred is always present as a kind of residue, a disturbance"[7] to any attempt to elide the pre- with the postmodern. Whereas postmodernism assumes that the other's property is always available for re-appropriation, the sacred is that which is recalcitrantly *un*available. A defence of the sacred can be read as a nostalgic gesture to preserve lost aura,[8] but for Ken Gelder, counter-practice is "the binding of the sacred to political resistance"[9] in ways that may involve an increasingly focused rather than a dissipated sense of both property and propriety.[10]

> [T]here would appear to be no clear intersection between a premodern binding of the sacred into localised strategies of non-disclosure and a postcultural mode of being that is ultimately global in its orientations, driven by availability and appropriation—where one resists modernity not through silence or secrecy, but by positive and productive interactions with it.[11]

What this suggests is that resistance to the reductive incorporation of the sacred object respectively as art and as commodity may be furthered by strategies of re-contextualisation (*i.e.* re-placing within an authentic context): the withdrawal of objects from public exhibition, for example, or their placement in "a new type of ethnographic museum"[12] where their ritual significance could be respected; the devising of regimes of cultural rights in which the customary laws of Aboriginal peoples could achieve some institutional force against the individualising structures of copyright law. It is important, however, to be attuned to the essentialism that may be involved in such strategies, or in the service of which they may become enlisted. As Eric Michaels has forcefully argued, Aboriginal artists are not exempted from the postmodern condition. Aboriginal art is a practice of *bricolage* in which indigenous cultural resources are consciously remade and transformed in the encounter with the forms, materials, techniques and institutions of the modern West: it is a "radical invention [which] emerge[s] only in dialogic space."[13] Indeed for Michaels, authenticity may be the Western mystification *par excellence*— and a highly convenient marketing device: "the discourse, the documen-

---

[7] K. Gelder, "Aboriginal Narrative and Property" (1991) Vol. 50(2/3) *Meanjin* 353–365, 361.
[8] S. During, quoted in Gelder, *ibid.* p. 355.
[9] *ibid.*
[10] See also H. Fourmile, "Some Background to Issues Concerning the Appropriation of Aboriginal Imagery" in *Postmodernism: a Consideration of the Appropriation of Aboriginal Imagery* (above n. 41, pp. 6–10); A. Marie, "Killing me Softly", above n. 93.
[11] Gelder, above n. 205, p. 361.
[12] Morphy, above n. 40, p. 25.
[13] E. Michaels, "Postmodernism, Appropriation and Western Desert Acrylics" in *Postmodernism: a Consideration of the Appropriation of Aboriginal Imagery* (above n. 1), pp. 26–34, 29.

tations, the display which are employed to contextualise the work promote only a generalised otherness, a *faux* alterity, a commodified inaccessibility."[14] The resourcefulness and ingenuity with which Aboriginal identities have been articulated with the demands and opportunities of the art world and the market must not be underestimated. The acrylic paintings of Central Australia, certainly, "have not been wrenched out of any proper context. From the very beginning they were intended to be seen 'under Western eyes'; they were made expressly to be appropriated (for a price) into another culture."[15]

Whether the appeal to the object's sacred essence constitutes a strategy of effective resistance or feeds yet another Western fantasy is a matter which cannot be decided in the abstract, or indeed by Western commentators: it is for those actively engaged in local contexts to determine. In general, however, the danger involved in such an invocation is that it risks arbitrarily ossifying both the meaning of Aboriginal art and the norms which regulate it. As Fred Myers has pointed out, "the available meanings to Aborigines of . . . [painting] activity are many. . . . [T]hey include painting as a source of income, painting as a source of cultural respect, painting as a meaningful activity defined by its relationship to indigenous values (in the context of "self-determination"), and also painting as an assertion of personal/socio-political identity expressed in rights to place."[16] For Aboriginal people themselves, at this point in their history, all of these meanings are important; all, for that reason, are 'authentic'. But further, the Aboriginal 'community' is as divided as any other, and the question of how art is to be evaluated is one on which people will disagree. For women, and others historically excluded from the instituted structures of authority within Aboriginal clans, for example, the modes of valorisation obtaining in the spheres of art and the market will often cut against those deriving from traditional sources, frequently to their advantage. Artistic reputation, and the income that comes with it, may therefore provide an alternative route to empowerment over that made available by the rite of initiation: in this context, the invocation of the sacred as the defining essence of the artistic product may well be problematic. It is because of tensions such as these that Aboriginal people are continually called upon to negotiate the contradictions between the available meanings of their artistic practices, and 'indigenous values' have not been immunised from change in this process. Indeed there are signs that, particularly where paintings are produced for sale, women are successfully asserting rights to paint in restricted contexts, thus gaining access to secret knowledge which has

---

[14] *ibid.* 30.

[15] M.R. Rubinstein, "Outstations of the Postmodern" (1989) *Arts Magazine* 40–47, 46. See also L. Taylor, "Making Painting Pay", (1996) 55(4) *Meanjin* 746; R. Benjamin, "Aboriginal Art: Exploitation or Empowerment?" (1990) *Art in America* 73–81; *cf.* Fry and Willis, "Aboriginal Art: Symptom or Success?", above, n. 98.

[16] F. Myers, "Representing Culture: the Production of Discourse(s) for Aboriginal Acrylic Paintings" (1991) 6(1) *Cultural Anthropology* 26–62, 34.

hitherto been regarded as the preserve of initiated men, and so partaking of political power in ways hitherto considered unimaginable. Rules and conventions as to who may paint what, and with what level of understanding, are therefore in a constant state of flux; moreover, these rules "are not uniform throughout the country, but can, and do, vary between groups".[17] Any attempt to codify them in a single regime of cultural rights, then, would confront the "danger of imposing uniformity where none exists and freezing Aboriginal practice at an arbitrary date".[18]

It would, however, head off the uncomfortable challenges which Aboriginal art currently presents to the doctrinal categories of copyright law. This art interrogates copyright's fundamental concepts and distinctions, and demands that their limits be seen neither as necessary nor inevitable, but as particular responses to specific problems, posed in particular ways. Oddly, the approach to copyright law that sees it as locked into a commitment to a now outdated Romantic aesthetic is complicit with the former view. This approach represents the structures of the law as frozen by its adherence to Romanticism and, therefore, monolithically resistant to change: "while [copyright] law participated in the construction of the modern 'author,' it has yet to be affected by the structuralist and poststructuralist 'critique of authorship' that we have been witnessing in literary and cultural studies for several decades."[19] Jaszi and Woodmansee have, it seems, given up on the capacity of what they describe as "mainstream intellectual property law" to facilitate "indigenous peoples' efforts . . . to control the exploitation of their heritage."[20] They call instead for "special regimes" for the protection of "folkloric works" and "works of cultural heritage"[21] emphasising "collective rather than individual entitlement."[22] As well as courting the dangers mentioned above, these solutions leave no room for a positive engagement with copyright law, and refuse the potential for such an engagement to transform its structures and procedures. The project of critique may well include a strategy of devising new regimes of rights which attempt, however crudely, to map Western legislation onto 'indigenous' systems of regulation. But it must also involve an interrogation of the limits that have been inherited from the past. Is it necessarily the case, for example, that works which are entirely derived from a pre-existing source lack originality?[23] Could an artistic work conceivably be copied by means of a verbal description?[24] The persistence of conflicting

---

[17] Anderson, "Aboriginal Imagery", above at p. 74, n. 56, p. 10.
[18] K. Maddock, quoted in Anderson, *ibid.*
[19] Jaszi and Woodmansee, above n. 1, p. 948.
[20] *ibid.*, p. 963.
[21] *ibid.*, p. 969.
[22] *ibid.*, p. 968.
[23] *Walter v. Lane* [1900] A.C. 539 (verbatim report of an orally delivered speech held to be capable of attracting copyright); *Express Newspapers v. News UK* [1990] F.S.R. 359.
[24] *Anacon Corporation Ltd. v. Environmental Research Technology Ltd* [1994] F.S.R. 659 (circuit diagram held to qualify both as a literary and an artistic work; the question of whether it could be copied by means of a verbal description was left open). "My first thought was that it would be absurd to

authorities and ambiguous precedents on these and other issues testify to the lack of closure within legal doctrine, despite the dogmatism with which its dictates tend to be enunciated. Johnny Bulun Bulun's case, indeed, is a striking example of how an imaginative legal strategy could unravel the sense of false necessity generated by the doleful prognostications published in the *Report on the Protection of Aboriginal Folklore* only eight years previously.[25]

There is a more fundamental tendency involved in the impulse to shift the problem of what lies beyond the limit onto another terrain: it rehearses yet again the *necessary* opposition between 'us' and 'them'; 'our' law and 'their' law. For the integrity of our law depends precisely upon its ability to banish any trace of theirs: any element of myth in our notions of authorship or ownership, of ritual in the practices through which we live these statuses, or of the sacred in our concept of the work; any notion that imitation and re-use might be the norm, rather than the antithesis, of authorial practice; any suspicion that the images that we produce might constitute our meanings and identities rather than merely expressing them. The finality of the legal determination in *Yumbulul*, which glibly dismisses the Aboriginal other as *absolutely* other, prevents us from confronting these questions, but at the same time it incites them. In particular, it invites an exploration of the myth of author-ity in Western culture, wherein the originary and originating individual is deemed to be a natural and given reality: the irreducible *a priori* of art and ownership alike. Western conceptions of aesthetic and legal personality, no less than the model of personality to which Terry Yumbulul had been acculturated, require and presuppose rituals of initiation, learning and habituation: different ethics of self-formation, by which these modes of subjectivity are embodied and lived. Thus the aesthetic ethos is "an ethic of withdrawal; . . . a means by which individuals set themselves apart from 'ordinary' existence and conduct themselves as subjects of a

---

regard a circuit diagram as a literary work, but the more one thinks about the ambit of that expression, as used in the Act, the more one is driven to the conclusion that provided it is all written down and contains information which can be read by somebody, as opposed to appreciated simply with the eye, the more one sees that that is just what it is. Similarly musical notation is written down, but needs expressly to be taken out of the definition of 'literary work'. But that which is not expressly taken out remains within it. What one has here is electrical engineer's notation." (*per* Jacob J. at 663). See also *Autospin (Oil Seals) Ltd v. Beehive Spinning* [1995] R.P.C. 683.
[25] At the time of writing, lawyers for Johnny Bulun Bulun's clan are seeking an injunction to prevent the unauthorised reproduction of one of his paintings by exploiting the vagueness inherent in the principle of equitable ownership of copyright. As Sir Mervyn Davies expressed this principle in *A&M Records v. Video Collection* [1995] E.M.L.R. 25, 33: "When A makes or creates a work for B and A becomes at law the owner of the copyright in the work, B will sometimes be regarded as the equitable owner of the copyright and entitled to have an assignment made in his favour by A. B will be so regarded when it is a necessary implication from the facts of the case that copyright should belong to B." Arguably, it is generally a "necessary implication" of the relationship between an Aboriginal artist and his or her clan that the reproduction rights in any paintings made in furtherance of ritual obligations belong to the clan. The application has been brought in the Federal Court in Darwin, before the same judge (von Doussa J.) who, in *Milpurrurru v. Indofurn Pty Ltd* (1994) 54 F.C.R. 240, held that where the unauthorised reproduction of Aboriginal works involves a breach of copyright, anger and distress suffered by the plaintiff artists "in [their] cultural environment" (*ibid.* at 277) could be taken into account in quantifying the damage suffered by them.

heightened form of being:"[26] Hunter identifies as among its leading features "inwardness, attentiveness to subjective states, intensification of imaginative experience, disregard for 'public' appearances, the identification of nobility with self-cultivation, dialectical thinking."[27] Legal personality, on the other hand, requires an ethic whose elements are quite opposed: calculation; instrumental action; the development of capacities for decision-making and contracting; accountability; enterprise. If these personae appear artificial—so obviously *learned*—in relation to Terry Yumbulul himself, perhaps the lesson to be drawn is not that Yumbulul's 'real' Aboriginal identity stands behind and prior to them, but that identity itself—whether Aboriginal, authorial, or proprietorial—is neither natural nor necessary, but historically produced and open to contestation.

*   *   *   *   *   *   *   *

Acknowledgements:

This paper owes its own conditions of possibility to a period spent as a Visiting Fellow in the Law Department at the University of New South Wales in Sydney in 1993. My thanks go to all the members of the Department for their hospitality and encouragement during my stay, and to the Institute for Commonwealth Studies in London which provided financial assistance towards the initial research. Special thanks go to Peter Anderson, Jenny Beard, Andrew Benjamin, David Brown, Colin Golvan, Chips Mackinolty, and Tim Rowse for their time and patience. All errors and omissions are the author's.

---

[26] *ibid.* p. 361.
[27] Hunter, above n. 13, p. 360.

3. Patenting Human Genetic Information. Is Nothing Sacred?

Baljit K. Dhadda

Research student at Queen Mary and Westfield College, London. B.A. History/Politics (Warwick), M.A. Gender and International Development (Warwick). The subject of her research is the patenting of transgenic products that incorporate human biological material.

Patenting Human Genetic Information.
Is Nothing Sacred?*

They've come to take our blood and tissues for their interests, not for ours . . . genetics is a violation of our ethics, it attacks our culture's worldview. We don't view our genes as protein, actions ready to be interpreted, for us our genes are sacred.[1]

I never imagined people would patent plants and animals. It's fundamentally immoral, contrary to the Guaymi view of nature, and our place in it. To patent human material . . . to take human DNA and patent its products . . . that violates the integrity of life itself and our deepest sense of morality.[2]

Introduction

The accelerating pace of patent applications for genetic inventions has been accompanied with lively debate and protest. Disparate social groups, including religious, indigenous and environmental groups, have attempted to thwart applications for the grant of patent rights to human genetic information. The grounds of protest have ranged from concern about the neo-colonial implications of granting patenting control over information derived from human bodies, to ethical and moral concern about the patenting of "life".[3] Attempts to assert patenting rights to information derived from living matter have clearly hit a sensitive social nerve as the ethics of this practice have been subject to international public, media and legal scrutiny.

To explore the debate concerning the ethics of patenting human genetic information, I shall focus on the work of the Human Genome Diversity Project, a research project which seeks knowledge of human identity and evolutionary history through genetics.[4] I shall stress the point that opposition to the patenting of human genetic information reflects concerns that are anterior to patent and ownership rights. These concerns are inextricably intertwined with the quasi-mystical notion that genetic information can disclose the essence of human being and identities.[5] An interesting dimension of this dispute lies in the assumption that genetic information can be conflated with life itself, which has

* Thanks to Dr Lynda Birke and Prof. Peter Fitzpatrick for their encouragement and support.
[1] Debra Harry for the Indigenous People's Diversity Network, cited (1995) 377, *Nature* 373.
[2] Isidoro Acosta (President of the Guaymi General Congress), cited in Rural Advancement Foundation International (RAFI), *Indigenous People Protest U.S. Secretary of Commerce Patent Claim in Guyami Indian Cell Line*, Press Release RAFI October 26, 1993.
[3] See RAFI (1993) above and *Science*, Vol. 270, 6 October 1995.
[4] I shall elaborate on the work of the Human Genome Diversity Project later in the paper.
[5] I am not suggesting that patents have not added to this controversy. My point is that the subject matter of human genetic information is shrouded with mystery and controversy in itself and requires attention in its own right.

been shared by opponents and proponents of the Human Genome Diversity Project alike. This supposition has been shaped, I suggest, by the scientific idea that the gene contains natural truths about human being, identity and origins. My aim is not to simply advocate the position that opponents to the patenting of human genetic information put forward, but rather to contest the naturalist presumptions that underpin this debate. In particular, I shall problematise the suggestion that genetic information can explain why specific population groups are endangered.

Describing the controversies

On October 26, 1993 the Rural Advancement Foundation International (RAFI)[6] issued a press release condemning a patent claim for the human cell line of a Guaymi Indian woman. Indigenous organisations joined protests against the patenting of human genetic information and raised concern over the ethics of patenting information derived from the human body. The patent application WO 9208784 A1 in 1993 followed the discovery of the T-lymphotropic virus Type 2 which is of medical interest for AIDS and leukaemia research.[7] The Guaymi patent claim is one of three internationally publicised disputes that has served to contest the ethics of patenting human genetic information.[8] The quasi-mystical, even sacred, qualities associated with the human gene is the focus for discussion.[9] More precisely, the question arises why the patenting of human genetic information has met with controversy.

At the outset it is important to grasp the importance of the contest over the drawing of the distinction between genetic information and genetic material. This distinction has proved difficult to maintain as indigenous organisations have interpreted the symbolic importance of the gene (including genetic information) as essential for self-definition and identity. John Liddle (for the Australian Aboriginal Congress), for example, has stated that "over the past 200 years, non-Aboriginal peoples have taken our land, language, culture, health—even our children. Now they

---

[6] The Rural Advancement Foundation International (RAFI) is an international research organisation that concentrates on the impact of developments in the biotechnological industry on the economies and peoples of the South. RAFI disseminates information to non-government organisations and governments and has drawn attention to the growing number of Northern patent applications for Southern genetic resources.

[7] RAFI (1993), above.

[8] The other two disputes involved the Hagahai patent application filed by the U.S. Department of Health and Human Services and the National Institute of Health for cell-lines derived from blood samples extracted in May 1989. RAFI report that in this case, a U.S. patent was granted despite objections from the Papua New Guinea Government. The Solomon Islands patent claim was filed in the name of the U.S. Department of Commerce in 1990 and RAFI research reports that the government of the Solomon Islands has asked the U.S. government to withdraw this claim. See RAFI (1993) above n. 2; *The Patenting of Human Genetic Material* RAFI, 1994; Cunningham, H. and Scharper, S., "Patenting the Primitive, Anthropological and Ethical Reflections on Indigenous Peoples and the Human Genome Diversity Project" paper presented at *Controlling our Destinies Conference*, University of Notre Dame, October 6, 1995.

[9] I shall be developing this strand of the opposition to the patenting of human genetic information rather than economic, religious or moral arguments.

want to take the genetic material which makes us Aboriginal people as well".[10] Secondly, although this dispute has focused on the issue of ownership and control of *information* derived from the human body, environmental movements have linked it with the patenting of physical resources and living matter such as land, plants and animals and has been described as a form of "biopiracy".[11] Geneticists and representatives of genome projects have sought to stabilise and reinforce the distinction between genetic material and information. Accordingly, Henry Greely (chair of the ethics subcommittee for the Human Genome Diversity Project) reminds us that "the patent does not patent a person. It does not even patent human genetic material. It's the cell line viral preparation derived from the cell . . . the idea that the U.S. government owns a person or his genetic material is absolute rubbish."[12]

The point that I shall develop in more detail concerns the representation of genetic information as "sacred". I shall argue that the distinction drawn between genetic matter and information obscures the point that modern geneticists have presented genetic information as the transmitter of the truth of human identities and origins. This position has added supra-scientific and quasi-mystical qualities to human genetic information. By focusing on the work of the Human Genome Diversity Project I shall contend that this dispute is being fuelled by the politics of representation.

By introducing a different register of meaning I shall suggest that the human body is a text and that genetic information functions to produce meaning in a corporeal language system. The gene represents a modern sign of human identity which signifies authentic human identities and origins. I shall proceed to deconstruct the claim that the gene can reveal authentic human identities and origins as the gene is located in a network of oppositions to produce multiple and contested meanings rather than a definitive self-same identity.[13] Furthermore, I suggest that the Project is entrenching and classifying differences between human groups through genetics and actively constituting Primitive human identities in opposition to Modern counterparts. A modern colonial encounter between the Modern and the Primitive is thereby being

---

[10] Cited in RAFI (1994) above n. 8. RAFI (1994) has also been critical of the Human Genome Diversity Project on the grounds that blood and tissue samples have not always been extracted with the prior informed consent of indigenous peoples. This point was also raised in *Moore v. Regents of the University of California* (1991) 793 P. 2d. 479; 15 U.S.P.Q. 2d 1753 (Cal. 1990) which I shall refer to later. I shall not be developing this point in this discussion.

[11] Shayana Kadidal, for example, provides an insightful analysis of the controversy provoked by the patenting of the neem plant in India which has been in use for centuries due to its variety of medicinal and agricultural uses. Kadidal discusses the award of a patent to an American company, W.R. Grace, for a method of improving neem oil extract. This patent was awarded despite the fact that most developing countries (including India) exclude agricultural and pharmaceutical inventions from patentability. An extended coverage of these issues can be found in Kadidal, S., "Subject-matter imperialism? Biodiversity, foreign prior art and the neem patent controversy" (1997) *IDEA—The Journal of Law and Technology, Vol. 37, No. 2*.

[12] (1995) Vol. 270, 17 *Science* 1112.

[13] Derrida, J., *Differance* in *Margins of Philosophy* (translated by Alan Bass) (the University of Chicago, 1982).

conducted through the Project's interpretation of genetic signification. The importance of this encounter lies in the ability of Moderns to perpetuate the naturalist myth that the Primitive is doomed to extinction by virtue of their genetic composition. This myth legitimises the destruction of endangered population groups by refusing to recognise that lived social and material interactions play an important part in determining life chances.

The Human Genome Diversity Project

The Human Genome Diversity Project is affiliated to the Human Genome Organisation (HUGO). HUGO seeks to both map and sequence the entire set of genes (the genome) found in humans and to store this information in a computer database with the aim of identifying the hereditary transmission of disease and physical characteristics of human beings (for an explanation of gene mapping and sequencing see below).[14] The Human Genome Diversity Project was conceived by the geneticist Luigi Cavalli-Sforza of Stanford University in 1991 who expressed concern that HUGO was concentrating on peoples of European origin and ignored the range of human diversity. In 1993 the HGD Project became affiliated to HUGO.[15]

The Human Genome Diversity Project (hereafter the Project or HGD Project) is an interdisciplinary research project that incorporates the work of geneticists, linguists, anthropologists and evolutionists. The Project studies endangered population groups who have been termed "linguistic isolates".[16] The genetic composition of linguistic isolates is held to further knowledge of human identity, history and origins. Cavalli–Sforza explains:

> The populations that can tell us most about our evolutionary past are those that have been isolated for some time, are likely to be linguistically and culturally distinct and are often surrounded by geographic boundaries . . . Such isolated population groups are being rapidly merged with their neighbours, however, destroying irrevocably the information needed to reconstruct our evolutionary history.[17]

Examples of selected population groups include the !Kung (from the Kalahari desert) and the Plains Apache (from Oklahoma).[18]

Patenting Human Genetic Information

A patent is an intellectual property right which confers intangible monopoly property rights to inventors for limited periods of time.

---

[14] Judson, H.F., A History of the Science and Technology Behind Gene Mapping and Sequencing (Eds. Kevles, D.J. and Hood, L. eds.) The Code of Codes, Scientific and Social Issues in the Human Genome Project, (Cambridge, Massachussetts, London, England, 1993) (First publication 1992, Harvard University Press, Cambridge, Mass., 1993).

[15] King, D., "The Human Genome Diversity Project" Genetics News January/February 1996.

[16] Human Genome Diversity Project Summary Document HUGO Europe 1993, at 13.

[17] King (1996) above n. 15, at 6.

[18] Cunningham and Scharper above n. 8.

Patents are a legal fiction designed to provide recognition, encouragement and rewards for innovation.[19] The historic roots of patents in the western world have evolved from monopoly trading rights in the Middle Ages. In England, for example, royal grants were granted which gave privileges to inventors and political supporters. This practice was formalised in the *Statute of Monopolies* (1624) which was designed to both curb the growth of market monopolies which had been granted as political favours and to continue to provide incentives to innovators. In section 6 of the Statute, the "true and first inventor" of "any manner of new manufacture" was awarded with a patent for a period of 14 years.[20] Patent legislation has developed at a rapid pace during and since the Industrial Revolution all over Europe and North America.[21]

In the U.S., the first Patent Act was enacted in 1790 for "any useful art, manufacture, engine machine, or device, or any improvement therein not before known or used".[22] An important amendment was provided in the 1952 Act which included patent provision for a "process" rather than "art". To qualify for patent protection the inventor is obliged to demonstrate the addition of human inventiveness for commercial application and is prevented from claiming patent rights to "abstract ideas", products of "nature" and "physical phenomenon".[23] These exclusions serve to reinforce the importance of demonstrating inventiveness as opposed to a discovery that does not have a practical or commercial utility. The scope of patentable subject matter in the U.S. has expanded to include products and processes derived from living matter.[24]

---

[19] See for example Merges, R.P., "The Economic Impact of Intellectual Property Rights. An Overview and Guide" (1995) 19 *Journal of Cultural Economics* 103–117, and O'Connor, (K.) "Patenting Animals and Other Living Things" (1991) 65 *Southern Californian Law Review*.
I do not propose to look critically at patents or the notion of an "inventor" in this paper. However, Jacques Derrida provides an interesting discussion of the revival of the concept of an "invention", and its status in patenting law. He points out that an invention relies on convention for validation, whilst the former simultaneously breaks with convention. Thus the nature of an invention, Derrida argues, is inherently transgressive and deconstructive. Deconstruction is presented as an inventive rather than a negative act that can question the traditional concept of "invention" which relies upon a myth of origins. Further reference to this argument can be found in Derrida, (J.), *Psyche: Inventions of the Other* (L. Waters and W. Godzich (Eds.) *Reading de Man Reading*. (University of Minessota Press, Canada, USA, 1989).
[20] Holyoak, J. and Torremans, P., *Intellectual Property Law*, (Butterworths, London, 1995) p. 6.
[21] For a historical overview of the development of patents see Holyoak and Torremans (*ibid*); they also provide an interesting economic discussion of whether patents encourage or stifle competition and their role in a free market economy. See also MacLeod, *Inventing the Industrial Revolution*. (CUP, Cambridge, 1988), Dutton, *The Patent System and Inventive Activity during the Industrial Revolution 1750–1852*, (Manchester U.P., Manchester, 1986), and Machlup & Penrose, [*The Patent Controversy*] (1950) 10 J.Econ. Hist. 1, 1950.
[22] O'Connor (1991) above n. 19, at p. 599.
[23] See Dhadda, B.K., *Taking the Blood and Flesh of Others. A Vampire Manifesto?* (Unpublished M.A. dissertation, The University of Warwick, 1996), and O'Connor (1991) above n. 19.
[24] A landmark decision came in the U.S. Supreme Court's decision in *Diamond v. Chakrabarty* (447 U.S. 303 (1980). In this case, Chief Justice Burger argued that biotechnological achievements should be rewarded even if such inventiveness is derived from products of living matter. A more detailed discussion of this case can be found in O'Connor, K. (1991) above. Legal affirmation of the principle of patenting human cell lines came in the publicised American case *Moore v. Regents of the University of California* [1991] 793 P. 2d. 479. For a discussion of this case see (I.) Kennedy and A. Grubb, *Medical Law—Text with Materials* (2nd ed., Butterworths, 1994) and Hoffmaster, The Ethics of Patenting Higher Life Forms, (1989) 4 *Intellectual Property Journal* 1.

The publicised American case *Moore v. Regents of the University of California*[25] affirmed the legal principle that living donors do not have property rights to biological material derived from their body.[26] This case involved the removal and patenting of Moore's cells. The patented cells were used to develop an anticancer drug and Moore claimed that he should receive financial benefits generated from the patent. The California Supreme Court ruled that the admission of property rights was inappropriate and could impede future medical research.[27] This case affirmed the patenting principle that inventors (rather than discoverers such as Moore) should be rewarded for the products of their intellectual labour.[28]

The HUGO position on patenting human genetic information reflects the principles outlined above. The HUGO Position Statement on CDNAs patents (January 6, 1992) states that "HUGO does not oppose patenting of useful benefits derived from genetic information. HUGO does, however, oppose the patenting of short sequences ... of unknown function". The HUGO opposition to the patenting of short sequences of unknown function corresponds to the stipulations of patenting law that products of nature should be excluded from being patentable subject matter and that inventors should have demonstrated that their products have commercial utility. This provision has served to exclude the patenting of DNA sequences that have been discovered but have an unknown utility. HUGO put forward the position that the patenting of unknown genetic sequences could impede future scientific research.[29]

The publicity that has followed the patenting of human cell lines by the Project has included the suggestion that the HGD Project is involved in a form of "biopiracy". Pat Mooney (representing RAFI) explains that:

what they [the Guaymi] object to is piracy, and the immorality of granting monopoly control over human cell lines. When a foreign government comes into a country, takes blood . . . to patent and profit from the cell line, that's wrong. Life should not be subject to patent monopolies.[30]

Sensitive to the controversy that surrounds the patenting of information derived from the bodies of endangered peoples, the HGD Project has modified the HUGO position. Its position on patenting states that, "(t)he

---

[25] [1991] 793 **P** and 2d 479; 15 U.S.P.Q. 2d 1753.

[26] Kennedy and Grubb, *Medical Law—Text with Material* (2nd ed., Butterworths, London, 1994).

[27] This case also addressed the legal point that the cells were withdrawn without prior informed consent.

[28] See also *Howard Florey/Relaxin* (1995) *Offical Journal of the European Patent Office* 388: Opposition by the Green Party to the Howard Florey Institute's patent for the DNA sequences of a naturally occurring substance obtained from the human ovary on "patenting life" grounds rejected because Opposition Division characterised DNA not as "life" but rather as a "chemical substance which carries genetic code."

[29] See also M. McGrath, *The Patent Provision in TRIPS: Protecting Reasonable Remuneration for Services Rendered—or the Latest Development in Western Colonialism?* [1996] 7 E.I.P.R.

[30] RAFI (1993) above n. 2.

patenting of any products which may be derived from the samples contributed to the HGD Project should include provision for the financial return on sales to benefit the sampled population or individual" (The Document (1993), p. 34). Despite this modification to traditional patenting rights, attempts that have been made to distribute financial gains with sampled populations have continued to meet with controversy. Medical anthropologist, Carol Jenkins (employed by the Papua New Guinea Institute of Medical Research), for example, worked with the Hagahai tribe for 10 years and attained consent for the patenting of any useful discoveries made. Jenkins and the Hagahai tribe came to an agreement that financial benefits derived from any future patent would be distributed with tribe members (Jenkins was a co-inventor and entitled to 50 per cent of the royalties which she had already agreed to assign to the Hagahai people). Following this research a human cell-line derived from a tribe-member was patented.[31] This patent continued to meet with opposition from environmental organisations despite the prior consent and attempts to distribute the financial benefits from this patent with tribe members.[32] In view of the above objections to the patenting of human genetic information, it appears that attention to the issues of financial remuneration alone is insufficient and that these modifications made by the Project fail to address all of the tensions that underpin this dispute.[33]

I shall suggest that the Project's attempts to assert property rights to genetic information through patent applications have proved particularly sensitive as genetic information has been isolated as the most important component of the gene by proponents of the Project and modern geneticists alike. Modern genetic frameworks thus inform both the *symbolic* construct of genetic information as the essence of human identity and being, as well as the controversy that surrounds the patenting of human genetic information.

The modern representation of a human essence found in the gene shares several classical philosophical and semiological precepts that I shall proceed to discuss and deconstruct. However, I want to begin by locating my reading of modern genetics within a Derridean understanding of the world as a text and, secondly, to apply the movement of "différance" to modern genetics.

---

[31] B. Cohen, "Whose genes are they anyway?" in (1996) Vol. 381, *Nature* 11.

[32] RAFI issued a press release accusing the scientists involved with this patent application of being "scientific vampires", even though Jenkins had discussed the idea of a patent with the Hagahai and agreed that the tribe would receive a share of the financial benefits ((1995) Vol. 270 *Science* 1112).

[33] Although opposition to the patenting of human genetic information has included religious, moral and economic arguments, I shall be concentrating on the argument that the patenting of human genetic information is unethical because DNA contains the essence of human identity and being.

"Différance"

Being/speaks/always and everywhere/throughout/language.[34]

An integral part of Derrida's work concerns the role and function of language. Language mediates our relationship with reality and any notion of reality is not possible without language. Language is, therefore, everywhere and the world that we inhabit can only be comprehended as a text that is inscribed with meaning through language systems. Dominant western philosophical precepts that have continued to exert an influence on diverse areas of thought including philosophy, linguistics and psychoanalysis are consistently questioned and challenged. Examples of such precepts include the notion that "truth" and "presence" are attainable through human knowledge systems. These claims are dismantled by emphasis on the importance of recognising that systems of signification filter our apprehension of reality.

The logocentric tradition that has dominated western philosophy since the Ancient Greeks is addressed and continually interrogated by the play of "différance". Logocentricism refers to both the privilege accorded to the order of "presence" by western philosophers and the related notion that the revelation of pure, self-present meaning and truth is possible. These presuppositions are known as the metaphysics of presence, which:

> is the determination of Being as presence in all senses of this word. It could be shown that all the names related to fundamentals, to principles, or to the center have always designated an invariable presence—eidos, arche, telos, energeia, ousia (essence, existence, substance, subject).[35]

The pervasive influence of the metaphysics of presence in western philosophical thought is exposed and dismantled through the movement of "différance".

By identifying the influence of logocentricism on classical semiology,[36] Derrida proceeds to introduce "différance". In classical semiology he states, "[t]he sign is usually said to be put in the place of the thing itself, the present thing, 'thing' here standing for meaning or referent. The sign represents the presence in the absence".[37] This position presupposes that an order of presence is possible and that the sign is "secondary and provisional . . . EWdue to an original and lost presence from which the sign thus derives".[38] This classical position thus prioritises the order of

---

[34] Derrida (1982) above n. 13, at p. 27.
[35] J. Derrida, *Structure, Sign and Play in the Discourse of the Human Sciences in Writing and Difference* (trans. by Alan Bass), (Routledge and Kegan Paul, London, 1985), at pp. 279, 280.
[36] Semiology is the study of signs and symbols in language (signifiers) and their relationships to referents (the signified).
[37] Derrida (1982) above n. 13, at p. 9.
[38] *ibid.*

presence and presumes that the process of signification is a movement towards a "deferred presence that it aims to reappropriate".[39] The presupposition that a lost presence can be retrieved or that access to a state of presence was ever possible is questioned. The position outlined does not result in an imperfection of meaning but recognises the imperfection of meaning that is inherent to any system of signification.

An alternative method for understanding the possibility of conceptualisation and signification through language is proposed as "différance". "Différance" is a neologism and is derived from the French verb "différer" (to differ). There are two distinct meanings attached to "différance"; to defer and to differentiate. The semantic composition of "différance" preliminarily announces three important themes that I shall develop. Firstly, the idea of suspension, spacing or an interval. The process of deferment serves to suspend time, whilst the process of differentiation implies a spatial interval between "things" (or "signs"— see later). Equally important is the notion of the polysemic nature of meaning inherent to "différance", and indeed, to any linguistic system. Finally, the logocentric confidence in speech as a natural and direct form of communication which is contained within the order of presence (unlike writing) is contested. The privilege accorded to spoken language is referred to as "phonocentricism", a privilege which marks the influence of the metaphysics of presence on western metaphysics. In contrast to the hierarchical opposition of speech to writing, Derrida maintains that all systems of signification are a form of writing. The fact that the difference between an "a" and an "e" in "différance" and "différence" remains inaudible in French, therefore, serves to question the philosophical conviction in a purely phonetic language.[40] To comprehend the differences between these terms, the listener relies on non-present elements that are external to the process of speech. The implication of this position is that speech is not any more direct, immediate or self-present than writing.

Derrida questions the provisional and secondary nature of the sign in classical semiology (*i.e.* the presumption that the sign derives from an earlier and lost presence and that the process of signification is a movement towards a deferred presence by insisting on an "originary différance". This means that "différance" precedes and resides within the sign to diminish any hopes of restoring either a complete identity or assured meaning. The implications of this position are that firstly, the sign does not represent a lost presence or a primary signified but is locked into the "systematic play of differences".[41] And secondly, the process of "différance" questions the "authority of presence, or of its simple symmetrical opposite, absence or lack".[42] Derrida thereby resists

---

[39] *ibid.*
[40] *ibid.*
[41] *ibid*, at 11.
[42] *ibid*, at 10.

the alternatives of presence or absence which are offered in western metaphysical frameworks and proceeds to reinforce the importance of recognising the play of "différance" (or the "(archi)trace"):

> The play of differences supposes, in effect, syntheses and referrals which forbid at any moment, or in any sense, that a simple element be present in and of itself, referring only to itself . . . Nothing, neither among the elements nor within the system, is anywhere ever simply present or absent. There are only, everywhere, differences and traces of traces.[43]

The attempt to fix a singular, self-present meaning or identity to a signified is not, therefore, possible because "différance" precedes the process of signification.

The work of Saussure is introduced and radicalized to develop "différance". The importance of Saussure's work lies in the fact that he:

> first of all is the thinker who put the arbitrary character of the sign and the differential character of the sign at the very foundation of general semiology, particularly linguistics...There can be arbitrariness only because the system of signs is constituted solely by differences in terms, and not by their plenitude. The elements of signification function not due to the compact force of their nuclei but rather to the network of oppositions that distinguish them, and then relates them one to another. "Arbitrary and differential," says Saussure, "are two correlative characteristics".[44]

The fact that language consists only of "differences *without positive terms*"[45] is one of the important points to emerge from Saussure's work. Derrida expounds on this point to state that philosophical discourse "lives in and on difference" which is evident from the logic of binary opposition which is entrenched in philosophical discourse such as "culture as nature different and deferred".[46] Differences between terms are thus produced through binary oppositions to generate meaning. Meaning is not produced by reference to a primary signified that is identical to the signifier but is generated from relations between terms.

Following the logic of "différance", the process of "différance" cannot be reduced to, nor conceptualised by, any notion of an "origin" as "there is no presence before and outside semiological difference".[47] The non-possibility of an origin is articulated in the following terms: "(d)ifférance

---

[43] J. Derrida, *Positions* (trans. by Alan Bass), (The Athlone Press, London, 1987), at 26.
[44] Derrida (1982) above n. 13, at 11.
[45] *ibid.*
[46] *ibid.*, at 17.
[47] *ibid.*, at 12. Although the position put forward to dismantle the idea of an "origin" seems to repeat the arguments made in relation to classical semiology, it is important to separate these points as they carry specific philosophical histories and it would be inaccurate to conflate the two areas.

is the non-full, non-simple, structured and differentiating origin of differences. Thus, the name "origin" no longer suits it".[48] The fact that "différance" *precedes* and continually inhabits the sign makes it impossible to locate a point of origin.

Derrida proceeds to introduce the notion of "archi-writing" (or architrace or "différance"). This refers to a system of writing that recognizes the time interval inherent to the present moment as any notion of presence resides within "the mark of the past element" and lets "itself be vitiated by the mark of its relation to the future element".[49] The notion of the architrace therefore relates the present "no less to what is called the future than to what is called the past" and does not fall into a simple presence-absence opposition.[50] The concept of archi-writing suggests the infinite divisibility of the "present" moment and the impossibility of grasping such "present" moments. Thus the classical movement towards a deferred presence that the secondary and provisional sign attempts to reappropriate is not possible as the past has never been present.[51]

In summary, Derrida introduces several themes which will inform and further my interpretation of the Human Genome Diversity Project's symbolic construct of genetic information. Firstly, the idea of the polysemic nature of meaning. That is, the impossibility of uniting a signifier with a single (or primary) signified as the sign is entrenched in a network of oppositions. Meaning is thereby generated from differences without positive terms as the sign is a place of difference rather than that of self-same identity. Any attempt to retrieve an absent present, therefore, and to fix a determinate signified is a non-possibility. Contrary to the logocentric traditions of western metaphysics, identity is generated from the movement of "différance" which is *relational*. And finally, Derrida's scrutiny of the authority of presence suggests the non-possibility of representing or of fully retrieving a lost presence which leads to the importance of recognising the non-possibility of an "origin" as "différance" precedes language and meaning.

DNA in modern genetics

What lies at the heart of every living thing is not a fire, not warm breath, not a "spark of life." It is information, words, instructions. If you want a metaphor, don't think of fire and sparks and breath. Think instead of a billion discrete digital characters . . . think about information technology.[52]

---

[48] *ibid.*, at 11. The violence of the concept of an "origin" is a theme developed by J. Derrida, in *Force of law: The "Mystical Foundation of Authority"* in D. Cornell, M. Rosenfeld, and G. Carlson, eds. *Deconstruction and the Possibility of Justice* (Routledge, New York, 1992). I am restricting this discussion to the themes developed by Derrida in "Différance" n. 13.

[49] Derrida (1982) above, at 13.

[50] *ibid.*

[51] *ibid.*, at p. 21.

[52] R. Dawkins, *The Blind Watchmaker* (Norton, New York, 1986), at p. 112.

A more important set of instruction books will never be found by human beings. When finally interpreted, the genetic messages encoded within our DNA molecules will provide the ultimate answers to the chemical underpinnings of human existence.[53]

Genetics is the scientific study of the transmission of heredity characteristics and genetic diseases such as sickle cell anaemia. The units of inheritance are called "genes" and are located in the chromosomal part of human cells. Human cells are the smallest and fundamental units of living things.[54] The discovery in 1953 of the double helix structure and physical substance of genes, Deoxyribonucleic acid (DNA), marked a landmark in the development of molecular biology. A further decade of research provided knowledge of the process of cell regeneration which is essential for life regeneration and sustenance. The so-called "Central Dogma of Molecular Biology" (the Central Dogma) presented the following linear sequence of information flow:

DNA-RNA PROTEIN

The DNA represents the information centre and is hierarchically positioned above the messenger RNA (Ribonucleic acid). RNA is presented as inherently unstable and, consequently, information is only stored in DNA (with the exception of "lower" life forms such as viruses).[55] This sequence of information flow posits DNA as the information centre and as the most important structural component of the Central Dogma and also promotes the idea that DNA contains information which can reveal the essence of human identity.[56] The Central Dogma represents the information centre housed in DNA as the most important structural components of both the gene, and by implication, of human identity.

The Project's understanding of human genetics and human evolution is informed by what is known as the neo-Darwinian synthesis. The neo-Darwinian synthesis refers to the modern combination and selection of themes from Charles Darwin's theory of natural selection and Gregor Mendel's theory of heredity. The synthesis is a distortion of Darwin's and Mendel's theories and it is important to emphasise the fact that the Synthesis does not represent the views of either Gregor Mendel or Charles Darwin. The key selected points taken from Darwin's theory of evolution are that where population numbers exceed the natural resources of the environment then individuals with a more favourable disposition will survive and reproduce at the expense of weaker individuals in a competitive struggle for scarce resources. Note that Darwin did not imply that population numbers always exceed resource supply. The so-called rediscovery of the Mendelian laws of inheritance in 1900

---

[53] James Watson (former director of HUGO) cited at p. 1, M.A. Rothstein, "Symposium, Legal and Ethical Issues Raised by the Human Genome Project" [1992], *Houston Law Review* 29.

[54] L.D. Hartl, J.S. McDonnell and J.S. McDonnell, *Our Uncertain Heritage. Genetics and Human Diversity* (2nd ed.) (Harper Collins Publishers, New York, 1985).

[55] Macer, D., *Shaping Genes. Ethics, Law and Science of using Genetic Technology in Medicine and Agriculture*, (Eubios Ethics Institute, 1990).

[56] *ibid.*

provided Darwinism with a theory of inheritance through the identification of heredity elements (later known as genes) as the location of change and stability in the species.[57] However, unlike the Synthesis, Mendel's work did not imply that major changes between biological forms could occur from genetic changes. The inclusion of the so-called "Weismann barrier" (from August Weismann) put forward the view that genes were insulated from direct environmental influence in the lifetime of an organism. The overall effect of the Synthesis is to suggest that genetic heredity composition and the hands of nature determine the life chances of living populations rather than lived material relationships, as the capacity to successfully adapt to environmental conditions is denied in the lifetime of an organism.[58]

The Central Dogma has been subject to criticism for reproducing a hierarchical Aristotelian world view through the perpetuation of a Mind-body opposition. This is evident from the subordination of matter (RNA) to the mind (DNA) and is a view evident, for example, from Aristotelian accounts of human reproduction in which the female is constructed as the supplier of matter whilst the male is the supplier of motion.[59]

Ho puts forward an alternative model of genetics called the "Fluid Genome".[60] The Fluid Genome presents reverse-information flow (RNA-DNA) as a necessary part of gene behaviour in all organisms (including "higher" life forms such as human beings). This model also problematises the concept of a stable gene identity with rigidly demarcated boundaries through the assertion that gene identity is necessarily fluid as genes constantly traverse boundaries and are constantly interacting with environmental influences (Ho does not suggest that gene boundaries are infinitely fluid).[61] The notion of a symbiotic gene identity and the movement inherent to Ho's account of gene identity contrasts with the static image put forward by the Central Dogma. The fluid genome stresses the point that genes are co-operative and cannot be defined in isolation from other genes and contrasts with the representation of gene identity as highly static, competitive, autonomous and individualistic by the Central Dogma.

The result of the neo-Darwinian synthesis is to portray a reductionist account of the genome, and particularly of genetic information, as determining all of the organisms traits and identity without the possibility for change in the lifetime of an organism. This account of gene

---

[57] For a fuller discussion of the new genetics and of the neo-Darwinian synthesis see S. Newman, "Carnal Boundaries: The Commingling of Flesh in Theory and Practice", in (L. Birke and R. Hubbard, eds.), *Reinventing Biology* (Indiana University Press, Bloomington and Indianapolis, 1995).
[58] Dhadda n. 23 (1996) above.
[59] Biology and Gender Study Group, "The Importance of Feminist Critique for Contemporary Cell Biology" in (N. Tuana, (ed.) (*Feminism and Science*), Indiana University Press, Bloomington, 1989), and Dhadda (1996) above n. 23.
[60] M, Ho, "Unravelling gene biotechnology" Paper given at the Tavistock Clinic (*The Politics of Attachment*) March 1995.
[61] The identification of so-called "jumping genes" that transgress gene boundaries was first made by Barbara McClintock. This is not a dominant, modern account of gene behaviour.

identity sharply contrasts with the Fluid Genome model. Successful adaptation to a competitive environment is projected as the key to long-term survival by the neo-Darwinian synthesis. According to the neo-Darwinian synthesis, therefore, the key to defining endangered population groups and understanding why those groups are endangered lies in the ability to decipher genetic codes which are found in the DNA.

Genetic codes are found along DNA molecules. Each DNA molecule consists of two intertwined strands which hold genetic information in the form of a genetic alphabet. Several thousand chemical letters are to be found in each gene.[62] Genetic codes consist of chemical subunits called nucleotides and are coded through the genetic alphabet A, T, G and C (deoxyadonesine phosphate, deoxythymidine phosphate, deoxy-guanosine phosphate and deoxycytidine phosphate respectively). Each word in a gene consists of three letters such as ACT. There are an estimated six billion nucleotides in a human cell.[63]

The order of these codes is significant because this is the only variable found in the double helix structure of DNA. The Project's attempts to sequence and map the human genome referred to both the processes of identifying the sequence of genetic codes and to the identification of the relationships and locations of genes within the human body.

A striking feature of genetic coding, sequencing and mapping is how these processes correspond with the structure of a language system. Interpretation of genetic codes requires knowledge of the genetic alphabet whilst the sequencing of genetic words and their relationships correspond with a sentence structure. The Central Dogma, I submit, represents genetic codes found in human DNA as signifiers of human identity.

To contest the symbolic representation of genetic information outlined I shall offer a Derridean reading of the Project. I shall suggest that firstly, the Project is entrenched in the metaphysics of presence through its commitment to the notion that an absent present can be retrieved by recourse to scientific truths. In this context, this view is evident from the claim that the truth of human origins and human identity can be retrieved from DNA. Modern geneticists are positing DNA as a modern sign of human identity. Contrary to these claims, Derrida suggests that the nostalgia for a lost presence and for a complete, definable and fixed human identity is impossible to satisfy as the being of a sign is always already "not there" and never to be found in its "full being".[64] The modern attempt to fix a determinate human identity is, therefore, an impossible task because of the multiple and contested nature of meaning which does not allow for a natural, immediate or singular correspondence between signifiers and signifieds such as human identities.[65]

---

[62] Hartl *et al.* 1985 above n. 54 at 25.

[63] See Hartl *et al.* above n. 54 and Judson above n. 14.

[64] Spivak at p. xvii, in J. Derrida, *Of Grammatology* (trans. Gayatri Chakravarty Spivak), (The John Hopkins University Press, Baltimore and London, 1976).

[65] Derrida (1976) above n. 64.

Finally, as I continue to illustrate, identity is dependent on differences and oppositions that can never be simply present.[66]

DNA and the movement of "différance"

To grapple with the question why the patenting of human genetic information has fuelled controversy, I have presented the argument that modern genetic paradigms reify DNA and that the reification of human DNA requires consideration prior to the issue of patenting. The representation of genetic information as sacred is borne from the conviction that a human eidos (essence) can be recovered by interpreting coded genetic inscriptions. The ability to decipher and control the interpretation of genetic codes thus confers the power to define human identity and difference. Such is the conviction in an enduring, timeless human essence that modern geneticists have held that genetic codes can reveal and retrieve a lost human presence by narrating a history of human origins. This construct of genetic information suggests that contests for property rights to human DNA have been not been spurred by attempts to control mere chemical codes, but rather by efforts to assert control over representations of human identities.

I am adopting the position that our comprehension of, and relationship with, the real world is inescapably mediated by human-made language. Language is neither "natural" nor "neutral" as it is culturally and historically bound. The meanings produced by language are, therefore, arbitrary. Accordingly, I will read the human body as a text. Human bodily texts are inscribed with meaning by genetic systems of signification. A modern genetic signification system is composed of signifiers and signifieds which produce meaning through relational terms.

The HGD Project's claim that human DNA can provide information about human identities and origins suggests that the genetic codes found in DNA serve as signifiers of human identities and origins. Genetic signifiers are comprised of the genetic inscriptions A, T, G and C which are to be found in DNA molecules (nucleotides). Human identities and origins represent the signifieds. I want to suggest that the gene is a modern sign of human identity. The fact that genetic codes only produce meaning through recognition of their sequencing and locations further attests to the position that modern genetics represents a modern system of signification as meaning is generated from the structured relationships between signs.[67] In other words, the function of, and meaning generated from, genetic signs is analogous to the mechanisms of a language system. It is crucial to reiterate the point that the meanings generated from genetic signification are neither natural nor neutral but are culturally and historically bound and that our comprehension of human identities is

---

[66] J. Culler, *Jacques Derrida* in (J. Sturrock, (ed.) *Structuralism and Since: from Levi-Strauss to Derrida*, Oxford University Press, London, 1979), at p. 163.
[67] I am referring to the processes of genetic sequencing and mapping which I referred to earlier at p. 104.

mediated by a human-made (rather than a natural or preordained) genetic language. The Project's interpretation of the neo-Darwinian synthesis and genetic codes does not, therefore, unravel natural truths or assured meanings about human identities or origins.

The Project's claim that DNA can reveal human history and retrieve the truth of human origins illustrates the pervasive influence of the metaphysics of presence. The genetic information of endangered populations is being posited as secondary to an "originary" and lost presence by the Project through the claim that the DNA (the signifier) of these peoples can recover knowledge of human origins (the signified). Furthermore, the Project's attempt to define determinate human identities through human genes reveres the classical semiological dream of grasping the full being of a sign. This dream is informed by the presupposition that a signifier (DNA) can be united with a primary signified (human identity).

The movement of "difference" shakes these classical precepts to their foundations. The Project's attempt to capture a moment of human origin fails to recognise the deferral of time and spatial interval which is inherent to the system of archi-writing (or "différance"). The movement of "différance" means that a sign cannot precede nor lie outside of semiological "différance" as the systematic play of the traces of differences produce meaning. The claim that DNA can fully retrieve the truth of human origins, therefore, is a non-possibility. Additionally, the fact that there is a deferral of time and a spatial interval between signs which are enmeshed in a play of differences and oppositions means that human identity is being defined through a systematic play of differences and oppositions between signs (human genes).

A significant effect of the movement of "différance" is that the sign indicates a place of difference rather than a self-same identity. Signs are thus implicated in a systematic play of differences *without positive terms*. This radically alters the function of genetic signs as these signs do not characterise human identities by what they are, but rather through opposition to what they are not. In this context, the genetic codes of "endangered" (primitive) population groups are being defined in opposition to what they are not—the genetic codes of "survivor" (modern) population groups. I am suggesting that a violent and hierarchical Modern-Primitive opposition is prominent in the Project's field of meaning.

Aboriginal Groups and the Human Genome Diversity Project

Aboriginal population groups are of particular interest to scientists involved with the Project as their genetic composition has not been affected by "admixture" (I shall refer to admixture as miscegenation) and are represented as more deeply entrenched in history.[68] Genetic samples

---

[68] Human Genome Diversity Project Summary Document HUGO Europe (1993), at p. 4.

taken from Aboriginal peoples have therefore been held invaluable for providing information about human identity, history and origins. Sampled population groups have been divided into five categories by the Project: populations that carry information regarding the "genetic composition of contemporary 'ethnic groups' ", language groups and cultures' such as the "origin of New World populations" and the "Bantu expansion",[69] populations that are "anthropologically unique" with "unique cultural or linguistic attributes",[70] populations that constitute "linguistic isolates" who can help to explain how "cultural evolution parallels the processes leading to genetic microdifferentiation",[71] populations that can help to identify the "genetic etiology of important disease"[72] and, finally, the Project stresses the urgency of sampling populations that are "in danger of losing their identity as genetic units" before this "information is lost forever".[73] The Project's interest in the latter group has sparked controversy as it expresses concern for the loss of genetic information rather than the fact that these populations are endangered.[74]

The aim is to develop a genetic and statistical database to record information about human identity.[75] Using language as a criterion for classification, the Project will distinguish 5,000 population groups with "distinct properties and possibly distinct gene frequencies".[76] This information is to be extracted from genetic samples which will be stored at repositories such as the American Type Culture Collection. The samples of blood, hair and cheek scrapings will be frozen in liquid nitrogen containers and with the application of procedures, such as a polymerase chain reaction, strands of DNA sequences can be replicated.[77]

Sensitive to the controversy and publicity that has followed the work of the HGD Project the Project's practitioners have contested the suggestion that it is classifying populations into racial groups. The Project's Summary Document (1993) articulates a clear direction for its work which is intended to combat racism and states that "in biological terms there is no such thing as a clearly defined race . . . populations are defined on a statistical basis rather than on the basis that each has entirely distinct and different genetic or physical characteristics".[78] This statement implies that the use of statistics precludes the possibility of classifying human populations into racial groups. The Document pro-

---

[69] *ibid*, at pp. 12–13.
[70] *ibid*, at p. 13.
[71] *ibid*.
[72] *ibid*. I will not be developing this aspect of the Project's work. A discussion of DNA based medical research can be found in Caskey, DNA-Based Medicine: Prevention and Therapy in The Code of Codes (D.J. Kevles, and L. Hood (eds.)), (Harvard University Press Cambridge, Massachussetts, London, England, 1992).
[73] HGD Project Summary Document (1993) above n. 68, at p. 13.
[74] King (1996) above n. 15 and RAFI (1993) above n. 68.
[75] HGD Project Summary Document (1993) above n. 68, at p. 1.
[76] *ibid.*, at p. 12.
[77] Cunningham and Scharper (1995) above n. 8.
[78] HGD Project Summary Document (1993) above n. 68, at p. 2.

ceeds to express concern that its genetic database could be subject to racist misinterpretation by attempts to classify human groups into racial groups and reiterates the Project's commitment to eliminating racism.

Restating the argument

A Primitive-Modern opposition has been entrenched through the Project's claim that endangered population groups are culturally, genetically, geographically and linguistically distinct from survivor populations (see earlier). Furthermore, endangered population groups have been presented as more deeply embedded in history by the Project's practitioners who have thereby underlined the spatial and time interval that opposes a Primitive to a Modern human identity. Moreover, the Project's interest in populations that have not been affected by "admixture" suggests that miscegenation represents a point of confusion as a Primitive-Modern division is broken down and synthesised. Hence the Project's argument that miscegenation obscures attempts to identify authentic human identities and to recover the truth of human origins. Miscegenation is thus presented as a form of genetic impurity. In sum, I am suggesting that a classification of human groups is being conducted through genetics which serves to naturalise and legitimise the endangered status of specific peoples.

4. The Question of Patenting Life

Brad Sherman and Lionel Bently

Brad Sherman
Senior lecturer in law at Griffith University, Brisbane, Queensland. LL.B. (Queensland), LL.M. (London), PhD (Griffith University). Formerly he taught at London School of Economics and was Hershell Smith Research Fellow at Emmanuel College, Cambridge. He has written in the *Modern Law Review, European Intellectual Property Review* (E.I.P.R.), *Social and Legal Studies* and *Oxford Journal of Legal Studies*. He edited, with Alain Strowel, *Of Authors and Origins: Essays on Copyright Law* (Oxford, 1994) and, with David Saunders, *From Berne to Geneva: Recent Developments in International Copyright and Neighbouring Rights*. He was also consultant to the Australian Government on Reforms of Performers' Rights.

Lionel Bently
Lecturer in Law at King's College London. B.A. (Cantab), Fullbright School, 1990. Formerly he taught law at Keele University. His academic interests include property, intellectual property and legal theory. He has written in the *Modern Law Review, European Intellectual Property Review* (E.I.P.R.), *Legal Studies* and the *Journal of Business Law*. In 1996 he edited with Leo Flynn, *Law and the Senses: Sensational Jurisprudence*, in the series of Law and Social Theory.

Learning Resources
Centre

The Question of Patenting Life*

Patents and Biotechnology

Looking back at the legal literature over the last decade or so, it is clear that the question of patent protection of biotechnology, while not new, has taken on a new significance: it has burst onto the legal agenda and in so doing secured itself a prominent place in the legal consciousness. The recent attempts to patent elements of the human body have ensured that this situation is unlikely to change for some time. While there are many points in common between the way in which the law has responded to biotechnology and the way it reacted to other technologies, there are certain traits associated with biotechnology which distinguish it from the other forms of subject matter that patent law has dealt with. These include the way in which the invention is described, the status of offspring, and the role that ought to be played by the research exemption.[1] A more general problem that faces applicants for biotechnological patents, particularly in relation to questions of non-obviousness and infringement, stems from the fact that the model of technology commonly employed by the law is mechanistic, whereas biological resources tend to be described in more functional terms. Although these features are important, the most obvious difference between the patenting of biotechnology and the patenting of other forms of technology is that it has led to the introduction of ethics into patent law. While the commodification of knowledge which is an inevitable consequence of the grant of intellectual property rights has been addressed at various stages in the history of intellectual property law, this is the first occasion in which ethical issues have been broached in any serious fashion.

One of the defining features of patent law, at least up until its encounter with biotechnology, was that it was treated as if it was hermetically sealed, closed off from external considerations. Modern patent law is characterised not only by its highly technical and specialised nature but also by its startling and marked isolation from matters cultural, political and ethical. With the exceptions of liberal theory and economic analysis, patent law has largely remained insulated from external debates and from historical and theoretical discussions: a trait which is reflected in the fact that patent law is continually presented as a neutral, inert system which is above or beyond ethical, political, or cultural concerns. Importantly, this image extends not only to a belief in the neutrality of the patent regime but also to the idea that the technical

---

* A version of this paper was previously published in K. Stern & P. Walsh, Property Rights in the Human Body (Centre of Medical Law and Ethics Occasional Paper No. 2).
[1] R. Merges, "Intellectual Property Rights in Higher Life Forms: The Patent System and Controversial Technologies" (1988) 47 *Maryland Law Review* 1051, 1056–8.

111

invention is itself intrinsically uncontroversial. This is reinforced by the fact that the image of patent law is understood and explained through the language of positivism and is thus premised on the absence of morality. In recent years, however, the isolated world of patents has been broken open and that which has so long been ignored and suppressed has forced its way back onto the legal agenda. The catalyst for these calls for a return to ethical values in patent law lies with the development of genetic engineering, the related attempts to patent the products of such research and the debates that this has spurred.[2]

What is most striking about the interaction of patent law and ethics is how uncomfortable the relationship has been and the difficulties that it has produced. While it may be cathartic for academics to lament the problems that arise in these circumstances, it offers little assistance in finding solutions to these important issues. It is our aim in this paper to explore some of the reasons why the law has experienced the problems that it has in accommodating and responding to the ethical. More importantly we also ask what is at stake in the interaction of the ethical and the legal that is threatened by this marriage. Before pursuing such questions, it may be helpful to offer some examples of the difficulties that patent law has experienced in its recent encounter with ethics.

Recent European Experiences

Article 53(a) of the *European Patent Convention* (EPC) states that patents are not to be granted for inventions the publication or exploitation of which would be contrary to public order or morality. Section 1(3)(a) of the Patents Act (U.K.) 1977, which is modelled on the EPC, states that a patent will not be granted for "an invention the publication or exploitation of which would be generally expected to encourage offensive, immoral or anti-social behaviour."

The first occasion in which Article 53(a) was juridically discussed at the European Patent Office (EPO) was in the 1989 *Onco-Mouse* decision.[3] In this case the Technical Board of Appeal (TBA) was asked to consider whether it was necessary to apply Article 53(a) when deciding the patentability of a mouse which had been genetically modified so that the mouse would develop cancer: a result which the applicant hoped would be useful in cancer research. Reversing the findings of the Examining Division, the

---

[2] For useful explanations of the scientific basis of the technology, see D.L. Burk, "Patenting Transgenic Human Embryos: A Non-use Cost Perspective" (1993) 30 *Houston Law Review* 1597, 1601–1615; J. de Vellis, "Ownership of Cell Lines" (1991) 65 *South California Law Review* 697; S.B. Maebius, "Novel DNA Sequences and the Utility Requirement: the Human Genome Initiative" (1992) *Journal of the Patent and Trademark Office Society* 651.

[3] *Onco-Mouse* [1989] *Official Journal of the European Patent Office* (Exam) 476; [1990] *Official Journal of the European Patent Office* 476, 490 (TBA); [1991] E.P.O.R. 525 (Exam). On this see V. Vossius, "Patent Protection for Animals" (1990) E.I.P.R. 250; L. Bently, "Imitations and Immorality: The Onco-Mouse Decision" (1992–3) *Kings College Law Journal* 145; S. Crespi, "The EC Directive on Biotechnology Patents—An Evaluation of the Ethical, Social and Political Objections" (1992) 4 *Intellectual Property in Business* 17.

Technical Board of Appeal held that ethical concerns needed to be taken into account in deciding issues of patentability. In particular, it said:

"[t]he genetic manipulation of mammalian animals is undeniably problematical in various respects, particularly where activated onco genes are inserted to make an animal abnormally sensitive to carcinogenic substances and stimuli and consequently prone to develop tumours, which necessarily cause suffering. There is also a danger that genetically manipulated animals, if released into the environment, might entail unforeseeable and irreversible adverse effects . . . The decision as to whether or not Article 53(a) of the EPC is a bar to patenting the present invention would seem to depend mainly on a careful weighing up of the suffering of animals and possible risks to the environment on the one hand, and the invention's usefulness to mankind on the other."

When this question was sent back to the Examining Division for reconsideration, it was held that the usefulness of the invention in cancer research outweighed any suffering that might be caused to the animal and, as such, that it was not an immoral invention and therefore was *prima facie* patentable.[4] The utilitarian approach adopted in *Onco Mouse* was applied in 1991 when the EPO warned the pharmaceutical company Upjohn that it would not accept an application to patent a mouse into which a gene had been introduced such that the mouse would lose its hair. In weighing up the benefit which flowed from the invention (the usefulness of the mice in experiments to cure hair loss) as against the harm suffered by the mice, the EPO asserted that the invention was immoral and thus would not be patentable.[5]

The next occasion on which the application of Article 53(a) was considered was in *Greenpeace U.K. v. Plant Genetic Systems NV*.[6] In this case, the opponents objected to the patent which had been granted for a genetically engineered plant on the grounds that it was inherently immoral and that it created environmental risks. Following the cost/benefit test suggested in *Onco-Mouse*, the opponents argued that the risks should be balanced against the benefits likely to accrue from the invention. The Opposition Division refused to apply the utilitarian test arguing that it was only necessary to consider the exclusion where the invention would be universally regarded as outrageous and an overwhelming consensus would exist to the effect that no patent should be granted. That is, it was only necessary to consider these ethical questions

---

[4] While this may seem like a satisfactory resolution of the conflict, there can be little doubt that the Onco-Mouse case raised questions with which the EPO felt extremely uncomfortable. Indeed the Onco-Mouse case attracted so much attention that the EPO is reported to have said that they wished someone would invent a genetically manipulated cat to eat the Onco-Mouse.
[5] *The Independent*, February 2, 1992.
[6] (1993) 24 *International Review of Industrial Property and Copyright* 618. L. Bently, "Sowing Seeds of Doubt on Onco-Mouse" (1994–1995) *Kings College Law Journal* 188.

once a certain (ethical) threshold had been passed. The upshot of this was that in most cases it would not be necessary to consider the morality of particular patents.

The *Greenpeace* decision highlights the difficulties that confront patent law when attempting to take ethical considerations into account. The most notable stumbling block to the inclusion of ethical issues that confronted the EPO lay in the attitude of the patent office to its own role and function. In its opinion, the patent system was primarily concerned with technical considerations. Consequently, the Opposition Division believed that it should not be involved in considering ethical concerns on a routine basis. These were matters for which it was not trained, which were outside its competence and which should only be considered exceptionally.

Even if the Opposition Division had been willing to consider ethical concerns, the case highlights a further difficulty in relation to the immorality exclusion. In an attempt to apply the utilitarian examination outlined in *Onco-Mouse*, the Opposition Division was faced with the problem that it was unable to quantify the objections raised against the patent that the test required. This was because the objections were abstract in nature, based on *a priori* principles, and not readily reducible to a quantifiable form. This was compounded by the fact that no evidence was submitted to support these claims. Instead, the examiners were asked to determine the opposition on the basis of personal philosophy or conviction. The Opposition Division rejected such an approach because it felt that this would produce "individual" or "arbitrary" decisions. Moreover, even if it were possible to convert abstractly formulated objections into more concrete quantities (for example, through the use of opinion poll evidence), the Opposition Division clung to the view that patent law was not a forum in which such opinions should play a role.

The approach advocated in the *Greenpeace* decision was adopted by the Opposition Division in the *Relaxin* case.[7] This decision concerned an opposition by the Green Party to the Howard Florey Institute's patent for the DNA sequences of a naturally occurring substance obtained from the human ovary, which relaxes the uterus during childbirth. There were three grounds of objection: first, that the use of pregnancy for profit was offensive to "human dignity"; secondly, that the applicant was involved in "patenting life", an activity which was intrinsically immoral; thirdly, that such patenting was equivalent to slavery. In rejecting the Green Party's objections, the EPO noted that the tissue used in the research was donated during the course of necessary gynaecological operations and thus had not offended "human dignity". Moreover, the Opposition Division characterised DNA not as "life" but rather as a "chemical substance which carries genetic code". The argument that the applicant was "patenting life" was thus misconceived. Finally, it rejected the Green

---

[7] (1995) *Offical Journal of the European Patent Office* 388; [1995] E.P.O.R. 541.

Party's assertion that such patenting was equivalent to slavery on the grounds that such an assertion misunderstood the nature of a patent. This was because, according to the Opposition Division, a patent does not give the proprietor any rights over a human being: all a patent monopoly provides is the right to prevent someone from practising the same.

As with the *Greenpeace* decision, the Opposition Division's decision in *Relaxin* further highlights the problems that confront patent law in accommodating ethical considerations. This was explicitly acknowledged by the Opposition Division in *Relaxin* when it commented that "[w]hether or not human genes should be patented is a controversial issue on which many persons have strong opinions . . . the EPO is not the right institution to decide on fundamental ethical questions". Furthermore, the case reveals the difficulty involved in translating the ethical concerns of the objectors into the language of patent law. Faced with a choice between a scientific understanding of DNA as chemicals and the social understanding of DNA as life, the former interpretation was preferred by the Opposition Division. The prioritisation of the scientific view of genetic process over the Green Party's approach illustrates the depth of the conflict between the logic of ethical objections and those of patenting, at least as currently understood.

Further analysis of the issue came with the decision of the Board of Appeal in *Plant Genetic Systems*.[8] While this decision, which has attracted many critics,[9] represents a more flexible approach to the incorporation of ethics into law, it still highlights the uncertainty and ambiguity that exists in this relationship. Noting that patent offices exist "at the cross roads between science and public policy", the Board of Appeal said that *ordre public* in Article 53(a) covers the protection of public security, the physical integrity of individuals as part of society and the protection of the environment. Accordingly, under Article 53(a), inventions the exploitation of which are likely to breach public peace or social order (for example, through acts of terrorism) or seriously prejudice the environment are to be excluded from patentability. The Board of Appeal added that the concept of morality is related to the belief that some behaviour is right and acceptable whereas other behaviour is wrong: a belief which was founded on the totality of the accepted norms which are deeply rooted in a particular culture. For the purposes of the EPC, the culture in question is one which is inherent in European society and civilisation. As such, inventions the exploitation of which are not in conformity with the conventionally accepted standards of conduct pertaining to this culture are to be excluded from patentability as being contrary to morality. After offering these sweeping and unhelpful references to European civilisation (which presumably now excludes the former Yugoslavia), the Board

---

[8] (1995) *Offical Journal of the European Patent Office* 545.
[9] For *e.g.* see J. Straus, "Patenting Human Genes in Europe" (1995) 26 *International Review of Industrial Property and Copyright* 920; Llewellyn, Article 53 Revisited [1995] E.I.P.R. 506, especially at 510–511.

of Appeal attempted to clarify the way in which Article 53(a) was to be interpreted. As well as casting doubts on the value of opinion poll evidence, they also said that the mere fact that the exploitation of a particular subject matter was permitted in some or all of the Contracting States would not automatically influence the ethical status of that subject, at least in relation to its patentability. The Board of Appeal added that while the morality provision was to be narrowly construed, and that it may be difficult to judge whether or not claimed subject matter was contrary to *ordre public* or morality, the provisions should not be disregarded. (Given the explicit wording of Article 53(a) it is difficult to see how they could have concluded otherwise.) The Board also observed that a balancing exercise was not the only way of assessing patentability: although it was an approach perhaps most useful in situations in which actual damage and or disadvantage existed.

Historical Reflections on the Problem of Accommodating Ethics

While ethics has in recent years been forced back onto the legal agenda, as the *Greenpeace* and *Relaxin* decisions make apparent, it has been as an uneasy and uncomfortable relationship.[10] With an EPC working party recently suggesting that there was no European definition of morality, the uncertain fate of the E.C. Biotechnology Directive, and the recent fiasco surrounding the opposition proceedings brought against the Onco-Mouse,[11] it seems clear that while in many other situations patent law has been able to accommodate alien concepts within its own logic and procedures, in its encounter with the ethical, patent law is now confronted with a set of problems for which it manifestly lacks not only an appropriate conceptual, procedural, or institutional framework, but also a suitable language to deal with ethical questions. While in other areas of the law there has been some success in quantifying factors such as risk to the environment or the harm and suffering caused to humans and animals, it has not been possible to translate similar considerations into a language that fits within the technical framework of patent law.

Although a number of explanations can be given as to why patent law experienced the problems that it has in accommodating ethical considera-

---

[10] Similar problems have also occured in other jurisdictions and in other fora. A notable example of this is the European Parliament's discomfort when dealing with ethical considerations in the Proposed E.C. Directive on the Legal Protection of Biotechnological Inventions. On the failure of the first version, see Roberts, "The Former Biotechnology Directive" (1995) (May) *Patent World* 27. A second proposal was produced by the Commission almost immediately and advice was taken from a Group of Advisers on the Ethical Implications of Biotechnology: see, *Research Fortnight*, October 16, 1996, at 15. At the end of November 1997, after much wrangling between the Council and Parliament, the second proposal was finally accepted. For the proposal, see Amended Proposal for a European Parliament and Council Directive on the Legal Protection of Biotechnological Inventions COM(97) 446 final—95/0350(COD) OJ C 97/C 311/05. This was reviewed in Ford, "The Morality of Biotech Patents: Differing Legal Obligations in Europe?" [1997] E.I.P.R. 315.
[11] Opposition proceedings involving 17 opponents as well as thousands of individuals were heard on November, 21–24 1995. No decision was given at the end of the hearing. See (1996) 3 E.I.P.R. D–90.

tions, we wish to concentrate on two specific factors. The first is that in patent law the invention is treated as a closed, secure and fixed entity. Questions such as how we are to understand what an invention is and how this is to be identified are taken as givens, as matters which are beyond doubt or question. Secondly, and closely related to this, is that in its dealings with the invention the law has done all that it can to avoid making qualitative judgements. Indeed, one of the defining characteristics of intellectual property over the last century or so has been the manner in which quietly but consistently questions of judgement have been replaced with what are taken as objective criteria. At every turn that which is perceived as judgemental, value-laden or subjective has been replaced by quantifiable, objective criteria.

While it may sometimes appear otherwise, it has not always been this way. Indeed, for many years the invention was treated in law as an open and fluid concept. While the invention is now almost universally treated as a thing, it was once seen more as a form of performance or action (albeit one that the law temporarily froze in time). Moreover, while we now take the nature of the invention for granted, it once had an uncertain ontological status. In particular, during the literary property debate that took place in the middle of the eighteenth century and the patent controversy in the middle of the nineteenth century, commentators, judges and jurists pondered on questions such as the metaphysical status of the invention and how the subject matter of patents differed from copyright.

In the same way in which the invention was once treated as an open and fluid entity, there was also a time in which the law was more than willing to pass judgement on particular patents. For example, for the duration of a patent to be extended beyond its normal lifespan the Privy Council Rules of 1835 specified that it was necessary for an applicant to show that the invention was meritorious, but unrewarded.[12] In turn, one of the chief aims of patent law reform in the nineteenth century was to ensure that only inventions of appropriate quality were patented. While we are now obsessed with the number of patents registered, at the time it was the quality of what was registered that mattered most. Indeed, the multiplication of patents was seen as an evil that needed to be remedied. To this end, consideration was given to techniques such as increasing the cost of registration and the introduction of a system of examination as a way of ensuring that inventions of a trivial or undeserving nature were not patented.[13] Concern with the quality of patents perhaps reached its

---

[12] Prior to 1835, patents were prolonged only as a result of special Acts of Parliament. After Lord Brougham's Act of 1835, however, this process was taken away from Parliament and conducted on the basis on Privy Council Rules. For an overview of this precursor to the Supplementary Protection Certificate, see John Waggett, *The Law and Practice Relating to the Prolongation of the Terms of Letters Patent for Inventions* (Butterworth, London, 1887).

[13] It was said in 1864 that one of the main problems that needed improving were first "that of the existence of a number of Patents for alleged inventions of a trivial nature; and in the second place, that of the granting of Patents for inventions which are either old or practically useless, and are employed by the patentees only to embarass rival manufactures." *Report of the Commissioners appointed to Inquire into the Working of the law Relating to Letters Patent for inventions* (1864) XXIX PP, i.

peak with the introduction of the requirement that the patentee needed to make a declaration that the invention was "of great public Utility,"[14] the aim of which was to prevent absurd and trifling inventions which would stand in the way of subsequent and really useful inventions from being patented.[15] Another situation where we witness the law's willingness to evaluate the invention was in terms of the way the categories of intellectual property were distinguished. In particular, the quantity and later the quality of the mental labour embodied in different creations was an important factor in distinguishing patents from designs, copyright and trade marks.

In the middle part of the nineteenth century, at the same time that intellectual property as a subject was maturing, these two trends were reversed. As the metaphysical debates about the nature of property which had dominated in the eighteenth and nineteenth century lost their cudos,[16] the invention, once seen as a form of action and as an open and fluid concept, came to be treated as a stable, unitary thing. Simultaneously, matters of judgment were either ignored or replaced by more quantifiable criteria. The nature of these changes are captured in Scrutton's preface to his then leading work on copyright published in 1883. Speaking of the period up until the middle period of the nineteenth century Scrutton said that any attempt to "reduce to principle the laws dealing with Copyright, or the similar laws of Patents and Trade-marks" ... "would naturally commence with an investigation of the nature of the property." Such an inquiry would have "at once lead the student into what has been called the 'realm of legal metaphysics'". While examinations into the nature of the invention as a species of intangible property had once been virtually obligatory, Scrutton felt excused from these fruitless forms of inquiry. As he said, "[f]ortunately, however, the necessity for this general preliminary investigation is obviated by the fact that practical agreement prevails amongst modern jurists as to the answer to be obtained."[17]

What Scrutton was hinting at here was the shift which had occurred in law away from the type of inquiry which focused on the nature of the invention to a situation where the invention was treated as a closed and stable entity. While these changes can be seen as a further stage in the reification of creativity which had long been a feature of intellectual

---

[14] Schedule 1 to the *Patent Law Amendment Act* 1852.

[15] Attorney-General, *Hansard*, Vol. 118, col. 1876, August 5, 1851.

[16] "This ground ... does not consist in any vague inference from the right of property in an invention, or the celebrated principle of a mans power to "do as he will with his own; but simply in the position, that a greater sum of good to the community will arise from encouraging men to go to the expense of invention" Anon, "Unreasonableness of Judge-made Law in setting aside Patents" (1835) 22 *The Westminster Review* 447, 471.

[17] Thomas Edward Scrutton, *The Laws of Copyright: An Examination of the principles which regulate literary and artistic property in England and other countries* (John Murray, London, 1883), 2–3. Earl Granville was even clearer as to the nature of the change, to the closure of the invention when speaking of the 1851 *Patents For Inventions Bill* he said that "Mr Bramwell, the ablest defender of patent right, although he does not distinctly abandon the ground of property, entirely lays it aside in his argument. Earl Granville, "Patents For Inventions Bill", (February 26, 1875) CXXII *Hansard* 916.

property law, it would be a mistake to see them solely in these terms. This is because the shift from action to thing, from labour to invention, marked an important change in the logic of intellectual property law; it saw the reconceptualisation of intangible property and with it the invention. One of the most notable manifestations of this was that it saw the gradual separation of the inventor from the invention. In particular, as the work was closed, the concept of mental labour, so important in conceptualising intangible property over the previous century disappeared. Edelman's comment that in the copyright system "the work is radically detached from the person of the author, and acquires an absolute judicial autonomy" and as a result "the author, as person, disappears in favour of his creation,"[18] applies equally to patent law. Coryton captured the nature of the move from creator to creation when he said that unlike other books on patent law, the principle around which his treatise was organised was the invention. As a result this meant that the "person of the Patentee becomes in comparison with it a subordinate idea."[19] The gradual exclusion (or perhaps more accurately the suppression) of the inventor, which came about with the closure of the invention, manifest itself in the shift of the focus of attention away from the "men of ingenuity" to the "men of capital". This was reflected in the *Patents, Designs and Trade Marks Act 1883* which allowed that an applicant "not an inventor may obtain Letters Patent." This provision was introduced to "meet the case of an inventor without capital desiring the assistance of a capitalist by giving him a share of the patent."[20]

As we have seen, in the eighteenth and early part of the nineteenth century the law had been more than willing to differentiate between different works on the basis of their quality: to discriminate against those inventions which it regarded as trivial or undeserving (such as the kalediscope). During the middle part of the nineteenth century, however, questions were raised as to whether it was appropriate for the law to engage in such speculative exercises. What began as doubts about the appropriateness of such decisions grew over time into a fear of judgement; a fear about qualitative decisions, a fear of the arbitrary and the individual. Rather than attempting to decide whether a particular invention was valuable, as it had so willingly done in the past, it was argued that the law should refrain from these modes of inquiry: an approach reiterated in the *Relaxin* decision.[21]

---

[18] B. Edelman "Une loi substantiellement internationale. La loi du 3 Juillet sur let droits d'auteur et droit voisins." (1987) 114 *Journal de droit international* 567–568.

[19] John Coryton, *A Treatise on the Law of Letters-Patent for the Sole Use of Inventions in the United Kingdom of England and Ireland: To which is added a summary of the Patent laws in force in the principal foreign states* (H. Sweet, London, 1855), iv.

[20] W. Lawson, *Patents, Designs and Trade Marks Practice* (Butterworths, London, 1884), ix.

[21] In so doing, intellectual property came to echo modernism's fear of the anxiety of being tainted by politics, morality and judgment. Andreas Huyssen, *After the Great Divide* (Indiana University Press, Bloomington, 1986), vii. This fear of judgment was one of the reasons why examination was not taken seriously until early in the twentieth century when the expert-examiner was able to decide upon the nature of the invention, design or mark.

A reason for this change in attitude was the growing belief that the law was ill equipped to make subjective, qualitative decisions.[22] The doubts about the laws ability to make qualitative judgements was summed up in the evidence given by the Master of the Rolls to the 1851 Select Committee on Patents when he said:

"I cannot imagine any way in which you can distinguish good inventions from bad ones; I have heard of so many inventions which having been looked on as perfectly wild and ridiculous, which have turned out afterwards to be most advantageous to the public; and on the contrary I have known many which have looked as if they were going to do very great wonders and would be of the greatest public service, which have turned out to be empty bubbles; so that I really think it would be almost impossible for any tribunal to distinguish a good invention from a bad one."[23]

Given that the only secure means by which the value of a machine or a new chemical could be judged was retrospectively,[24] an option usually not available, the law became suspicious of such modes of inquiry.[25] In a period in which patent law was being attacked by the likes of Macaulay and lampooned by Dickens, all was done to ensure it was not brought into further disrepute. Rather than leaving itself open to the charge of having rejected a invention on the basis that it was non-meritorious, and later being proved wrong, the law attempted to distance itself from such questions. In short it opted for a form of technological agnosticism.[26]

These changes were both part of and reinforced by more general changes that were taking place at the time. For example, in addition to developing a fear about making incorrect decisions, drawing on *laissez faire* ideas recently championed by political economists, commentators came to mock attempts by the law to regulate taste, morality, industry, honesty and public opinion.[27] The growing suspicion of attempts to

---

[22] "The spirit of our institutions is to leave the public the utmost latitude for judging itself upon the questions of merit; and it may, therefore, be concluded that there are no suffcient reasons for making the questions of merit any ground to refuse acknowledgement of the rights of invention". Society of Arts: Extracts from the First Report on the Rights of Inventors, *Select Committee on Patents* (1851) XVIII PP Appendix C. "the intrinsic merits of an invention the public at large are the best and only judges". *ibid.*

[23] Question asked of The Master of the Rolls & Solicitor General *Select Committee on Patents* (1851) XVIII PP 655. The "patent office had abandoned the issue of utility to the market by the end of the nineteenth century. Patent scholars and judges recognised that the purpose of patents was to confer a predictable, enforcable right of exclusion, not to decide which inventions promoted the betterment of society". George J. Armstrong, "From the Fetishism of Commodites to the Regulated Market: The Rise and Decline of Property" (1987) 82 *Northwestern University Law Review* 79, 95.

[24] "Nothing but subsequent experience can afford an adequate test of the utility or inutility of an invention". Lord Overstone, *Report of the Commissioners appointed to Inquire into the Working of the law Relating to Letters Patent for Inventions* (1864) XXIX PP 85.

[25] "We must select the good from the bad by trial alone, for the best judges of these matters cannot determine *a priori* which will turn out good, and which will fail." John Farey, *Select Committee on the law Relative to Patents for Invention* (1929), 132.

[26] Strictly speaking it was not that these qualitative processes disappeared so much as they migrated to other areas of patent law.

[27] John Coryton, *A Treatise on the Law of Letters-Patent for the Sole Use of Inventions in the United Kingdom of England and Ireland: To which is added a summary of the Patent laws in force in the principal foreign states* (H. Sweet, London, 1855), 17.

evaluate the quality of inventions was reinforced by the moves towards legal science and positivism which took place in the law towards the end of the nineteenth century; intellectual fashions which had a visible impact on intellectual property law at the time.[28] The belief in the neutrality of patents was reinforced by the proliferation of patent treatises which took place over the course of the nineteenth century. As Simpson says, in "a legal world in which the modern concept of authority, attached peculiarly to judges, has begun to emerge; the text writer, unless he himself is a judge, possesses as an individual no authority derived from office. Consequently his views are important only if they are unoriginal . . . and if their authority derives solely from their substance":[29] a view which spilled over into the content of the treatises.[30] Closely associated with the closure of the invention and the attempted exorcism of judgment was the demand for intellectual property to be placed in a form so that it could be rendered calculable. The problem with this, however, was that labour was not readily susceptible to quantification. The particular difficulty which the law faced in modernising intellectual property law was that there was "no measure of the amount of labour". This was because "the work of a lifetime may be concentrated into a page of mathematical symbols. The distinction in the old acts between casts and engravings from natural or artificial objects only led to vexations and difficulties; so have the questions that have arisen as to works of mental industry or original invention". The response by patent law to these problems was to adopt the principle that "no distinction lay between the inventions of the man of genius, the plodder, and the accidental finder, the luck labour and inspiration give an equal right".[31] As we have seen, the law also responded to the fact that labour (and creativity) could not easily be measured by moving away from the labour embodied in the creation towards the object itself. While labour could not be calculated, the closed work and the contribution that it made could.

The closure of the work and the attempted exorcism of judgment brought with it a number of changes. It led, for example, to increased attention being given to the economic dimension of patents: to questions such as the compulsory working of patents (particularly those taken out

---

[28] Scrutton explicitly drew upon Austin's jurisprudence to argue that all rights "in the strict sense of the word, result from the command of the Sovereign, and have no existence prior to such command". Thomas Edward Scrutton, *The Laws of Copyright: An Examination of the principles which regulate literary and artistic property in England and other countries* (John Murray, London, 1883), 4.

[29] A.W.B. Simpson, "The Rise and Fall of the Legal Treatise: Legal Principles and the Forms of Legal Literature" in *Legal Theory and Legal Histrory: Essays on the Common Law* (The Hambeldon Press, London, 1987) 273, 279.

[30] As Davies said of his *Digest on Patents*, published in 1816, it was written "to avoid using language of our own, but shall chiefly make use of the language of the learned judges, referring to the cases in which they have made the observations stated". J. Davies, *A Collection of the Most Important Cases Respecting Patents of Inventions* (W. Reed, London, 1816), 415.

[31] T. Turner, *Recent Amendments of the Law for Patents for Inventions* (Elseworth, London, 1851), 32.

by foreigners) and the impact of patents on particular industries.[32] It also saw a move away from a concern with the *quality* of patents granted to a concern about the *quantity* of patents granted. Hand-in-hand with this was an increased reliance placed on external, measurable criteria; to this end, the patent office began to publish statistics of the number of patents granted, the technologies for which they were issued and the gender of the applicants. Even those concepts introduced to regulate the quality of inventions were subject to change. For example, the utility of inventions, once determined by judging the quality of the invention (often in advance of its use) shifted to more quantifiable criteria: to the consequences of the invention.[33]

For our purposes, the most important change brought about as a result of the closure of the work and the exorcism of judgment is that it created an atmosphere which was hostile to ethics. One reason for this was that the closure of the invention and the related closure of patent law as a legal category played an important role in marginalising non-legal concerns. Perhaps the most important explanation for the difficulties that have arisen in incorporating ethical questions into the law lies with the fact that one of the changes associated with the closure of the invention was that the intangible property was re-conceptualised so that it became detached from naturalistic explanations. Patent law came to be grounded in its own logic, with no reference to foundational, naturalistic explanations. While the invention was once closely tied to such modes of argumentation, with the closure of the invention the circle of normative judgment closed without passing through a domain of nature, divinity or metaphysics;[34] it led in short to the secularisation of patent law. To use the language of systems theory, the closure of the invention played an important role in bringing about the conceptual and normative closure of patent law.

While in themselves the closure of the work and the exorcism of judgment offer some assistance in explaining why the law experienced the problems that it has in dealing with ethics, they do not explain what is at *stake* in this interaction, what it is that is being challenged by the introduction of ethics onto the legal agenda. Perhaps most importantly of all they cannot tell us what is likely to be lost (or at least upset) by these new arrangements. A reason why the introduction of ethics into patent law has generated so many problems is that it asks the law to inquire into and pass judgment on the invention: to undo the practices the law spent the last century or so refining. While this is important, it is not the reopening of the invention in itself which is so troubling. Rather, what is

---

[32] It was reported that the introduction of the requirement that patents be compulsorily worked in the U.K. (s.27 of the Patents and Designs Act 1907), helped to generate "new factories costing £500,000 . . . giving employment to seven thousand men, and resulting in the payment of wages to £8,000 weekly". Anon, "Compulsory Working of Patents" (April 29, 1911), *The Manchester Chamber of Commerce Monthly Record*, 98.
[33] Under this view "the utility . . . of the change was ascertained by its consequences". T. Webtser *Law and Practice of Letters Patent for Inventions* (Crofts and Bleakdown, London, 1841, 45).
[34] Alain Pottage, "The Autonomy of Property", unpublished, 1.

at stake in the introduction of ethical criteria are those things which flow from and depend upon a closed invention. What is so troubling about the introduction of ethics, and a reason for the approach adopted at the EPO, is the belief that by opening up the invention, the turn to ethics will undermine those practices which depend upon the invention as a closed and stable entity.

One factor which flows from the closed nature of the invention and the certainty and security that this provides is that it means that patents are more readily accepted as a part of the commercial currency: that they can be included in the balance sheets and incorporated in the performance indicators of researchers, companies, and universities. More importantly, the closure of the invention plays an integral role in the efficient operation of the registration system. Like the encyclopedias of the eighteenth century, the patent registration systems was motivated by a desire to transfer technical knowledge into a more manageable and useable form.[35] In order for the registration system to operate effectively, for its final output to be useful, it was necessary that its practices and agents be trusted. In turn, the acceptance of the patent as a reliable and trusted indicator of the existence, legitimacy and value of intangible property depended on elaborate, plausible and sustained record-keeping.[36]

While a number of factors contributed to the establishment of an effective workable registration system, one factor stands out above the rest: the fact that the invention was treated as a closed and stable entity.[37] The reason for this was that one of the consequences of the closure of the invention was that there was no longer a need to look beyond the patent grant; users were able to rely upon the paper inscription and as such could place their trust and faith in the surface of the document. In short, the closure of the invention made it easier for the patent to be trusted, relied upon and used. Although patents never provided the same level of security as offered by title to land or money, the closed invention was nonetheless a central component of the registration system. It led to more defined patterns of standardisation, and in so doing ensured that the documents which patents agents routinely dealt with could be trusted and relied upon.[38] Put differently, the strength of registration came from the fact that there was no need to question what lay behind the paper inscription—the surface of the document.[39] The efficacy of the registra-

---

[35] See Richard Yeo, "Reading Encyclopedia: Science and the Organisation of Knowledge in British Dictionaries of Arts and Sciences, 1730–1850" (1991) 82 *ISIS* 24.

[36] Harriet Ritvo, "Possessing Mother Nature: Genetic capital in eighteenth century Britain" in (eds.) John Brewer and Susan Staves), *Early Modern Conceptions of Property* (Routledge, London, 1995) 413, 419.

[37] B. Latour, "Drawing things together" in (eds.) Michael Lynch and Steve Woolgar, *Representation in Scientific Practice* (MIT Press, London, 1990), pp. 45–47.

[38] If "you look at the face [of a watch] you can see the time at a glance. If you open the back and look at the machinery, it would puzzle a clever man to guess how it operated, and he would turn with a sigh of relief to an hour glass" Registrar Brickdale, quoted in Alain Pottage, "The Originality of Registration" (1995) 15 *O.J.L.S.* 371, 378.

[39] If anything needed to be done at all, the document would have to be interpreted.

tion system was ensured by the closure of the invention because it meant that users of the patent did not need to question the patent.[40]

It is now possible for us to return to the question posed at the start of this paper: what is at stake in the introduction of ethics into patent law? It should be clear by now that the answer to this question is nothing less than the efficiency of the registration system. By asking the law to question the nature of the invention, to open the invention up to qualitative scrutiny, ethics strikes at the heart of these processes. In the same way in which weak patent examination processes undermine the trust placed in the final product so too the opening up of the invention to qualitative judgment potentially undermines the registration system. In this sense the conflict associated with the patenting of genetically modified organisms can be seen not only as one between environmental groups and industrialists but also as one between ethical modes of thought and the sanctity of the inscription and the registration processes that depend upon it.

The security required by the registration system is also undermined by the second demand made as a consequence of the introduction of ethics into patent law: namely that the invention be judged. In particular, by asking patent law to evaluate the invention, it serves to undermine not only the image of the neutrality but also the universality of the patent system. This image, clearly influenced by the idea of the invention as a closed and inert object, has played an important role in both ensuring the efficacy of the patent system and also in transporting the regime throughout the world.[41] Like the technology that it sets out to regulate, patent law is supposed to transcend the local; a machine or a genetically modified seed is the same whether considered by the law in Germany, Britain, or India. A recent example of this is to be found in Article 27(1) of the *GATT/TRIPS* agreement which provides that "patents shall be available for any inventions, whether products or processes, in all fields of technology . . . patents shall be available and patent rights enjoyable without discrimination as to the place of invention, the field of technology and whether products are imported or locally produced".[42] While the universality of patents is now being asserted through human rights regimes, the introduction of ethical questions into patent law and, as those in the India, Papua New Guinea and Chile attest, the push towards the globalisation of patent law have served to highlight the political, cultural and economic nature of patent law.[43]

---

[40] In the same way in which the economy presupposes and depends upon an object which is trusted, mobile and secure—money—the patent registration system also relies upon a fixed and stable entity: a situation which was facilitated by the closure of the invention.

[41] This is because as with other more commercial areas of law, patents are more readily translated into a language or form that can cross boundaries.

[42] For many, the legitimacy of patent law is based upon the idea that it operates in a neutral apolitical way, without discrimination or prejudice, to reward and stimulate scientific progress. Paradoxically, one of the consequences of the interaction of patents and biotechnology is that it highlights the folly of those who believe in and promote the idea of the neutrality of patents.

[43] In principle, by asking patent law to evaluate biotechnological inventions, ethics calls into question the status of all inventions.

While our aim in this chapter was to identify what was at stake in the interaction of patent law and ethics, this should not be read as a defence of patents nor as an apology for the present impasse. Rather what it should suggest is that if ethics is to be taken seriously, it is necessary for us to rethink patent law.[44] A useful starting point in this process would be to acknowledge that one of the reasons why ethics has proved so problematic is that these questions are treated, in the tradition of applied jurisprudence, as something external to law, as something which is beyond the scope of legal doctrine. If we are to move away from the applied jurisprudence model which has served this area of law so poorly, if ethics is to be embodied within rather than appended to the administrative and legal process, there is a need to re-imagine patent law and to rethink what we understand by patent doctrine.[45] Importantly, this needs to be done in such a way that it does not merely reproduce the model that currently marginalises ethical questions.[46] Moreover, there is a need to realise that what is at stake in the interaction of patents and ethics is not only patent protection of the products of biotechnological research, but also a particular way of thinking about patent law itself. It is here that we witness the true novelty of the interaction of patent law and biotechnology.

---

[44] Or as Lord Hoffman would have it, to determine the nature of patent law's "specialised epistemology". *Merriele Dow Pharmaceuticals v. Norton & Co* (1995) 33 *I.P.R.* 1.

[45] Contrast, Llewellyn, "The Legal Protection of Biotechnological Inventions: An Alternative Approach" [1997] E.I.P.R. 115 (proposing use of plant variety system as a model for patent reform, and arguing that "the issue of morality, if it is to be retained, should be stated as more appropriately belonging to regulatory bodies which would arguably be better fora for objectively deciding and enforcing concepts of morality.").

[46] Although the concern of this paper is not to review the Directive, it is notable that recitals explicitly refer to ethical principles as a "supplement" to the standard, see, Amended Proposal for a European Parliament and Council Directive on the Legal Protection of Biotechnological Inventions COM(97) 446 final—95/0350(COD) O.J. C–97, C–311/05.

5. A Few Thoughts on Copyright Law and the Subject of Writing

Victor Tadros

Lecturer in Law, University of Aberdeen. B.A. Hons (Oxon.). He has taught at Birkbeck College London and King's College London. He is in the process of completing a doctorate on the implications of Foucault's work on law and legal theory. He has published articles in the Oxford Journal of Legal Studies. He organised a panel at the Critical Legal Conference 1997 with Sionaidh Douglas Scott entitled "European Community Law and Ethics". His interests include legal theory, law and psychiatry and criminal law.

A Few Thoughts on Copyright Law and the Subject of Writing

That there has been a tension between two different sets of ethical principles in copyright law has been well documented in the literature. Copyright cases, as Paul Edward Geller has put it, are informed by two sets of norms: *market place norms* and *authorship norms*. The former, he argues, "require rules to maintain a reliable market in products of the mind",[1] whereas the latter "dictate rules to empower authors to control the use by others of their self-expression".[2] The former treat writing as an object within the economic system whereas the latter treat writing as a manifestation of self that must be protected by right. Discussion of these norms has generally proceeded without an effective evaluation of the ethical relationship between writing and the subject and, in this article, I would like to develop such an account.

In order to do this I would like to explore the forms of subjectivication,[3] to use a Foucauldian concept, involved in each system of norms; that is, to determine what kind of subject is produced when writing is considered either as an expression of the author's self or as an object of the market-place. For when we evaluate the ethics of different legal and practical approaches to writing we are not just concerned with the notion of justice or rights, we are concerned with the stimulation, production and reinforcement of a certain paradigm of subjectivity. That is, we are concerned with a way of understanding or experiencing ourselves and others as beings. Writing, unlike other objects of production, has a fundamental relationship to subjectivity. It both constructs a narrative of the subject which can be acted on[4] and provides an experience of self-expression, a revealing of oneself to the world. Consequently, in dealing

---

[1] In P.E. Geller, *Must Copyright Be For Ever Caught Between Marketplace And Authorship Norms?* in B Sherman and A. Strowel, *Of Authors and Origins: Essays on Copyright Law* (Oxford University Press, Oxford, 1994) p. 159.

[2] *ibid.* p. 159.

[3] Foucault, it should be noted, is critical of the notion that there is a single form of subjectivity that can be found throughout history. Rather, the subject, for Foucault, is produced by networks of power, knowledge and self-hood which are historically immanent. See, for the clearest example of this thought, Foucault's interview entitled *An Aesthetics of Existence* in which he states that "I do indeed believe that there is no sovereign, founding subject, a universal form of subject to be found everywhere. I am very sceptical of this view of the subject and very hostile to it. I believe, on the contrary, that the subject is constituted through practices of subjection, or, in a more autonomous way, through practices of liberation, of liberty, as in Antiquity, on the basis, of course, of a number of rules, styles, inventions to be found in the cultural environment" (*An Aesthetics of Existence* in L.D Kritzman (ed.) *Michel Foucault: Politics Philosophy Culture: Interviews and Other Writings 1977–1984* (Routledge, London, 1988), pp. 50–51. This thought also underpins my ethical evaluation of copyright norms from the perspective of the type of subject which they produce. Foucault's own term for the production of subject is *assujetissement*.

[4] See M. Foucault, *Discipline and Punish* (trans. A. Sheridan), (Penguin, London, 1977), pp. 189–191.

with the ethical principles of copyright, we are dealing with a way of delimiting and controlling the kind of subjects that we are and wish to become. And as we shall see, the law has a significant role to play in codifying these forms of experience. This is an ethical history which Geller's language of norms overlooks.

This essay is divided into three parts. Firstly, I would like to consider the ethical relationship that is developed between the author and writing, using two famous essays by French theorists to open my discussion: Roland Barthes', *Death of the Author* and Michel Foucault's, *What is an Author*? Then I would like to consider thought in the market place using some concepts from Heidegger's essay entitled *The Question Concerning Technology*. Finally I would like to develop an alternative account of the relationship between writing and the self from Foucault's late work and, in particular, the essay entitled *Self Writing*. If some of my text seems quite derivative I hope that the last section will help to explain why I have chosen this form.

Authorial Hermeneutics

Authorship is the name which is given to a relationship between the literary text and its writer, a relationship which has dominated Western culture from the late eighteenth century. In this understanding the text is regarded as a reproduction, more or less accurate, of the internal thoughts, soul or being of its author. A chronological gap is posited, at least in theory, between the "being" of thought and its manifestation in the text. The text is regarded as both the only manifestation of the soul of the author that we have and yet an entirely inadequate manifestation of this soul. For the attempt by the author to translate his soul onto the text is always fraught with the danger of misinterpretation or misrecognition.

In this conception of the relationship between text and writer, then, the author is regarded as a unity, a "body of thought". And the role of the critic is to re-establish this unity by making commensurate all of the contradictions, slippages and multiplicities of the text. On this theme, Foucault has commented:

> The author . . . constitutes a principle of unity in writing where any unevenness of production is ascribed to changes caused by evolution, maturation, or outside influence. In addition, the author serves to neutralize the contradictions that are found in a series of texts. Governing this function is the belief that there must be—at a particular level of an author's thought, of his conscious or unconscious desire—a point where contradictions are resolved, where the incompatible elements can be shown to relate to one another or to cohere around a fundamental and originating contradiction.[5]

---

[5] M. Foucault, *What is an Author*? in D.F. Bouchard (ed.), *Language, Counter-Memory, Practice* (Cornell University Press, New York, 1977), p. 128.

Authorship, for Foucault, must be studied as a function of discourse, a function which governs both the mode of interpreting texts and their categorisation. That is, authorship does not, or does not only, refer to the real writer behind the text, it functions in discourse as a way of dividing texts from each other, creating a difference both in the status accorded to each as well as establishing different modes of interpretation for them. Those texts that have authors are to be studied in a different way to those not given authors.

The conception of authorship as a unity behind the multiplicity of the text came under attack in French literary theory of the 1960s, particularly in the work of Roland Barthes. "Having buried the Author", Barthes wrote in his famous essay, *The Death of the Author*, "the modern scriptor can . . . no longer believe, as according to the pathetic view of his predecessors, that his hand is too slow for his thought or passion and that consequently, making a law of necessity, he must emphasise this delay and indefinitely 'polish' his form".[6] The view which Barthes objected to was the notion that writing is always a translation of thought, that thought must precede writing, that the text is a mere uncertain representation of the sovereign subject of the author. Rather, for Barthes, we should understand the text as a production of discourse itself. Reference to authorial intention, thought Barthes, should play no part in the analysis of texts. Texts, in Barthes view, should be seen as the product of an anonymous language itself.

But, contrary to Barthes view, I would like to argue that "this naturalistic" conception of the author is not just an illusion or a discursive trick. The dissemination of the authorship paradigm not only created a way of seeing and interpreting particular texts. It also gave a particular form to the experience of writing and of being a writer. If, as Barthes suggested, the modern "scriptor" can no longer believe that he is merely translating his pre-existing thought or being, that does not deny that a real experience, which as we shall see can be called "ethical", was not once present in the production of texts. In other words, whilst we can follow Foucault in considering authorship as a "function of discourse",[7] that does not say that a material experience of "being an author" was not itself developed as a result of this discourse. It is not sufficient for Foucault to suggest that the "aspects of an individual, which we designate as an author (or which comprise an individual as an author), are projections, in terms always more or less psychological, or our way of handling texts"[8] because the concept of authorship is not just function to aid textual interpretation, it also functions to construct a particular experience of writing, albeit an experience which is riddled with para-doxes. In considering the ethical relationship between a writer and a text that is created by the "author-function", then, we need to consider the

---

[6] R. Barthes, *The Death of the Author* in *Image Music Text* (Trans. S. Heath) (Fontana Press, London, 1977) p. 146.
[7] *ibid.* p. 124.
[8] *ibid.* p. 127.

right to the text that is established through the coincidence of a particular mode of handling texts and a particular experience of writing.

This experience of writing can be called an "authorial hermeneutics" by which I mean the practice which involves the author in the activity of attempting to make manifest in the text the truth of his being. Writing is not, as Barthes suggests, merely produced by an anonymous language. For this, as Foucault argues, would assign "the empirical characteristics of an author to a transcendental anonymity"[9]; it would emasculate the experience and the activity known as writing as though this has had no bearing on the text. Literature, at least that literature to which, traditionally, we have assigned authors, is attributed a certain value and has to it attached a certain right not just as an illusion of discourse but because of a belief and a practice through which the author attempts, necessarily unsuccessfully, to recreate himself in the text.

The relationship between text and writer that is established by the term "authorship" is, as Foucault suggests, ethical.[10] And it gains its ethical dimension both from the priority that is given to certain texts to which we assign authors as well as a certain experience, with which we are all more or less familiar, of "being an author". Authorial hermeneutics, then, is the experience of attempting to manifest ones soul, being or truth in text. It involves not just unfolding one's "interior" thoughts onto the outside but investigating oneself, "digging deep within oneself" in order to discover what "is" the primordial self. Western literature, for Foucault at least, has the form and character of the confession. He develops this theme in *The History of Sexuality Vol. 1* where he characterises Western literature, since the Middle Ages, as a literature "ordered according to the infinite task of extracting the depths of oneself, in between the words, a truth which the very form of the confession holds out like a shimmering image".[11] The act of writing is a profound expression of being and, whilst this act dominates the writer by tying him to a subjectivity that he can never truly know, it nonetheless establishes a certain right to the text. The text is ethical both because of the self that it expresses and the form of activity that constitutes this expression.

The moral right which an author has to his text is more or less equivalent to the right that he has to himself, a right to defend himself against infiltration and defamation, his right against being treated as a slave, as an object, without his consent. This is manifest most obviously in the French concept of *droit morale* or moral right, inalienable rights of the author recognised in French case law in the nineteenth century.[12] A *droit morale* is a right which far outstrips that accorded to any other object of his creation, to a table or a chair. It far outstrips a right to

---

[9] *ibid.* p. 120.
[10] *ibid.* p. 116.
[11] M. Foucault, *The History of Sexuality Vol. 1: An Introduction*, (Trans. R. Hurley), (Penguin, London, 1978), p. 59.
[12] As embodied in the Berne Convention Art. 6, *bis*.

remuneration for his labour. It is a right to himself as self, as accorded by the sacred moment in which he manifests himself. As Le Chapelier has famously put it "the most sacred, the most legitimate, the most inviolable, and . . . the most personal of all properties, is the work which is the fruit of a writer's thought".[13] Furthermore, this is a right which one can never absolutely give up. One can never entirely divest oneself of such a right through contract in just the same way as one could not absolutely contract one's self away as one does with an object. A text is more than just a property, it is a "bringing to the light of day" of oneself. And as such, its protection is (or was) a sacred duty of the law.

Even if we can no longer believe in the unity of the subject that is expressed in the text, that does not mean that we should devalue entirely the paradoxical experience of writing in law. And to evaluate the ethical content of the law (effectively), once we have signalled the "death of the author" we must be aware of the ethical value of authorship that has been lost. Foucault claims that "we should re-examine the empty space left by the author's disappearance".[14] But in order to do this we must not devalue the ethical value of writing, authorised by a hermeneutics of self, that we have lost in revealing all of the paradoxes inherent in this traditional model of authorship. And this should be borne in mind when I ask, in the next section, "what is the new value of writing once we have read the author his last {w} ri(gh)t[e]s?"

Texts and Technology

The ethical relationship which I have described between a writer and his text would be wholly inadequate to characterise the way in which texts are circulated and manipulated in modern society. A simple right to one's thought as an expression of self is not, and probably never has been, embodied in the law without being supplemented by the normative structure of the market. If the subject has become fragmented, if the author, as the unitary origin of writing, is dead, that is not to say that the law has not inherited a normative system instituted by that traditional model, but neither is it to say that the way in which texts are distributed, translated and manipulated in the market place is entirely, or even mostly, dependent on such a model of authorship.[15] Just as in modern literature there has been a fragmentation of the subject, so in the market

---

[13] Quoted in J. Ginsburg, *A Tale of Two Copyrights: Literary Property in Revolutionary France and America* in B. Sherman and A. Strowel, (eds.) *Of Authors and Origins*, p. 144. As Ginsburg points out, this quote has been taken out of context. Once the work is published, Le Chapelier contended that its main principle would be in the "public domain". Nevertheless, if this shows that there was a competition between *droit morale* and the public domain, this is not to discredit the ethical value that was accorded to the works of an author. The rights accorded to the author, as Ginsburg points out, still operated as an exception to what we have called "market place norms" in Le Chapelier's view.
[14] M. Foucault, *What is an Author?*, p. 121.
[15] The introduction of the authorship paradigm, as Geller notes, was instituted into a market place that preceded it and to which it was always to a certain extent subject (P. Geller, *Must Copyright Be For Ever Caught Between Marketplace And Authorship Norms*).

place the relationship between writer and text is no longer, and probably never has been, dependent on the unity known as "a sovereign author". On the contrary, at least since the beginning of this century, the necessities of the market have played a part in breaking up this unity by the deployment of its own more fluid concepts. We can understand some of the fragmentary relationships between individuals and texts if we consider the element of "right" that is present in the term "copyright."

A copyright is not just an ultimate power which one holds over a certain expression of thought. Like many uses of the word "right", this type of characterisation covers a thousand ambiguities. A right "to" an expression is at once a right to remuneration from that expression, a right to publish and a right to take (legal) action against those others that falsely appropriate that expression. It is a right against those that would parody it, misrepresent it, transpose it. To have a right to an expression is not merely to "own" that expression, it is to have the capacity to control its manipulation, to govern its distribution. It does not necessarily mean that one must posit an essential relationship between an expression, a thought and a subject. A right, considered in terms of capacities, need not be limited to the profound productions of "authors", it may be attributed to any expression of thought. This is the first way in which the word right has been divorced from an object attached to a sovereign subject. A right is a potential for action that one "holds" in reference to a particular expression without it being necessary to deploy any concept at all concerning the mode of production.

There is also an ambiguity in this word "holds". The function of the word "holds" is determined by the type of body to which such a right can be assigned as well as the way in which it can manipulate the object of that right. In the case of a text, a right can, in the simplest case, be assigned to an individual who is regarded as an author of a text. But even in this case it is unclear exactly *what it is* in that individual to which the right is assigned. Is it the continuing subsistence of his body? Is it the continuing mind from which the work originated? Is it to another right, the right to use a certain proper name? All the familiar problems of personal identity seem to arise with regard to this simplest case of authorship and whilst, in practice, we need not determine exactly what we mean by the term "individual" in relation to the holding of a right, nevertheless, our doubts about the subsistence of the identity of a writer seems to put in question the relationship between the writer and his text both epistemologically and in law.

These problems only multiply themselves in the case of dual or multiple authors. In that case it may be that parts of the text are assigned to particular authors or that the whole is written jointly by the two. In the former case ambiguities may arise as to whether it is the writer of the individual part or the both of them that holds the right to individual parts of the text. Is the text a unity to which the parts are secondary or is it the parts that make up different unities that are collected into a particular multiplicity known as the book? In the latter case, even if the book is considered as a unity, it is a unity that reflects a multiplicity.

Whilst it is simple to say that the right is held by both authors, it becomes clear that this cannot be by virtue of the unity of which the text is a translation.[16] Again, in the case where an individual assigns to himself a ghost writer, is it the one who produces "the phrases" or who formulates the expressions in a material form that is assigned the right to the text or is it the "originator of the thoughts" that are merely transformed into the finished text?[17] And what if the writer cannot be considered to be any particular individual at all but rather a company or a computer with multiple programmers who can no longer be identified, and certainly no longer related to the text.[18] Whatever legal solutions have been provided to these problems can only exacerbate the dissolution of the author as the unitary subject in whom a text finds its origin and meaning.

In this world of writing even individuals have taken on the model of the conglomerate, of the machine with multiple parts, of fragmentation. Perhaps the most illuminating example of this possibility occurs at the beginning of Deleuze and Guattari's *A Thousand Plateaus* in a description which they give of a previous book which they wrote together:

> The two of us wrote *Anti-Oedipus* together. Since each of us was several, there was already quite a crowd. Here we have made use of everything that came within range, what was closest as well as farthest away. We have assigned clever pseudonyms to prevent recognition. Why have we kept our own names? Out of habit, purely out of habit. To make ourselves unrecognizable in turn. To render imperceptible, not ourselves, but what makes us act, feel, and think. Also because it's nice to talk like everybody else, to say the sun rises, when everybody knows it's only a manner of speaking. To reach, not the point where one no longer says I, but the point where it is no longer of any importance whether one says I. We are no longer ourselves. Each will know his own. We have been aided, inspired, multiplied.[19]

---

[16] The criteria for joint authorship are laid down in s.10(1) of the Copyright, Designs and Patents Act 1988 where it is stated that "'a work of joint authorship' means a work produced by the collaboration of two or more authors in which the contribution of each author is not distinct from that of the other author or authors".

[17] In general in English law it has been held that the former is regarded as author (*Donoghue v. Allied Newspapers Ltd.* [1938] 1 Ch. 106) although some doubt is cast on this principle by the case of *Najeria Heptulla v. Orient Longman Ltd* [1989] F.S.R. 598 where it is stated that "it is difficult to comprehend, or to accept, that when two people agree to produce a work where one provides the material . . . and the other expresses the same in a language which is presentable to the public that the entire credit for such an undertaking . . . should go to the person who has transcribed the thoughts of another. To me it appears that if there is intellectual contribution by two or more person, pursuant to a pre-concerted joint design, to the composition of a literary work then those persons have to be regarded as joint authors". However, as we shall see, this distinction is not really dependent on that between thought and expression but as to what level of abstraction of a particular thought/expression the court is willing to protect. For reasons of certainty, it would seem, the level of abstraction of an thought/expression which is considered in law a relationship of identity is kept fairly narrow.

[18] On rights in computer generated works see Pamela Samuelson, *Allocating Ownership Rights in Computer Generated Works* [1986] Vol. 47, *University of Pittsburgh Law Review*, 1185.

[19] G. Deleuze and F. Guattari, *A Thousand Plateaus*, (Trans. B. Massumi) (Athlone, London, 1987), p. 3.

And in such a world, what can have happened to the language of rights? To what does the copyright refer? What function does it have? What subjectivity does it refer to and help to create? Once the unity of the author has departed, the writer is fragmented, the one becomes many and the right becomes . . .?

I would like to begin my analysis of the nature of this right with the observation that a copyright is a right to thought. As far as traditional approaches to copyright go this thought, or expression, is a controversial one.[20] Nevertheless, insofar as I have been using the term expression, I would maintain that I could just as easily have substituted the word thought. For the distinction between thought and expression in copyright law can no longer be regarded as the distinction between the original or authorial *meaning* of an expression and the actual sentence which forms it. This difference is foreclosed by the arguments of Barthes and Foucault considered above. If thought is, following Foucault, now *thought on the outside*, thought which does not rely on a pre-existing subjective state to justify or unify its meaning, so this distinction between thought and expression apparently dissolves.

So what does it mean, then, to use the difference between thought and expression in the law? It is merely a strategy to foster a degree of legal certainty; in other words, it is a technique to make thought *functional*, to make thought technologically convenient. By using the distinction between thought and expression one ensures protection only of that which the law can successfully delimit with sufficient certainty. And this means dividing up thoughts until one is as close as possible to an indivisible element without losing the originality of the text. By allowing legal protection only to those phrases that have a minimal level of variation from the original text, the law minimises the potential for conflict between those claiming the identity of thoughts and those claiming their difference. The level of abstraction known as "the idea" is too ambiguous for the law; when one has two different expressions of the same idea it is unclear to the law whether there is one thought or two, engendering infinite possibilities of legal conflict. By limiting the protection of "thought" to the protection of "expression" the law reduces its problematic from the comparison of ideas, with a flexible expression, to the comparison of word order, which is far less flexible. Only carefully delimited variations, such as translations, are protected in law for this reason.

---

[20] The distinction between idea and expression was expressed as an idea in *Donogue v. Allied Newspapers* [1938]. The distinction was codified in the United States in the Copyright Act 1976, s.102. In subsection (b) it is stated that "in no case does copyright protection for an original work of authorship extend to any idea, procedure, process, system, method of operation, concept, principle, or discovery, regardless of the form in which it is described, explained, illustrated, or embodied in such work".

But this does not take away from the fact that it is thought that the law is ultimately protecting, for expression, and the publication of expression, is the only social manifestation of thought. Thought simply cannot take place in the public domain without its expression. Once we have introduced all of the slippages between expression and the abstract unity of the idea, a theme common to post-structuralist thinking, the idea itself becomes reduced to the possibility of its expression. The law, then, attempts to distinguish not between thought and expression, but between *the same expression or different expressions*, or, what amounts to the same thing for law, *the same thought or different thoughts*. The distinction between thought and expression does not draw a difference which can be maintained by the distinction between the unity of meaning and the multiplicity of its possible expressions. It draws a boundary around which statements, for purposes of law, will be regarded as identical and which will be regarded as different. So where I have used the term "expression" I would now like to substitute the word "thought" for it is thought that is the subject of copyright law and which copyright law protects.

Now, by ascribing the term "right" to a thought what does one do to the nature of thought? What does thought become once it becomes the subject of a right in the modern sense of the term? As we have seen, the term "right" denotes a potential for action. And this potential for action is flexible in two senses. First, its nature is flexible. Once a thought forms a complex with a right, that thought can be transferred or manipulated in the market place. It can be sold, transferred, withheld, acted upon, and manipulated. In some senses, then, a thought relates to its owner, either single or multiple, in the same way as any other object of production. In some ways having a right to a thought is like being the owner of a car; one is free to do with it what one will, so long as one is acting within the boundaries of the criminal law. In another sense, though, this metaphor of the car is insufficient. For the right to manipulate thought is not just controlled by the criminal law. The right to control thought is limited by contract, by the elements of inalienable rights that are still maintained, by the intricacies of copyright law, by a whole series of laws that govern its use. The model of car ownership is insufficient then, because the right to thought is not just determined by the circumstances in which action can be taken against an individual for his transgressions, it is also determined by a whole set of internal rules that determine the circumstances for its use and assignment, rules that determine the complete nature of the thought-right complex. Thought, then, takes the model of the hire-car; one's right over it is in principle temporary, subject to the rights of others, limited by the terms of contract and statutory controls.

Secondly, a right is flexible in its point of attack. It has often been argued that a right is a relationship between individuals. However, this is quite inadequate and for two reasons. Firstly because the determination of exactly *which* individuals this right operates between can never be known in advance. The right is rather a right against any potential aggressor. And secondly because this aggressor may take a form which has not been predicted in advance. A right to thought can be operated against a company, a group, an individual or a computer. And to this extent a right is like a patrol. When one is ascribed a right over a thought one has the potential to determine activities over that thought in much the same way as a military unit has the potential to determine activities over a piece of land. A right and a thought, then, form a complex. And the right expresses a relationship not between individuals but between one individual, group or multiplicity and a thought. The nature of the right determines the extent to which that thought can be mobilized.

As a consequence of the ascription of right certain capacities are attributed to the bearer. The capacity to bring an action, to prevent publication, to control repetition, and all of the traditional rights given to authors. But potentially also the capacity to divide the right to that thought, to leave it in a will, to assign it, to destroy it. Once it is assigned a right a thought becomes like a piece of technology, available for use. And this availability for use has certain limitations. The technique by which a right is assigned and its boundaries determined, then, is no longer (just) individualised, it is controlled by law. In taking up a right to that thought we become what Deleuze calls "dividuals", as opposed to individuals.[21] The right to control the manipulation of that thought is no longer invested in the unity that provides its natural origin. It is taken up by anybody and only to the extent that it has been assigned or ascribed to it by a legal process.

If thought has become technological, it is copyright law, by making thought the subject of rights, that has assimilated thought into the technological sphere and has codified it. But what does it mean to assimilate thought into technology? It means that thought no longer represents man; it is no longer regarded as a description of the nature of man *in itself* (although it may describe, or attempt to describe, man). Thought, rather, becomes ready for use. The energy of thought is unlocked by the market place. It no longer remains dormant as the description of a pre-existing subject. Thought, through copyright law, becomes a form of energy that can be manipulated. It is more than just a thing, it is a tool, a "for-which". Copyright law is what Heidegger calls a challenging, a challenging to the *natural* quality of thought; to the positing of thought as natural. "That challenging happens", as Heidegger writes, "in that the energy concealed in nature is unlocked, what is unlocked is transformed, what is transformed is stored up, what is stored up is, in turn, distributed, and what is distributed is switched about ever anew".[22] Thought itself is standing in reserve, ready to be manipulated. It

---

[21] See G. Deleuze, *Postscript on Control Societies* in *Negotiations* (Trans. M. Joughin) (Columbia University Press, New York, 1995).
[22] M. Heidegger, *The Question Concerning Technology* in *The Question Concerning Technology and Other Essays* (trans. W. Lovitt) (Harper, New York, 1977), p. 16.

is no longer tied to a natural author of whom it would be the expression. It is a potential which can be set in motion by those that are assigned a right.

What does Heidegger mean by this term "standing in reserve" or "standing-reserve" which I have borrowed? The contrast which Heidegger draws is between a piece of technology as an object and as "standing-reserve". "Whatever stands by in the sense of standing-reserve no longer stands over against us as object" he writes.[23] The whole of technology, in the modern world, has this quality for Heidegger; technology is no longer to be considered as an object to be determined by its qualities. It is to be considered as a function to be determined by its use. The example he gives is of the airliner:

> Yet an airliner that stands on the runway is surely an object. Certainly. We can represent the machine so. But then it conceals itself as to what and how it is. Revealed, it stands on the taxi strip only as standing-reserve, inasmuch as it is ordered to ensure the possibility of transportation. For this it must be in its whole structure and in every one of its constituent parts, on call for duty, *i.e.* ready for takeoff.[24]

In describing thought as standing-reserve, then, I am alluding to the way in which it has become technological. And as such, its ontological status is determined by *use*, use for profit, use for interviews, for curriculum vitae, for status, for titles, for reference, for consultation. For it is as it exists for use that we *care* about technology. Thought no longer has the paradoxical, but ethical, status of the natural revealing of man, of the author. It is no longer a sacred object whose value is in its natural meaning that remains to be uncovered and stabilised. Its value is in *what it can do* and as such it *is* what it can do.

But who achieved this transformation? In one sense it was thought itself. For without the energy of thought, of thinking this or that, the transformation could never have been effected. And yet there was no particular thought that directed the *overall* transformation. Thought as technology multiplied itself. For once a decision had to be made concerning *who would get the profits* (the ghost writer? the computer programmer? the corporation?), thought could only reach a compromise, it could only make a decision one way or the other. But whichever decision it made, the nature of thought was still in the process of a subtle transformation to which thought was a party but not as the main protagonist. It was technology, by making such decisions necessary, that harnessed the energy of thought, that assimilated thought, in the transformation of itself. For once writing became technological, once the experience of writing was no longer limited to an ethical duty to be carried out in solitude as a revealing, but was the subject of a technological transformation, thought was soon to follow. And, as technology effected its own reproduction and its own continuing complexity, thought itself could only function to coordinate that technology, to order it. It could not take control of it.

Technology is out of control, or rather it is self controlling. Thought does not have the capacity to reserve technology. Technology makes thought a capacity, assimilates thought into its own games of distribution. Thought has the capacity to make use of this or that but, just as man, it does not have control over the reserving of technology itself. The continuous event of reservation is not an activity which is governed by thought. Thought, like man, is challenged to exploit its own energies, it is already set in reserve to manipulate itself through the language of rights. If thought acts upon itself, it can only do so as possession. "If man is challenged, ordered, to do this [to exploit the energies of nature]," Heidegger writes, "then does not man himself belong even more originally than nature within the standing-reserve?".[25] So we can say of thought that, by being assimilated into the law as a right, it has become standing-reserve. Thought, acting upon itself, can only manipulate itself in this or that way. It can never assimilate itself *as a whole* to be within its own control and, consequently, it can never transform its ontological status. The subject cannot take on an ethical relationship to thought once thought is in the market place. It can only put itself in the position to manipulate thought. Or, more accurately, it only exists as a position for the manipulation of thought.

As a consequence of the mobilisation of thought in the market place, it has become, at least to a certain extent, dissociated from the experience of being. Thought itself has become set free, it has been appropriated by a market dominated by the production and satisfaction (often almost simultaneous) of desire. The text has lost the mythical quality that it once had when one attempted to operate on it a hermeneutics; an operation through which one would attempt to discover the unity of being and meaning behind the text. The text, and thought as carried through its various modes of production, has become a simple product of labour, a product that can be manipulated and used according to its own system of rights, a system within which subjects only provide potential as energy, as subjects of desire. The value of the text, as far as being is concerned, has been relegated as a problem. We now have only the most limited experience of determining a mode of being through the text. We are caught within a market in which the production of the new, the readable, the erotic, the popular, has replaced the desire for truth, the spiritual foundations of the text. The ethics which Foucault assigned to the author function has not been replaced by a new ethics of the text, it has been replaced by the autopoiesis of desire.

So let us return to Foucault's comment concerning the death of the author. "We should re-examine the empty space left by the author's

---

[25] *ibid.* p. 18.

disappearance,"[26] Foucault suggests, "we should attentively observe, along its gaps and fault lines, its new demarcations, and the reapportionment of this void; we should await the fluid functions released by this disappearance".[27] But in examining this space we have found nothing to replace the ethics that was once established by the author function. The space is truly empty in an ethical sense. The functions that have replaced the notion of the author are truly fluid, but they have the fluidity of the market. The text, now, is just another piece of technology to be manipulated according to the law of rights. And in this law nothing is sacred, nothing determining but desire, a desire that is constantly stimulated to the point of excess. All that we have achieved, in Foucault's terms, is a liberation from the dominating function of the author. But we have done nothing to determine the ethics associated with freedom.

As Foucault said in a late interview, "[the] act of liberation is not sufficient to establish the practices of liberty that later on will be necessary for this people, this society and these individuals to decide upon receivable and acceptable forms of their existence or political society".[28] And, he goes on "to say the things somewhat schematically, there would be desire, pulsation, taboos, repression and interiorisation. It is in lifting these taboos, *i.e.* in liberating one's self, that the problem would be solved. And there, I think that we are completely missing the moral problem . . . which is the practice of liberty. How can one practice freedom?".[29] This moral problem, it seems to me, also faces us with regard to authorship. Foucault's demand, in *What is an Author?* that we should "await the fluid functions released by this disappearance" of the author seems to me entirely inadequate. These functions have been released, thought has been appropriated by the market forces of desire upon which authorship was a dominating limit. But in doing so the moral problem of the relationship between the text and the subject has been lost. The text has lost almost all of the ethical relationship that it had to subjectivity. In all of the frenzy to break down the barriers surrounding the text, the whole ethical problem of how to conduct ourselves in an age of textual freedom has been forgotten.

A New Ethics of the Text in the Late Foucault

Foucault was concerned throughout his work with the relationship between writing and the subject. Firstly in *What is an Author?* he attempted to describe the way in which the "author-function" determined the modern construction of the author as a subject and a source for the interpretation of texts. Later, in *Discipline and Punish* he went on to characterise the production of the subject as narrated by disciplinary

---

[26] *c.f.* n. 12.
[27] M. Foucault, *What is an Author?* p. 121.
[28] M. Foucault, *The Ethic of Care for the Self as a Practice of Freedom* in J. Bernauer and D. Rasmussen (eds.) *The Final Foucault*, (Massachusett, MIT Press, Cambridge, 1987) p. 3.
[29] *ibid.* p. 4.

institutions in the form of the examination.[30] Finally, in a late article, recently translated under the title *Self Writing*, he attempted to show a relationship between the text and the subject in Greco-Roman culture. In this section I would like to consider this final essay in order to develop a relationship between writing and the subject that would not take the dominating and paradoxical form of the sovereign author. In short, the relationship between the subject and the text which I would like to institute is not one in which the subject is regarded as the origin of the text but rather one in which the text has a part to play in the ethical formation of subjects. In this scheme, the valorisation of the text is not for its origin in a sovereign subject but rather its potential for shaping a new and more ethical form of subjectivity. But before undertaking this analysis we ought briefly to consider the place of this essay in Foucault's project towards the end of his life.

The essay *Self Writing* is an extension of Foucault's work on techniques of the self. Through these techniques one takes oneself as a field of actions, one learns how to constitute or shape oneself as an ethical subject. In Foucault's words, there is a problematisation as to "the manner in which the individual could form himself as the ethical subject (*sujet moral*) of his actions (*ses conduites*)".[31] In this relationship between the subject and himself, Foucault suggests that "the act of writing for oneself and for others—came, rather late, to play a considerable role" (SW: 208).[32] Whilst it was important to read it was also important to write. And this not in order that one could express the hidden truth of oneself, an obligation that would be fulfilled by the form of diaries and confessions in later western societies, but in order that one could bring "present to hand" wise thoughts for use, meditation and the shaping of the self. This function of writing, Foucault, following Plutarch, has called "ethopoietic"; "it is an agent of the transformation of truth into *ethos*".[33]

It should be noted that the form of writing that Foucault refers to introduces a relationship between the subject and truth as strong as the relationship that he develops in *What is an Author?* However, this relationship operates in the opposite direction. In *What is an Author?* the text provides evidence of the truth of the author. The text, being a manifestation of his inner soul, was considered a reflection, however inadequate, of the being that preceded it. Now, in writing, as an activity of Greco-Roman society, there is also a relationship between the subject and truth. However, in this society it is the truth of the outside that leads

---

[30] As Foucault writes, "the examination that places individuals in a field of surveillance also situates them in a network of writing; it engages them in a whole mass of documents that capture and fix them. . . . A 'power of writing' was constituted as an essential part in the mechanisms of discipline" (M. Foucault, *Discipline and Punish*. (Trans. Sheridan.) Penguin, London, 1977), p. 189. This power of writing made each individual a case, a narrative which directs future operations of power.

[31] M. Foucault, respectively *The Care of the Self*. (Trans. R. Hurley) *Le Souci de Soi* (Gallimard, Paris, 1984), p. 95 and p. 117.

[32] M. Foucault, *Self Writing* (trans. R. Hurley) in P. Rabinow, (ed.) Michael Foucault, Ethics: The Essential Works 1, (Penguin Press, London, 1997), p. 208.

[33] *ibid.*, p. 209.

an individual to form, shape or constitute his own being or directs him in the activity of forming, shaping or constituting that being.

Hence, in *What is an Author?* Foucault wrote of the "manner in which a text apparently points to this figure who is outside and precedes it"[34] suggesting a form of narrative in which, in the activity of writing, the author attempts as closely as possible to bring to the light what is already inside himself. On the other hand, in the writing of truths, as they were constituted in the private journals known as *hupomnemata*, the aim was not to express the truth of oneself, to bring forth the hidden, but to repeat the "already-said",[35] the wise statements which one could utilise to aid the formation of an ethical self. Foucault wrote the following of the *hupomnemata*:

> they do not constitute a "narrative of oneself"; they do not have the aim of bringing to the light of day the *arcana conscientiae*, the oral or written confession of which has a purificatory value. The movement they seek to bring about is the reverse of that: the intent is not to pursue the unspeakable, nor to reveal the hidden, nor to say the unsaid, but on the contrary to capture the already said, to collect what one has managed to hear or read, and for a purpose that is nothing less than the shaping of the self.[36]

In the chronological link between writing and the subject, then, Foucault suggests that the movement should be reversed. It is not that, in signalling the death of the author, we should break all links between the text and the subject. Rather we should see the text as a potential for the formation of the ethical subject. If Barthes signalled the "birth of the reader"[37] he only gave it a birth, not an education, an evolution or a development. The reader does not, in Greco-Roman culture, constitute the unity of the text, the site of meaning. Rather he constitutes himself as a harmony of true and wise texts.

In ancient Rome writing was not just an occupation that one did for oneself. As in modern Western society, writing can have an audience. In both the Greco-Roman culture and modern Western society, writing is given the role of "bringing forth oneself", of making oneself apparent in the world. However, once again, this "bringing forth of oneself" takes different forms in each culture. As we have seen, Foucault suggests that

---

[34] M. Foucault, *What is an Author?* p. 115.

[35] The idea of the "common-place book" of the Renaissance provides a more recent example of this kind of textual practice in which phrases are collected in such a way that the notion of the author becomes entirely inappropriate; see, for a detailed analysis, M. Thomas, *Reading and Writing the Renaissance Commonplace Book: A Question of Authorship?* In M. Woodmansee and P. Jaszi (eds.) *The Construction of Authorship* (Duke University Press, London, 1994). See also Yeo. *Ephiaim Chamber's Cyclopaedia (1728) and the Tradition of Commonplaces* (March 1996) J.H.I. 157. It should be noted that the commonplace book was not generally concerned with philosophical or ethical texts but with literary phrases. This practice has been continued by Samuel Beckett.

[36] M. Foucault, *Self Writing*. (Trans. R. Hurley). In P. Rabinow, (ed.) *Ethics: the Essential Works 1*, (Penguin Press, London, 1997), pp. 210–11.

[37] R. Barthes, *The Death of the Author*, p. 148.

modern Western literature takes the form of a confession, a revelation of the hidden in oneself. If the Greco-Roman culture also made the self manifest through writing, this was not because the text could constitute his hidden interior but because the text could make present the absent both to oneself and others. And this "making present" did not take the form of a revealing of hidden elements. Rather it was a way of setting oneself up to oneself for observation and examination by oneself and one's peers.

This relationship between writing and the self becomes clear from Foucault's analysis of Roman correspondence. As Foucault puts it, "the work the letter carries out on the recipient, but is also brought to bear on the writer by the very letter he sends, thus involves an "introspection"; but the latter is to be understood not so much as a decipherment of the self by the self as an opening one gives the other onto oneself".[38] Writing, whilst it takes the form of a revealing, then, does not operate as a way of unfolding the secrets hidden in the depths of ones soul. It operates by recounting ones actions and impressions, the experiences that one has had. So, for example, Seneca recounts to Lucilius the events of every day in full, thus committing himself to live under the gaze of others. And his correspondence could include "an account of the everyday banality, an account of correct or incorrect actions, of the regimen observed, of the physical or mental exercises in which one engaged".[39] This is not to say that correspondence merely describes external events; as Foucault writes, it is an account not just of the actions but of the impressions that accompany them: hence the introspective quality referred to. But this is done not so that one can extinguish one's desires but so that one can perfect one's technique of living. Correspondence, then, is not a quest whereby one reveals what one is but rather an accounting of a style of living so that one can perfect this style, this technique of the self.

Conclusion: A New Ethics of Writing

In the modern world of writing we have a constant obligation to produce the new, to develop new themes and variations of themes. Either one must write something new or not write. As we have seen, Foucault, in an account which has certain ironies given his own project, suggests that the "already-said" should replace the unsaid as the subject of writing. Rather than an injunction against repetition, which makes of the "already-said" a form of property, we should valorise certain forms of repetition. For a text does not belong to an author as the origin of its formation, it belongs to a reader/writer who determines his own mode of being by it (or more than belonging to him, for this would still be to use the language of appropriation and technology, it becomes him or he becomes (immanent to) the text).

---

[38] M. Foucault, *Self Writing*, p. 217.
[39] *ibid.*, p. 219.

In Greco-Roman writing, unlike in the Western experience of literature there was no obligation constantly to express the new or the interesting. As we have seen, writing could be quite banal, an expression of the already-said, an expression, down to the most minute and trivial details, of what one has done. The constant desire for originality which is stimulated by modern thought-technology had only a limited value in Greco-Roman culture. In the culture of the Ancients it was the self rather than the text that constituted the ethical evaluation of writing. Writing is for the self as an experience of becoming, of stylising one's existence, rather than an expression or fulfilment of desire. The sovereign author reveals his desire through the text. Technological writing fulfils a desire which it creates through the text. In Greco-Roman culture, if there is a relationship between thought and desire it is that through writing one can become a master of one's desire, so that one can develop a style of living and a style of self that one can call ethical.

Consequently, rather than making "authorship norms" and "market-place norms" commensurate, we should aim at displacing both with a series of what Foucault might have called "ethopoietic norms", norms whereby the legal protection of texts is directed at where they can go and with what ethical value rather than where they come, where the labour of production becomes less important than the labour of utilisation. It is only in the development of such norms that we can truly be said to have replaced the sovereign subject with a form worthy of the terms "norma-tive" and "ethical". And it is only by doing this that we would be in a position to evaluate, in an ethical sense, what, if anything, should become of copyright law.

6. Equal Treatment for Artists Under Copyright Law and the E.U.'s *Droit De Suite*

Simon Hughes

Currently employed by the Authors' Licensing and Collecting Society as a researcher for a European Union funded project concerning electronic commerce with particular emphasis on the trading of intellectual property rights. Holds a LL.B degree (Brunel University) and a LL.M degree in Intellectual Property Law (QMW, London). He has published in the E.I.P.R.

Equal Treatment for Artists Under Copyright Law and the E.U.'s *Droit De Suite*[1]

I. Introduction

a) The Problem

Imagine three people: A, B, and C. Imagine each is considered a creative genius in their respective field and as a result each has achieved widespread fame among almost all sectors of the British public and, to varying extent, also international acclaim. Through the legal mechanisms in place both A and C have been afforded the possibility of earning vast sums of money, thus rewarding their creative and intellectual efforts. Their work has made them both multi-millionaires. In contrast, due to the lack of a similar legal mechanism being in place, B, while being able to make a very good living, has not been afforded the possibility of joining the heights that A and C have reached.

A is a writer. It could be Jeffrey Archer,[2] who receives a royalty for every copy of one of his books sold and also a royalty for every time one of his books is borrowed from a public library.[3] C is a composer or songwriter or both. It could be Phil Collins,[4] who (ignoring his role as a performer for present purposes) receives a royalty on every record sold, and via the Mechanical Copyright Protection Society also receives royalties for recordings made by broadcasters and suppliers of background music to clubs, pubs, restaurants, and so on. In addition, Collins would receive further royalties from the public performance of his songs from the Performing Rights Society, irrespective of whether or not the actual performance is by Collins himself. B is a painter. It could be

---

[1] This article is based on research carried out for an LL.M. extended essay submitted to the University of London July 1, 1997. The author is indebted to Professor J. Lahore for his extensive help during the preparation of the essay. The author is also grateful to Professor J.A.L. Sterling and Professor G. Dworkin for their assistance and encouragement.

[2] Archer is ranked at 360 in The Sunday Times list of the richest 500 people in Britain in 1997 with an estimated worth of at least £50 million. The annual royalties from Barbara Taylor Bradford's book sales are estimated to be about £1 million ranking her ahead of Jeffrey Archer at 305 in the list with a total worth of £60 million. Internet Web site: address htt://www.sunday-times.co.UK/news/pages/infotimes/500richest.

[3] The Public Lending Right Act 1979 provides an author with a royalty of 2p for each borrowing of one of their books from a public library up to an annual maximum of £6,000.

[4] Ranked at 172 in *The Sunday Times* list, Collins has an estimated worth of £105 million. Paul McCartney, whose solo and music publishing copyrights are valued at £100 million, was ranked 37 in the list with a total worth calculated at £420 million.

Francis Bacon,[5] who is only able to benefit from the first sale of his work. There is no legal mechanism to enable him to receive a royalty every time one of his paintings is resold in the U.K. or every time his work is exhibited for public display. However, if B was George Beuys, a German artist, he would have been afforded the possibility of being able to benefit from every sale of his work. As with Francis Bacon, he would receive the purchase price for the initial sale of the work but, in addition, he also would receive a royalty for each subsequent resale of his work in Germany.[6]

This highlights a double anomaly in the law. First, the discrimination in the treatment between different categories of creators: some being able to fully participate in the success of their work and others who are prevented from this participation following the initial sale of their work. Second, the discrimination in the treatment of creators within the same category which arises from differing legal provisions which apply. This is accentuated within the E.U. where some Member States employ the legal mechanism for artists to participate in the resales of their work and other Member States do not; thus offending the aims of a single market and equal treatment for all the citizens of the E.U.[7]

b) The Solution

The European Commission has initiated the removal of this anomaly by proposing a Directive to harmonise the legal mechanism; Proposed Directive "on the resale right for the benefit of the author of an original work of art".[8] This legal mechanism is commonly referred to as *"droit de suite."*

c) The Debate

The question concering the introduction of a *droit de suite* has been one of the chief debates concerning the art world over the last two decades. During this time proposals to introduce a *droit de suite* have been rejected

---

[5] Bacon died in 1992 with a gross estate valued at £11 million. It is interesting to note that no fine artist (painter, sculptor etc.) appears in The Sunday Times list. Ironically the steady rise in art values is one of the reasons given for the rich becoming richer in the list (Article, The Rich Get Richer, The Sunday Times, htpt://www.sunday-times.co.UK/news/pages/infotimes/500richest). To turn the screw further, the composer of musicals, Andrew Lloyd Webber (net worth estimated at a staggering £550m and rising), is considered to be one of the prominent private art collectors in the world owning a Picasso valued at £18 million and a Canaletto valued at £10 million; both far in excess of what these artists earned during their lifetimes.
[6] As Beuys is now deceased the royalties are received by his heirs for the remaining duration of his copyright.
[7] As a result of the Phil Collins decision national treatment must apply—a painting by Bacon sold in Germany would attract the German *droit de suite* provision, and conversely, a painting by Beuys sold in the U.K. would not attract any *droit de suite* provision. See page 34 below.
[8] COM(96) 97 final.

in the U.K., Australia and the USA.[9] The move by the E.U.'s legislative process has reopened the debate with added fervour and if and when adopted may prove to be a catalyst to the introduction of *droit de suite* provisions throughout the world.

In this debate two issues arise: First, Should there be a *droit de suite*? Does a sophisticated legal system in a world approaching the second millennium need a *droit de suite*? Is it just that without such a provision an artist can not economically benefit from copyright law in the same way as an author or composer can benefit? Second, if the question of existence is answered in the affirmative, what form should a *droit de suite* take? How should it be drafted? Most papers written on the subject concentrate only on the existence question paying no or only scant regard to the question of form.[10] This may be considered as being short-sighted. The two questions are inextricably linked. If the case for the existence of a *droit de suite* succeeds then the justification for its existence must shape the form that a *droit de suite* takes.

In attempting to answer these questions this paper will first examine the French origin of the right, its objectives, and the theoretical justifications for its introduction. It is then useful to consider the subsequent development of the *droit de suite* through the Berne Convention, further developments in France, and its introduction and refinement in Germany. This is followed by an appraisal of the United Kingdom's fervent opposition to the introduction of a U.K. provision, which is primarily based on the fear that its introduction will result in an almost wholesale transference of the London art market to non *droit de suite* countries, notably to the United States and Switzerland.[11] This paper will then

---

[9] See the Report on Copyright and Designs Law (Cmnd. 6732) (1977) ("The Whiford Report"), discussed below from page 26; the Australian Copyright Council, *Droit de Suite*: The Artist's Resale Royalty and its Implications for Australia (1989) ("Australian Copyright Council Report"); and the U.S. Copyright Office's Report *Droit de Suite*: The Artists Resale Royalty (Washington: Register of Copyright 1992) ("U.S. Copyright Office's Report"). For a summary of the latter see also *Droit de Suite*: The Artist's Resale Royalty, Copyright Office Report Executive Summary (1992) 16 *Colum.-VLA J.L. & Arts* 381; and Perlmutter, S., "Resale Royalties for Artists: An Analysis of the Registrar of Copyrights" Report (1992) 16 *Column.-V.L.A.J.L. & Arts* 395.

[10] See for example, with regard to the U.S. R. Hauser, "The French *Droit de Suite*: The Problem of Protection for the Underprivileged Artist under the Copyright Law" [1959] 6 *Bull Cop. Soc.* 94 ("Hauser"); N. Siegal, "The Resale Royalty Provisions of the Visual Artists Right Act: Their History and Theory" (1988) 93 *Dickinson Law Review* 1; T. Goetz, "In Support of the Resale Royalty" (1989) 7 *Cardozo Arts & Ent. L.J.* 249 ("Goetzl"); G. Edelson, "The Case Against an American *Droit de Suite*" (1989) 7 *Cardozo Arts & Ent. L.J.* 260 ("Edelson"); L. Neumann, "The Bern Convention and *Droit de Suite* Legislation in the United States: Domestic and International Consequences of Federal Incorporation of State Law for Treaty Implementation" (1992) 16 *Colum.-VLA J.L. & Arts* 157; M. Reddy, "The *Droit de Suite*: Why American Fine artist should have the Right to a Resale Royalty" (1995) 15 *Loyola of Los Angeles Entertainment Law Journal* 509; and with regard to Australia: S. Ricketson, "Moral Rights and the *Droit de Suite*: International Conditions and Australian obligations" [1990] 3 ENT L.R. 78; and with regard to the E.U.: T. Shapiro, "*Droit de Suite* An Author's Right in the Copyright Law of the European Community" (1992) 4 ENT L.R. 118 ("Shapiro"); N. Smith, "*Droit de Suite*—The Case Against the Initiative of the European Commission" [1996] 63 Copyright World 25 ("Smith"). Despite recommending against the introduction of a *droit de suite* the Whitford Report, the Australian Copyright Council Report, and the U.S. Copyright Office's Report did go on to consider the substantive provisions that a *droit de suite* should contain if it were to be introduced.

[11] The recognised standard abbreviations "UK" and "US" will be employed and although it is recognised that the United Kingdom did not exist at the time of the signing of the Berne Convention for the sake of consistency that the "UK" shall also be taken to mean Great Britain.

attempt to critically examine the proposed European Commission Directive to introduce a European Union wide *droit de suite*.[12] The Commission's study and its deliberation over the existence question is then explained.

The paper will then consider the possible form of the *droit de suite*. Existing *droit de suite* laws need to be examined and experience drawn from them utilised to formulate a model provision. The substantive proposals of the approved Directive are discussed. The paper suggests a number of amendments to the proposed Directive based on the evaluation of the French, German, Berne Convention, and other *droit de suite* laws, with a view to produce a workable and effective E.U. *droit de suite* provision that will not harm the London art market and will therefore be acceptable to the U.K.

d) Definition

Droit de suite is "one of the copyright concepts least understood in common law countries" remarked the editor of a copyright journal in 1959![13] In simple terms *droit de suite* is the right of an artist to receive a royalty payment from subsequent sales of their original work; hence the English language term, resale royalty right. The Explanatory Memorandum of the proposed Directive defines *"droit de suite"* as the right for the author, or after his death the right for his heirs or other beneficiaries, to receive a percentage of the price of a work—being usually a work in the field of the graphic and plastic arts—when it is resold by public auction or through an agent.[14] A literal translation of the French term, *"droit de suite"*, the "right to follow on" or the "right to follow up", derives from real property law in France.[15] The application of this term to the area of copyright (properly called "authors' right") reflects the high regard held for creative works in France.

The use of the term is not without its critics. One commentator remarked that the term was "invented somewhat hastily . . . by a rather far-fetched analogy with mortgages on real property" and it was not surprising that it was not understood by foreign jurists who tended to reject it without further examination of the concept behind the term.[16]

---

[12] The recognised standard abbreviation "E.U." will be employed and for the sake of consistency it shall be taken to mean the European Union in all its previous forms (EEC, E.C.).

[13] [1959] 6 *Bull Cop. Soc.* 91.

[14] Explanatory Memorandum (henceforth referred to as the "Memorandum"), I.1.

[15] Hauser, 97. Here, as under common law systems, a distinction is made between personalty (simply understood as being moveable property but including shares in land) and realty (property in land and titles). While under the French Civil Code the maxim "possession equals title" applies to personalty (Article 2279), with a taker cutting off all rights of the true owner except if taken by theft or found when the owner vindicates his right within three years, this maxim does not apply to realty. In the case of rights to realty the owner may pursue the realty in the hands of a taker, even a bona fide one. This right, which only exists in relation to realty is the *"droit de suite"*. The right also applies to creditors; in particular to mortgagees.

[16] F. Hepp, "Royalties from works of Fine Art. Origin of the concept of *droit de suite* in Copyright Law" [1959] 6 *Bull Cop. Soc.* 91 ("Hepp"), 91.

Synonyms for *"droit de suite"* include resale right, resale royalty, resale royalty right, follow-up right, art proceeds right, and compulsory profit sharing.[17] In this paper, for consistency, the original French term, *"droit de suite"*, will be employed.

II. The French Origin

The origin of the *droit de suite* concept as applied to works of art can be traced back to an article published in the *Chronique de Paris* on February 25, 1893 by a French lawyer, Albert Vaunois. His idea was that the artist should be given a share of the resale price based on profit made rather than on the resale price. The issue was then raised in 1896 by a second French lawyer, Edouard Mack, in his report to the Berne Congress of the International Literary and Artistic Association.[18]

In 1903 the *Société des Amis du Luxembourg*, was created in Paris with one of its dual purposes being to lobby for the enactment of a *droit de suite*. A draft bill was produced in 1904. This was followed by a high profile media campaign to win over public opinion which eventually,[19] after being delayed by the First World War, led to a Fine Arts Commission report being presented to Parliament in 1919.[20] A year later the Société had achieved its goal. On May 20, 1920 a law based on the 1904 draft bill was enacted.

A. The 1920 french law

The 1920 Law entitled "an artist to share in the sales price of his work as it later passes from buyer to buyer by claiming a statutory percentage".[21] Artists could claim a percentage of the gross price agreed at a public sale conducted by public officers in relation to the sale of their original work, providing the gross price was at least FF1,000. The public officer (*Commissaire-Priseur*) was usually an auctioneer, though in theory could also be a notary or a bailiff. Being based on the sale price meant that a sum would be payable even when the seller was selling at a price which was lower than that at which the seller had himself paid when purchasing the work.

The artist could claim the *droit de suite* directly or through a collecting society such as the Union of Artistic Property. This Artists' Union, which formed and then grew through the amalgamation of several bodies of artists, proved overwhelmingly to be the most popular means of collection. A natural consequence of this was that almost all French artists joined the Union. The Secretary General of the Union reported that there

---

[17] Edelson, 260. Edelson asserted that the resale royalty was an "Orwellian misuse of language".
[18] Hauser, 96.
[19] See 1904 edition of *L'Eclair* and *L'Humanité*, and articles of Jacques Duhr in *Le Journel* of 1908 and in *Le Siecle* of 1909; as cited by Hauser, 96, n. 8.
[20] Parliamentary Documents, Chamber of Deputies, Session of Sept. 2. 1919, Annex 6794 (1919).
[21] Hauser, 97.

is no record of an individual artist claiming his right directly under this 1920 law.[22] The *droit de suite* applied for the same duration as copyright; that is throughout the life of the artist and then for the benefit of his successors in title, which in 1920 included his heirs or legatees by testamentary disposition,[23] for 50 years. As with moral rights, the *droit de suite* was made inalienable.

A ministerial decree of December 17, 1920 set out the formal procedure to be followed when claiming the royalty. An artist or a designated agent had to claim the *droit de suite* in a particular work by inserting a declaration, at any time, to this effect in the *Journal Officiel*. This had the ancillary, and highly beneficial, effect of providing for a means of authenticating works of art.[24] Public auction houses were obliged to keep a register of sales recording the price paid for each work and then had to collect and pay the sums due to the artist within three months of the sale.

In practice, as the Artists' Union became the sole collecting agency, the Union's less formal procedure supplanted the official procedure. The Union used the auction house register, sales catalogue and also trade papers to calculate and supervise the collection of the *droit de suite*. The Union sent the auction house a statement of claim. After having collected the *droit de suite* sum from the seller, the public auction officer entered the sales price and the sum due under the *droit de suite* and returned the statement with the amount due to the Union which then, in turn, paid the artist or the heirs. The Union therefore became the sole agency of enforcement, suing through the courts if necessary.[25]

Three ambiguities arose from this law. First, "original" was not defined other than to distinguish it from a mere copy. This left doubt as to whether works of art that were reproduced in limited numbers such as lithographs, engravings, woodcuts, and medals would be covered. A conservative interpretation would deem only the original plate, "the cut", to be the original which would be a curious result as "the cut" is rarely ever sold at auction.[26] In practice the question of whether limited edition copies would be covered by this law is immaterial owing to the relatively high minimum sales price threshold.

The second ambiguity concerned the uncertainty over whether manuscripts, architectural works, or works of art attached to buildings such as murals were included. The right did not apply to manuscripts as they are not works of art *per se*;[27] though it may be argued that illustrated manuscripts merited inclusion. Nor did it apply to jewellery, photo-

---

[22] Hauser, 100.
[23] R. Plaisant, "The *Droit de Suite*" (1969) *Copyright* 157 ("Plaisant, R."), 158.
[24] In fact, some commentators believe that the primary purpose of this procedure and of the DDS was to authenticate works of art and protect the market from traffic in fake works of art. See Henri-Gabriel Ibels noted in Candau. *Du Droit De L'Artiste Sur Le Prix, De Revente De Ses Oeuvres* (Thesis 1916), cited in Hauser, 100.
[25] As the formal declaration was unnecessary under the Union's procedure, the additional benefit of being able to authenticate works of art was removed.
[26] Hauser, 98.
[27] Plaisant, R. (1969), 157.

graphs, and tapestries. The reason in the latter case was alleged to be because of the practical difficulty in determining the identity of the artist.

The third ambiguity followed directly from the second point: there was no express provision for joint works. A 1924 decree introduced a complex set of rules dealing with this situation. This was overtaken by the Artists' Union's procedure. A Union expert divided the total sale price between co-artists according to the value of each contribution and then from each respective share calculated the sum due under the *droit de suite*.

A further inadequacy was that the minimum sale price threshold was set at a high level, resulting in only a few artists benefiting. This was altered in 1922 when a sliding scale (1 per cent—3 per cent) was introduced and the threshold lowered to FF50.

B. Theoretical justification

Why was there thought to be a need for a *droit de suite* in France in 1920? Three reasons were suggested.

I. The Poor Artist Theory

A young and unknown artist sold his work at a low price. Years later the artist in old age struggles in poverty in his squalid garret surrounded by his cold and hungry family. Meanwhile the artist's work has become much sought after and changed hands for huge sums; astute art collectors are made wealthy through prudent resales of the artist's early works.

This picture is intensified when the artist is dead and his wife and children reduced to begging in the gutter. There is the much cited case of Millet's granddaughter selling flowers in the street to survive while his painting, the Angelus, originally sold by the artist for FF1,200 was resold for FF1,000,000.[28] This problem may have been accentuated as a result of the First World War and one recent commentator stated that the 1920 Law was "to assist widows of artist who were killed" in the war.[29] Other artists who met with hardship in their mature years include Degas, Bollin, Cezanne, and Gauguin. A painting sold by Degas for FF500 was resold in 1912 for FF436,000 when the artist, then 80, was living in very modest circumstances.[30] Bollin committed suicide to escape his financial hardship having sold 160 water colours for as little as 12 francs. After his death the same paintings were changing hands for FFl,500–2,000 each.[31] It was argued that a *droit de suite* would alleviate the impoverished lives of these artists and their families.

[28] Duchemin, Le *droit de suite* des Artistes (Paris: Paris & Thuillies 1948) ("Duchemin"), 17.
[29] Fry, R., "Copyright and the Resale Royalty" [1992] 136(9) S.J. 212, 212.
[30] P. Katzenberger, "The *Droit de Suite* In Copyright Law", (1973) 4 IIC 361 ("Katzenberger"), 365.
[31] Duchemin, 17.

However meritorious the claim for a *droit de suite* on this basis, such a provision may not have been the best means to alleviate the suffering of the starving artists. A more effective solution would have been the introduction of welfare benefits and state subsidies for artists, or even government regulation of artists' agreements with galleries. To provide a *droit de suite* as a humanitarian gesture "may therefore be nothing more than sentimentalism".[32]

2. The Equality of Treatment Theory

A second argument employed to support the *droit de suite* was that it would operate to redress the discrimination against artists within the law of copyright. Copyright enabled prolific writers of the nineteenth century such as Scott, Thackeray, and Dickens to earn fortunes through the receipt of royalties for books sold.[33] Composers received royalties from the sale of records and sheet music and from performances of their work.

The value of the artist's creation lies in the uniqueness of the original creative tangible object itself. The artist's income derives from a one off sale of this original work rather than from any intangible right to reproduce or perform it. The pecuniary interest in the work is generally exhausted at the time of the first sale. Contrast this with the author's manuscript. Value is not contained within the pages of the original manuscript, but derives from the exploitation of the work through reproduction, performance, or transmission. Thus, the present copyright system, because of the different manner of exploitation of art works, discriminates between artists and other creators of copyrightable works. This may be a more general criticism of copyright law and its historical development which has resulted in the present classification.

As an adjunct to this theory, the unequal bargaining position between an unknown writer and a publisher almost always results in the writer signing away his early works on unfavourable terms but later success will enable him to mitigate this as he is able to recoup some of the profit made on his work through royalties. The royalties allow participation in the future profits of the work. The unknown artist is also in a similarly weak bargaining position. However, in his case, no matter how popular his early works become, he is not able to recoup any share of the profits.

The *droit de suite* provides a means for the artist to share in the further exploitation of his work and in doing so redresses the balance between artists and other creators of copyright works. It is irrelevant whether or not the resale occurs at a profit for the seller. The artist is simply receiving a royalty on the resale of his art in the same way as the writer receives a royalty on the sale of further copies of his books. This theory has formed the basis for many of the national *droit de suite* laws. It has

---

[32] S. Ricketson, *The Berne Convention for the Protection of Literary and Artistic Works; 1886–1986,* (Kluwer, London, 1987) ("Ricketson (1987)"), 412.
[33] D. Thomas, *Copyright and the Creative Artist, Research Monograph* (Institute of Economic Affairs London, 1967), 19.

the advantage over the "increase in value approach" in that it appears less like a tax and therefore adheres more to the traditional conception of authors' right.

The *droit de suite* should parallel the royalty an author receives when a literary work is reproduced and published or the royalty received by a composer for public performances of a musical work. It should act as a fair reward and encourage the artist to create further works.[34]

A fully developed equality of treatment theory demands not only the existence of a *droit de suite* but also some form of exhibition right allowing the artist to fully exploit his work once it has left his control; usually after the first sale. The U.S. Federal Copyright Code contains an exhibition right enabling an artist to receive a fee from galleries and museums which display his work.[35] This right is, however, exhausted by the first sale of the work.[36] If this "first sale doctrine" was removed, then the artist (and heirs) would be able to receive fees for the entire duration of his copyright; akin to the royalties a writer receives. A variant on this would be to allow the owner to pay a licence fee to the artist for the exhibition of the work. A statutory set fee would save the owner having to negotiate the terms with the artist. Another possibility is a commercial rental right. Future owners of a work would pay a fee to the artist for any commercial rental of the work. All of these provisions would enable an artist to fully participate in the typical manner of exploitation of his work—exhibition.[37]

3. Increase In Value Theory

A third argument employed was that the increase in the value of the artist's original work was attributable to the growing fame of the artist and his subsequent work and as the artist is responsible for these factors, he should be entitled to a share in the increased value. The seller has done little to contribute but may participate in spectacular windfall profits and therefore should return a portion of these profits to the person responsible for them, the artist.[38] This basis is also more just to the middlemen, collectors, dealers, and auctioneers, than the equality of treatment approach, as it would imply that there would not be any payment due for a loss making resale.

However, it was asserted that the seller's astuteness in his earlier purchase of the art work deserves to be rewarded too, both for his artistic

---

[34] However, in taking no account of loss making sales the *droit de suite* may appear unfair to the seller. If the sale is at a profit the astute art dealer deserves a reward for his foresight and for the risk he made with such a precarious investment. From a commercial perspective, the exhaustion of all the artist's pecuniary rights when he sells the original work appears just and practical. Furthermore, some jurists view the singling out of the artist and his heirs as inequitable; see Hepp, 92.

[35] Copyright Code of 1976, s. 106(5).

[36] s. 109(c).

[37] Each of these possibilities would generate their own problems, discussion of which is beyond the scope of this paper. See M. Kretsinger, "*Droit de Suite:* The Artist's Right to a Resale Royalty" (1993) 15 *Hastings Comm/Ent L.J* 967.

[38] This may seem more justified when the seller is a business person, without necessarily having any interest in art, playing the art market in a similar manner to gambling on the stock exchange.

taste and for his courage in making such a risky investment. External factors may have partly contributed towards the increase in value and these should not be overlooked. The value may vary considerably according to public taste and fashion and the artist who directed his work at such a market would be able to benefit from a relatively high first sale price. As the fashion changed the work may fall from popularity, or even be forgotten after the artist's death, and this may be reflected in lower resale prices. While at the other extreme, great masterpieces are often not recognised at the time of creation and only come to prominence long after the artist's death when they are out of copyright and thus not touched by a *droit de suite*. A *droit de suite* based on this theory would appear more in the nature of a tax, functioning in a similar way to Capital Gains Tax, rather than an aspect of copyright law.

4. Respective Weight Of The Theories

All three theories were offered as justifications for the 1920 Law but the greatest weight was placed on the equality of treatment theory. This is illustrated in the preamble to the bill which concludes, "it is not alms we ask, but a property right".[39]

5. International Development

Thirteen months after the 1920 French Law was passed Belgium enacted a similar *droit de suite* provision.[40] This provided an artist or his heirs and successors in title with a payment of between two and six per cent of the sale price of an original work of art sold at a public sale. Czechoslovakia was the next country to introduce a *droit de suite* in 1926,[41] followed by Poland in 1935,[42] Uruguay in 1937,[43] and Italy in 1941.[44]

III. The Berne Convention And Droit De Suite

A. Background

The original status of the Berne Convention, as established in 1886, was that of a voluntary agreement between the signatories providing a basis for international copyright protection.[45] Its declared aim was to "protect,

---

[39] Parliamentary Documents, Chamber of Deputies, Ordinary Session, second sitting, January 23 1914, Annex 3423, 150 (1914). If it were "alms" that were sought then an improved socail benefits system or state funding of artists may be more effective in achieving this objective rather than a *droit de suite*.

[40] Law of June 25, 1921.

[41] Law of November 24, 1926 Article 35.

[42] Law of March 22, 1935.

[43] Law of December 17, 1937, Article 9.

[44] Law of April 22, 1941, Articles 144–155.

[45] The Berne Convention for the Protection of Literary and Artistic Works was signed on September 9, 1886 by Belgium, France, Germany, Great Britain, Italy, Spain, Tunisia and Haiti. The first six all being colonial powers, extending the scope of the Berne Union across the globe. For example, the accession of Great Britain with its colonies and self-governing dominions, which included Australia, New Zealand, Canada and Nova Scotia, the cape colony and Natal, and India, accounted for a population in excess of thirty million.

in as effective and uniform manner as possible, the rights of authors in their literary and artistic works".[46] The majority of the founding member states did not have a common law system of copyright paralleling the U.K. but a quite different civil law concept of author's right. This is based on a human right and consists of both economic and moral rights. Thus, from the outset there already appears to be a contradiction between the copyright approach of the U.K. and the author's right approach of continental Europe.

This was overcome by the adoption of the principle of national treatment contained in Article 5. Article 5(1) sets out that: every author of a Berne Convention country has the same rights in all other member countries as the nationals of those countries, "as well as the rights specially granted by this Convention". This latter clause has the effect of laying down the rights contained in the Convention as a minimum requirement even if they are not provided for within the national law. Article 5(2) states that where national laws make the grant of protection subject to formalities, these formalities shall not apply to the foreign author. The overall effect of Article 5 may mean that national law treated foreign authors better than national authors and thus would lead to the adjustment of national law, to increase protection to the Berne Convention minimum, promoting the Berne Convention aim of harmonisation. However, not wishing to oversimplify the deep rooted effects of signing the Berne Convention, Porter notes that in a "subtle but profound sense G.B. had entered into a convention based on a philosophy not yet properly accepted into British law, that of author's right".[47]

The Berne Convention came into force on December 5, 1887 and contained a provision for periodic revisions at 20 year intervals.[48] The first major revision was in Berlin in 1908 which extended the duration term to life of the author plus fifty years.[49] Though, under the reciprocity principle the term of protection claimed was not to extend beyond the term of protection in the country of origin of the work.[50]

B. The 1928 Rome revision

The 1928 Conference, following a motion proposed by the French and supported by the Belgian and Czech delegations, considered a *droit de suite* for the first time.[51] Subsequent discussion led to a modified, and less demanding, resolution being adopted; the U.K. delegation abstained from the vote. The resolution read:

> The Conference expresses the desire that those countries of the Union which have not yet adopted legislative provisions guaranteeing to the

---

[46] Berne Convention 1886, preamble.
[47] V. Porter, *Beyond The Berne Convention, Academia Research Monograph* (John Libbey, London, 1991), 3.
[48] Article 17.
[49] Article 7.
[50] Article 7(1), 7(2). See page 19 below.
[51] Desbois, *Rapporteur General*, Actes Rome Conference on Berne Revision May 7–June 2, 1928 (Berne: International Office 1929), 103.

benefit of artists an inalienable right to a share in the proceeds of successive public sales of their original works should take into account the possibility of considering such provisions.[52]

C. The 1948 Brussels revision

The 1948 Conference was delayed by the slow ratification of the 1928 revision and by the Second World War. The wording of the Berne Convention was redrafted, changing its status from a voluntary international agreement to one which imposed legal requirements on its members.[53]

The 1928 motion formed the basis for a proposed new Article 14bis, drawn up by the Belgium Government.[54] The intention "was to gain acceptance for *droit de suite* as part of copyright, rather than as something separate".[55] The British argued that "the time was not ripe for its adoption into U.K. law".[56] The Norwegians, Fins and Dutch also opposed the Article. The Dutch argued that the right did not properly belong to copyright and thus should not be included in the Berne Convention.[57] A compromise was reached in which the Article was amended to restrict its operation to states with *droit de suite* provisions on a reciprocal basis. The amended Article 14bis was adopted as follows:

(1) The author, or after his death, the persons or institutions authorised by national legislation shall, in respect of original works of art and original manuscripts of writers and composers, enjoy the inalienable right to an interest in any sale of the work subsequent to the first *disposal* of the work by the author.

(2) The protection provided by the preceding paragraph may be claimed in a country of the Union only if legislation in the country to which the author belongs so permits, and to the *degree* permitted by the country where this protection is claimed.

(3) The procedure for collection and amounts shall be a matter for determination by national legislation.

This is the Berne Convention provision that remains today as Article 14ter. The two words; "disposal" and "degree" have been replaced with "transfer" and "extent". Much is left to national legislation including the question of whether a state should indeed have a *droit de suite*, as even with ratification of the current 1971 text the adoption of such a provision remains voluntary.

---

[52] *ibid.*, Resolution 3. See also Ricketson (1987), 413.
[53] Article 2(4).
[54] Ricketson (1987), 414.
[55] *ibid.*, 415.
[56] Plaisant, M., 367; reported in Ricketson (1987), 415.
[57] *ibid.*, 366; reported in Ricketson (1987), 416.

1. Article 14ter

The right under art 14ter(1) is inalienable, and is akin to the moral rights under Article 6bis.[58] The provision departs from the French Law and also from the intention displayed in the preparatory work,[59] in that public and private sales are not differentiated. The use of the word "interest" indicates that the right applies to both profitable and loss making sales, following the French Law. Paragraph (2), however, allows for the possibility of national legislation restricting the right to profit–making sales.[60] The works covered extend beyond that covered by the French Law to include manuscripts, reflecting the national *droit de suite* laws of a few countries.[61] It is left to national legislation to determine who has the right after the author's death.[62]

Article 14ter(2) contains the principle of substantive reciprocity rather than the general Berne Convention basis of national treatment,[63] a very rare derogation from the fundamental principles of the Convention.[64] Reciprocity can be summed up by the phrase "get as you give": each state need only give to foreign authors the protection which is given to domestic authors in that foreign state. Berne members with greater protection need only give a term of protection equivalent to that of the author's country of origin. In contrast, under national treatment a state would be obliged to grant this higher level of protection even if the foreign author's state had a lower level of protection.[65] Thus, for example, the U.K. was not obliged to recognise the *droit de suite* of a French artist whose work was resold in London and conversely France did not have to confer *droit de suite* on a British artist.[66]

---

[58] However, as the right entitles the author to an "interest" in subsequent sales of his work, it is clear from the preparatory work for the Brussels Conference that this was considered to be a "pecuniary interest"; see Ricketson (1987), 416. It can also be argued that this provision originated from the 1920 French Law which may be interpreted as conceptualising the *droit de suite* as being more in the nature of a moral right.

[59] Belgium Government proposal, Plaisant, M., *Rapporteur General*, Berne Documents of the Brussels Revision Conference June 5–26, 1948 (Berne: International Office 1951), 364.

[60] This is the system adopted in Chile, Czechoslovakia, Italy, Portugal, Turkey, and Uruguay.

[61] Czechoslovakia, Portugal, Turkey, and Uruguay.

[62] Articles 7, 7bis.

[63] Reciprocity also applies to terms of protection, Article 7(8). For example: prior to the Term Directive (see page 55 below and the Collins decision page 34 below), U.K. authors publishing in Germany would only receive the same duration of copyright granted by U.K. law (life plus 50 years) and not the longer German duration (life plus 70 years).

[64] R. Plaisant, "*Droit de suite* and Droit Moral under the Berne Convention" (1988) *Colum.—VLA J.L. & Arts* 157 ("Plaisant R."), 158.

[65] For relations between member countries of the Universal Copyright Convention (UCC) (established by UNESCO, in Geneva, in 1952 as a less stringent alternative to the Berne Convention) who are not members of the Berne Convention, Article II of the UCC provides for the principle of national treatment. The *droit de suite* is not mentioned but under Article II it would appear that a foreign artist, whose country of origin is a UCC member, can claim national treatment for *droit de suite* purposes. Though, this has been disputed on the grounds that the UCC only applies to traditional areas of copyright; a view which is supported by the fact that the *droit de suite* was not mentioned in the formation of the UCC; see imer-Reimer, *GRUR Int.* (1967), 431, at 599. The UCC does not apply to countries which have signed the Berne Convention. Article XVII of the UCC gives the Berne Convention precedence; thus the effects of the UCC are reduced.

[66] For further comment and criticism of 14ter see Ricketson (1987), 417–423.

IV. European Developments

A. France: The 1920 law revisited

There were only four reported decisions concerning the *droit de suite* under the 1920 Law.[67] This probably reflects the success of the Artists' Union reaching an effective working agreement with the auction houses. In 1959 it seemed fairly clear that "the practical supervision and operation of collection under the *droit de suite* until the present time has been successful."[68]

1. The 1957 Revision

In 1957 the French author's right system was recodified.[69] This afforded the opportunity to fine–tune the *droit de suite*. The devaluation of the franc led to the minimum resale price threshold being set at FF100 (10,000 old francs—about $20) and the sliding scale was scrapped in favour of a single 3 per cent rate.

The right was extended to apply to all sales made "through the intermediary of a merchant";[70] a term later broadly interpreted to include purchases by galleries and agents for private individuals,[71] thus covering private sales for the first time. A proposal for a ministerial decree setting out the procedure for applying the *droit de suite* to private sales was never finalised because of the practical difficulties of tracing all private sales and then enforcing a *droit de suite* on an often reluctant art dealer. A compromise agreement between the Artists' Union and the Art Dealers' Union was reached in which dealers "consented to pay certain sums of money that will permit a better functioning of the social security system benefiting authors,"[72] ensuring that the *droit de suite* continued only to be collected from public sales.

The beneficiaries of the *droit de suite* were limited to the artist and his heirs; testamentary dispositions were no longer permitted. However, the wording of the provision was far from clear and led to litigation concerning the devolution of Claude Monet's *droit de suite*.[73] In this case, after Monet's death in 1926, the benefit of the *droit de suite* passed to his son. On the death of his son, in 1966, a Parisian museum was made the beneficiary under the son's will. Following the sale of a painting, Monet's niece (his son's first cousin) claimed the payment under the *droit de suite*. The auctioneer refused to grant the payment to the niece who then

---

[67] Hauser, 102. One of these cases brought to light a sharp practice among a group of disreputable art dealers. The heirs of the artist whose work was at issue were able to enforce their *droit de suite* in a fictitious sale. *Le Douanier Rousseau*, Gaz. du Pal., Feb. 13, 1931.

[68] Hauser, 101.

[69] Law of March 11, 1957.

[70] *ibid.*, Article 42.

[71] Desbois (1957) *Le Droit d'Auteur* 211.

[72] Plaisant R. (1969), 158.

[73] *Tribunal de Grande Instance* of Paris, July 3, 1968: *Jurisclasseur Periodique*, 1968, 15569.

proceeded to court. Plaisant states that following established case law there were two possible grounds for not allowing the niece's claim:[74] either the *droit de suite* was a pecuniary right and must therefore follow the law of succession, in which case the niece would be prevented from inheriting from the son because of his bequest to the museum, or the purpose of the right was to provide maintenance to the artist's close relatives, in which case a distant niece should not necessarily benefit as the law grants such relatives neither the benefit of maintenance nor a share of the estate.

The tribunal of first Instance took an entirely different line deciding in favour of the niece under the 1957 Law. This decision affirmed that a relation who did not inherit from the artist and who was prevented by will from inheriting from the first heir still received the benefit of the *droit de suite*, interfering with and disrupting the law of inheritance. A more satisfactory solution, Plaisant suggests, would have been to deny the *droit de suite* being disposed of by will but to allow the benefit of it being denied by will. Instead the Tribunal "violated the spirit of that law as well as the law of inheritance in general".[75]

The ambiguity concerning the definition of original was not dealt with nor was the question concerning manuscripts, architectural work, or works attached to buildings.

2. The Current Law

The 1957 Law was replaced in 1992 by a Law covering all aspects of Intellectual Property.[76] The *droit de suite* is categorised as an economic right and applies to graphic and three dimensional works,[77] but not to manuscripts nor any of the works that are expressly excluded. The threshold level is not contained within the code but in a regulation, presumably to make it easier to update in accordance with inflation and currency changes.

B. Outside France

Following the introduction of a *droit de suite* in France and its inclusion in the Berne Convention other countries started to adopt similar legislation[78] Not all countries with the provision have actually implemented the right or developed collection and payment procedures. The German copyright system is widely perceived as being one of the most modern and comprehensive in the world.[79] For this reason it is helpful to examine the *droit de suite* provisions employed in Germany.

---

[74] R. Plaisant, (1969), 159.

[75] *ibid.*

[76] No. 92–597 of July 1, 1992, as amended by Law No. 92–1336 of December 16, 1992.

[77] Article L. 122–8.

[78] See E. Ulmer, "The *"Droit de Suite"* in International Copyright Law" [1975] 6 IIC 12; and International Chamber Of Commerce, International Art and Trade Law, International Sales of Works of Art Volume IV (Deventer: Kluwer 1993).

[79] Professor Gerald Dworkin, International and Comparative Copyright lecture, Kings College, London, December 12, 1996.

C. Germany

The *droit de suite* was introduced into Germany (then the Federal Republic of Germany) by the Copyright Act of 1965.[80] The provision was similar to that of the French Law. It gave an artist a right to claim from the seller one per cent of the gross sales price of a resale conducted through an auctioneer or dealer of their original work, providing the gross sale price was at least DM500. The right relates only to "the original of a work of fine art" and expressly excludes architectural works and works of applied art.[81] Without this express exclusion the latter two categories of work would have fallen within the *droit de suite* owing to their inclusion in the code's definition of "fine art".[82] As with the French Law, a sum would be payable even when the seller was selling at a loss.[83]

The artist himself or a collecting society could claim the right and BILD-KUNST was formed for this purpose. The right exists for the same duration as copyright: life of the artist and then for the benefit of his successors in title. This, unlike the French Law, followed the general rules of succession allowing heirs or legatees by testamentary disposition to inherit the benefit for seventy years.[84] As with moral rights, the *droit de suite* was made inalienable.

Two difficulties arose from this law. The one per cent rate meant that a claim was hardly worth making as most sales were for less than 10,000 marks and many were below the 500 mark threshold.[85] The second difficulty was in pursuing a claim against a seller whose identity was often unknown, his anonymity preserved in his contract with the auctioneer or dealer who relied on their privilege and professional obligation to secrecy. The artist had no claim against these intermediaries.

These two difficulties led to the passing of the 1972 Copyright Amendment Act. The rate was increased to five per cent and the threshold at which the *droit de suite* takes effect was lowered to DM100. The five per cent rate was still rather modest as the dealer's commission was usually 15 per cent.[86]

A 1971 German Federal Supreme Court ruling obliged auctioneers in public sales to provide details of the seller or to pay the *droit de suite* themselves.[87] While making it easier for artists to enforce their right in

---

[80] Article 26.
[81] Article 26(1), (8).
[82] Article 2(1)4. "[P]lans for such work" also falls within the definition but are not excluded probably because if "plans" are ever sold the saleprice is unlikely to be above the threshold level.
[83] It is interesting to note that before the Law was enacted consideration was given to the right only applying to the seller's profit. Both the 1932 and 1959 draft bills were based on this concept. The Parliament decided in favour of a sales based right because of the practical application and enforcement of the right.
[84] See also R., Plaisant, (1969), 158.
[85] W., Nordemann, "The 1972 Amendment of the German Copyright Act" (1973) 4 I.I.C. 179 ("Nordemann (1973)"), 180.
[86] *ibid.*
[87] Decision of June 7, 1971 G.R.U.R. 519. This concerned the widows of two expressionist painters, Karl Hofer and Max Pechstein, *cf* 65 claiming their *droit de suite* benefit against two auction houses.

auction sales the decision did not help with private sales. This loophole was closed by extending the information right to all art dealers.[88] Dealers could avoid divulging information by paying the sums due. For ease of administration this right may only be asserted through a collecting society.[89] The artist has to maintain surveillance of the market to be aware of sales of his work and then be in a position to enforce the information right. The practicality of this has been questioned.[90]

A collecting society, or an auditor, has the right to inspect the accounts of a dealer where there exists reasonable doubt as to the accuracy or completeness of the information provided.[91] This may be ineffectual as the dealer may chose the auditor who may not make "special efforts on behalf of the collecting society to uncover the tricks of a clever book keeper".[92] It could also be argued that the mere existence of this right will have the effect that all information given is correct and comprehensive. "It is therefore expected that the enforcement of the *droit de suite* is now assured in Germany."[93]

The current German provisions covering copyright stem from the 1965 Law as amended by the Law of June 9, 1993. The *droit de suite* is not contained within the moral rights or exploitation rights but is categorised separately in a section headed "Other Rights of Authors".

Four problems still remain:

- The distinction drawn between works of pure art and works of applied art causes a problem. Sales of applied art are usually of copies and thus the *droit de suite* would not have applied anyway. However, it seems sensible for the sale of an original work of applied art to attract the *droit de suite*. In line with other *droit de suite* provisions architectural works are not covered. Furthermore, the right does not apply to manuscripts, jewellery, photographs nor to tapestries, which are not "original works of fine art".[94]
- There is no definition of "original". This is particularly a problem concerning prints, sculptures and works produced by modern techniques employed by artists.
- Private sales are excluded.
- Although, the 1972 amendments have gone along way to improve the situation, enforcement still remains a problem.[95]

---

[88] Article 26(3),(4).
[89] Article 26(5).
[90] Nordemann (1973), 181.
[91] Article 26(6).
[92] Nordemann (1973), 182.
[93] Katzenberger, 377.
[94] Article 26(1).
[95] For further discussion see also W. Nordemann, "The '*Droit de Suite*' in Article 14ter of the Berne Convention and in the Copyright Law of the Federal Republic of Germany" (1977) *Copyright* 337.

V. U.K. I: The Historical Background

The current statute covering copyright, the Copyright, Designs and Patents Act 1988, does not contain a *droit de suite*. However, such a provision has been discussed in several governmental papers.

A. The Whitford committee report of 1977

The Whitford Committee was set up to consider the ratification of the 1971 Paris text of the Berne Convention. It is the only in depth governmental study of the effects of introducing a U.K. *droit de suite*.[96] The Committee, in its 1977 report,[97] recommended that the U.K. should not introduce a *droit de suite* law giving several reasons that can be reduced to three main objections.

1. The Whitford Objections

a) Inefficacy

It was argued that in countries having a *droit de suite* only a small number of artists benefited significantly. Whilst well-known artists received large sums, most artists received very little.[98] Figures were given for the total sums collected in France for 1966 (£47,000) and world-wide for 1972 (little over £100,000).

b) Procedural and Administrative Difficulties

The Committee found that only small amounts were involved and collection was expensive.[99] Schemes were only effective where collecting societies operated and policed sales. The Art Registration Committee suggested that the right should be administered by a public body because of the "apparent inability of artists to organise themselves".[1] A suggestion by the Federation of British Artists and the Royal Society of British Sculptures that the right should only arise "in respect of appreciation beyond inflation" would have made the right complicated to administer.[2] The only truly independent body which made a submission, the Law Society, considered the right difficult to administer and enforce and foresaw little demand.[3]

---

[96] The Gregory Committee Report of 1952, Report of the Copyright Committee (Cmnd. 8662) (1952), which resulted in the 1956 Copyright Act ratifying the Brussels revision of the Berne Convention, did not consider the *droit de suite*.
[97] Report on Copyright and Designs Law (Cmnd. 6732) (1977).
[98] *ibid.*, para. 797.
[99] *ibid.*, para. 796.
[1] *ibid.*, para. 800.
[2] *ibid.*, para. 799.
[3] *ibid.*, para. 798.

c) Economic Effect

Whitford found that it was not clear that the lack of a U.K. *droit de suite* had a distorting effect on the European art market.[4] This finding was probably influenced by lobbying on behalf of the London art market. The non-distortion argument may have been be a front for the desire to protect the home market and its financial interests.

2. The Whitford Committee's Suggestions For A U.K. Droit De Suite

Despite the Committee's reservations, it did go on to consider the possible implementation of a *droit de suite* in the U.K. A number of issues were raised:

- Should artists be left to administer the right themselves? The Committee answered in the affirmative seeing no reason why the right should be treated differently from all other aspects of copyright.[5]
- Should the right be made inalienable and if so for how long? The Committee felt that the principle beneficiaries of the right would be heirs or assigns (if alienable). It also found that the "present climate of opinion is against inherited wealth" and that it would be contrary to normal practice in U.K. copyright law to provide inalienable rights.[6] As for duration, the right should not extend beyond the full copyright period; at that time, life plus 50 years. But comment was passed that it would be "purely fortuitous" if the artist or heirs received any income during this period.[7]
- To what sales should the right apply? Although logic demanded that the right should apply to all sales, for practical reasons the Committee felt that it must be limited to public sales. The Committee then acknowledged that this might result in sales being driven underground.
- To what works should the right apply? The Committee found that there was no logical reason for not applying the right to all artistic works including sculptures, drawings, engravings, photographs, architectural works, and "works of artistic craftsmanship" as well as paintings.[8] But practical reasons might necessitate some restriction; the Committee did not elaborate further.
- Should the right apply whether or not there is an increase in value? The Committee thought that justice demanded that the right should only apply "if a profit in excess of inflation is made". Though, the Committee also envisaged that a case could be "made

---

[4] *ibid.*, para. 801.
[5] *ibid.*, para. 802.
[6] This "normal practice" has since changed. The Copyright Designs and Patents Act 1988 introduced inalienable moral rights into the U.K.
[7] Report on Copyright and Designs Law (Cmnd. 6732) (1977), para. 802.
[8] *ibid.*, para. 803.

167

out for subsequent purchasers to claim contribution from the artist if they resell at a loss".[9]

- What should constitute "an original" for *droit de suite* purposes and should the right apply to limited editions? These questions were not answered by the Committee other than to comment that there was no logical reason to exclude manuscripts or limited edition books.
- At what rate the *droit de suite* levy should be set? The Committee, again, posed the question but did not proceed to provide an answer.

3. The Whitford Committee's Conclusion

The Committee concluded that *droit de suite* was "not necessarily fair or logical and that the main lesson to be drawn from the experience abroad is that *droit de suite* is just not practical either from the point of view of administration or as a source of income to individual artists and their heirs".[10]

B. The 1981 green paper

The 1981 Green Paper refers to the E.C. Commission's recommendation for the introduction of a Directive on the basis of Article 100 of the EEC Treaty to ensure harmonisation of the application of *droit de suite* throughout the Community.[11] This would provide an opportunity to re-examine the subject in greater detail. In conclusion the Green Paper reiterates the finding of the Whitford Report that the "arguments in support of *droit de suite* are not considered sufficiently logical, equitable or compelling to warrant its introduction".

C. The 1986 white paper

The 1986 White Paper conceded that certain bodies have argued that it is inequitable to deny artists a *droit de suite* on the grounds that:

- subsequent sales may take place at prices much higher than the first sale price; and
- writers and composers derive a continuing financial benefit from their works through royalties and performing rights.[12]

It noted the following arguments against a *droit de suite*:

- It would only be possible to exercise the right in relation to public sales. This would lead to an increase in clandestine private sales

---

[9] *ibid.*
[10] *ibid.*, para. 804.
[11] Reform of the Law relating to Copyright, Designs and Performers' Protection (Cmnd. 8302) (1981). The recommendation was contained in Community Action in the Cultural Sector, Supplement 6/1977 Bull.EC, 16.
[12] Intellectual Property and Innovation (Cmnd. 9712) (1986), 19.13–19.16.

(here it is assuming that all sales are to be included). Alternatively, it would drive sales away from auctioneers and dealers which, in the committee's view, would have an adverse effect upon the artists.

- According to logic, as artists benefit from profit they should also bear a share of any loss.
- Benefit to artists would not outweigh the complexity and expense of administration. The Paper concluded that "because no significant new arguments have emerged in support of recognition of the right since publication of the 1981 Green Paper, the Government does not intend to introduce a *droit de suite*."

VI. The European Union And The Proposed Directive

A. The history

The E.U. first considered a *droit de suite* in 1977 and then again in 1982.[13] Despite both proposals being approved by resolutions before the European Parliament no further action was taken.[14] The main reason forwarded for this lack of action was the strength of the powerful "anti-*droit de suite* lobbies".[15] There was no mention of a *droit de suite* in the European Commission's Green Paper on copyright in 1988.[16] However, in the follow up to the Green Paper, the Commission undertook to conduct a study which included the question of advisability of a Community initiative on a *droit de suite*.[17] As part of this study the Commission conducted a series of consultative questionnaires and held public hearings in 1991, 1994 and 1995.

B. The findings of the european commission study

The Findings of the European Commission Study were presented under the following headings:

1. Analysis of The Relevant Market.

The relevant art market is delimited by the exclusion of an artist's sale of his work and by the date of the artist's death. The former because such sales are logically excluded from a *droit de suite* and the latter because this determines the duration of copyright and consequently the duration

---

[13] Community Action in the Cultural Sector, Supplement 6/1977 Bull.EC, 16, see page 30 above; Stronger Community Action in the Cultural Sector, Supplement 6/1982 Bull. E.C., 24.
[14] O.J. 1979 C–39/50, O.J. 1983 C–342/127.
[15] Gautier, "The Single Market for Works of Art" [1990] 144 R.I.D.A. 12, 34.
[16] Copyright and the Challenge of Technology—Copyright Issues Requiring Immediate Action, COM(88) 172 final.
[17] Working Programme of the Commission in the Field of Copyright and Neighbouring Rights, COM(90) 584 final, chapter 8.5.

of the application of *droit de suite*. The duration confines the market to contemporary and, exceptionally, to modern art. However, since the study, the implementation of the Term Directive extending the duration of copyright (to life plus 70 years) has increased the size of the market potentially affected by a *droit de suite*,[18] stretching it further into the realm of modern art.[19] The statistics provided in the study should be modified to account for this change.

The key players on the market are: dealers, galleries, auction houses, major collectors and the state. High value works attract internationally mobile players searching for the location offering the best return. The E.U. art market is therefore influenced by the world market. Owing to the lack of statistics, it is difficult to calculate the exact size of the world art market. The only accurate figures available are those for auction sales and external trade. The Commission estimated the world art market for 1989 to be in the range of ECU 25–60 billion (approximately £2,050–5,000 million).[20] The magnitude of this range illustrates the difficulty of the calculation. The main buyers were: the United States (50 per cent, Japan (25 per cent), and Europe (20 per cent).[21] OECD figures show that, for 1992, works of art originating in Belgium, France, Germany and Spain were sold mainly in the U.S., the U.K. and Switzerland.[22]

As regards public auction sales the Commission was able to provide more detailed findings. From a peak in 1989/90 sales fell in 1991/92 and have since began to recover.[23] Sales were dominated by Sotheby's and Christie's and by the U.S. and by the U.S. and U.K. In 1994, 50 per cent of Sotheby's sales took place in North America, 32 per cent in the U.K. and 14 per cent in continental Europe.[24] This comprised 6 per cent of contemporary works and 14 per cent of modern and impressionist works;[25] a relatively small proportion. For 1992 and 1994, a similar pattern emerges from Christie's sales, with the U.S. and U.K. accounting for more than 80 per cent.[26] From 1989 to 1993 between 5.6–9 per cent of Christie's turnover derived from contemporary works and in 1989 and 1990 between 39.4–35.3 per cent derived from modern and impressionist works.[27]

In addition to the *droit de suite*, other factors influencing the art market include social security contributions for artists, sales commission, tax on profit, and VAT.

---

[18] Council Directive (EEC) No. 93/98 of October 29, 1993. See Antil, J., & Coles, P., "Copyright Duration: The European Community Adopts 'Three Score Years and Ten'" [1996] 7 E.I.P.R. 379.
[19] In 1997, the *droit de suite* could touch all artists except those who died before 1926 (the term being calculated from the end of the year of the artist's death).
[20] Memorandum p. 4, para. 4.
[21] *ibid.*
[22] *ibid.*, para. 5.
[23] *ibid.*, para. 6.
[24] *ibid.*, p. 5, para. 7. The respective figures were $666.3 million, $430.4 million, and $177.9 million.
[25] *ibid.*
[26] *ibid.*, p. 6, para. 8. A combined total of £524.5 million in 1992 and £585 million in 1993.
[27] *ibid.*

2. The Legal Position

a) The Berne Convention

The Commission noted that the diversity between *droit de suite* provisions or the lack of such a provision was partly due to the Berne Convention.[28] The Berne Convention leaves states free to decide whether or not to have a *droit de suite* and permits a broad interpretation in the operation of such a provision.[29]

b) Application of *Droit De Suite* In The Member States

The study considered how the *droit de suite* operated in the eleven states of the E.U. that provide for the right.[30] It concluded that there were numerous differences and that the right was not implemented in all states.

c) The Situation In The Other Member States

The *droit de suite* does not exist in four Member States.[31] Austria had not introduced a *droit de suite* provision when its 1994 Copyright Act was being reformed because of the decision in the Phil Collins case.[32] In Collins the court rejected the application of reprocity between Member States; national treatment must apply.[33] Austria considered that it was unacceptable that a *droit de suite* should be conferred on nationals of Members States, such as the U.K., which did not recognise the right. As regards the position of the U.K., the study simply reiterated the conclusions of the Whitford Report.[34]

d) The Situation In Third Countries

The study proceeded to consider the position in third countries falling within four groups.

   1) *Western Europe.* Switzerland had rejected the introduction of a *droit de suite* provision in its 1993 law reform on economic grounds; seeking to encourage itself as a location for art sales. In Norway and Iceland a small percentage of the sale price is channelled into an artists' solidarity fund.

---

[28] *ibid.*, p. 7.
[29] See p. 158, above.
[30] These states being France, Belgium, Italy, Germany, Portugal, Luxembourg, Spain, Denmark, Greece, Finland, and Sweden.
[31] Austria, Ireland, the Netherlands, and the U.K.
[32] Memorandum p. 12. Judgment of the Court of Justice, October 20, 1993, Joined Cases C–92/92 and C–326/92. *Collins v. Imtrat Handelsgesellschaft GmbH* [1993] E.C.R. 545.
[33] See p. 159, above.
[34] See p. 166, above.

2) *Central and Eastern Europe*. Most central and eastern European states now recognise a *droit de suite*.[35]

3) *The U.S.* The Copyright Office rejected introducing a Federal *droit de suite* in 1992 concluding that there were insufficient economic and political justifications.[36] However, it is on record as stating that it may reconsider its position in the event that the E.U. proceeded with harmonisation of *droit de suite*.[37] Only California has implemented state *droit de suite* legislation.[38]

4) *The rest of the World*. Many other countries have *droit de suite* legislation but fail to collect royalties.[39]

3. The Need For Action

a) Economic Impact of the Disparities, Distortion of Competition

The Commission is bound by the objectives concerning the functioning of the internal market as set out in Article 7a of the Treaty. The internal market is defined as "an area without internal frontiers in which the free movement of goods, persons, services and capital is ensured." Substantial differences between Member States in the existence and operation of *droit de suite* may interfere with the free movement of goods and distort competition which may harm the functioning of the internal art market. The Commission reported that there was a "noticeable shifting of sales towards countries where no royalties are collected or where taxes are lower".[40] The countries that have benefited are the U.S., the U.K. and Switzerland. The Beuys case is cited,[41] in which a German sold works to another German in London saying DM71,000 in royalty payments. Some art dealers feared that the introduction of a EU wide *droit de suite* would adversely affect the competitive position of the E.U. art market; sales would be lost to the U.S. and Switzerland.[42]

The Commission also recognised that the non-existence of a *droit de suite* was not the only factor influencing the location of art sales.[43] It went

---

[35] These include: Bulgaria, Estonia, Hungary, Latvia, Lithuania, Poland, Slovenia and now Romania.
[36] U.S. Copyright Office Report. In addition to the papers cited at footnote 10, see also Gautier, "The Single Market for Works of Art" [1990] 144 *R.I.D.A.* 12; L. DuBoff, "Artists' Rights: The Kennedy Proposal to Amend the Copyright Law" (1989) 7 *Cardozo Arts & Ent. L.J.* 227; M. A. Leaffer, "Of Moral Rights and Resale Royalties: The Kennedy Bill" (1989) 7 *Cardozo Arts & Ent. L.J.* 234; R. Mayer, "California Art Legislation Goes Federal" (1993) 15 *Hastings Comm/Ent L.J.* 981.
[37] *ibid.*, p. 149.
[38] California Civil Code S. 986.
[39] These include Algeria, Brazil, Burkima Faso, Chile, Congo, Costa Rica, Ecuador, Guinea, Ivory Coast, Madagascar, Morocco, Peru, the Philippines, the Russian Federation, Senegal, Tunisia, Turkey and Uruguay.
[40] Memorandum p. 14, para. 3.
[41] *ibid.* para. 7. BGH, Judgment of June 16, 1991—IZR24/92, GRUR 1994,798. See Case Comment: Germany: Copyright Act, s.26—"Joseph Beuys Works" [1993] 24(1) I.I.C.139; and K. Pilny, "Germany: copyright—application of the *droit de suite* of an artist against the vendor requires that the sale took place at least partly in Germany" [1995] 17(4) E.I.P.R. D94.
[42] *ibid.*, p. 15, paras 9, 10.
[43] One factor being the different tax arrangements that apply to art sales in each member state. This has recently been addressed by Directive 94/5/EC harmonising VAT throughout the E.U.

on to consider the costs incurred in auctioning a work in France and comparing this to the costs incurred in exporting the work and auctioning it in Switzerland and concluded that auction sales in Switzerland were not always more favourable than in France.[44] This was supported by a similar comparison between auction sales in Germany and Switzerland or the U.S. (New York). The Commission concluded that the *droit de suite* affected competition both within the Union and with third countries.

b) Subsidiarity And Political Desirability

In considering the impact of the Phil Collins Judgment,[45] prohibiting the application of reciprocity between Member States, the Commission acknowledged that a *droit de suite* would be payable to nationals of all Member States including those which did not have the provision. Equality at national level would therefore only be achieved by either Member States repealing their *droit de suite* provisions, or by introducing a harmonised *droit de suite* provision. Most Member States were in favour of the latter.[46]

c) The Appropriate Legal Basis

Article 100 of the Treaty of Rome would require the Council to act unanimously while under Article 100a a qualified majority would be sufficient,[47] thus allowing a provision to be passed more easily and with fewer amendments. The reason for harmonising *droit de suite* provisions is to assist the functioning of the internal market which is the very purpose for which Article 100a was introduced and thus the Commission found Article 100a to be the appropriate legal basis.[48]

C. The main provisions of the proposed directive

The European Commission published the proposed Directive in March 1996 and presented it to Parliament in April 1996. The proposal was then forwarded to the Committee on Legal Affairs and Citizens' Rights for report and to the Committee on Culture, Youth, Education and Media for opinion. A report, recommending 27 amendments, was tabled in February 1997.[49] The proposal, embodying most of the amendments, was approved in April 1997.[50] The terms "proposed Directive" and

---

[44] Explanatory Memorandum, p. 18, para. 15. But for France the figures did not take *droit de suite* payments into account.
[45] See p. 34 above.
[46] Memorandum p. 19, para. 3.
[47] Article 100a, as amended by the Treaty on European Union 1992, following the procedure set out in Article 189b.
[48] Memorandum p. 21, para. 7.
[49] European Parliament Report, Committee on Legal Affairs and Citizens' Rights, February 3, 1997, A4–0030/97 (henceforth referred to as the "European Parliament Report)".
[50] European Parliament Minutes of the sitting of April 9, 1997 (henceforth referred to as the "European Parliament Minutes)."

"approved Directive" will be employed to distinguish between them in the following analysis.

The *droit de suite* would:

- exist for as long as the work being sold is subject to copyright protection;
- apply to pictures, collages, paintings, drawings, engravings, prints, lithographs, sculptures, tapestries, ceramics and photographic works;
- apply to all public sales, in a commercial establishment or with the involvement of a dealer;
- have three different rates (4 per cent–1 per cent); and
- afford reciprocal treatment to nationals of third countries.

VII. A Critical Analysis of the Approved Directive

The substantive provisions of the approved Directive will now be examined and, where relevant, reference will be made to the proposed Directive. Throughout the Directive reference is made to the author. Article 1 makes it clear that it is only the author of an original work of art, in other words an artist.

A. Subject matter

The subject matter, an original work of art,[51] is specified in the approved Directive to ensure that the right is applied uniformly. This is defined to include:

> works intended to be viewed such as pictures, collages, paintings, drawings, engravings, prints, lithographs, sculptures, glass, tapestries, ceramics and photographs, provided they are made by the artist himself or are copies considered to be original works of art according to the relevant legal provisions in each Member State, but which may under no circumstances be more than twelve in number.[52]

The proposed Directive included manuscripts and may have been seen as defining the matter laid down in the Berne Convention which simply expressed that original works of art and original manuscripts were to be included. Evidence for this is to be found in Recital 1 of the proposed Directive which reiterated these two heads without further elaboration. The Memorandum stated that "on the basis of Article 14ter of the Berne Convention . . . the Directive determines the subject-matter of the right".[53] This provided a broad class extending beyond what is included in both the French and German provisions. In the approved Directive

---

[51] Article 1.
[52] Article 2.
[53] Ch. V, p. 21, para 1.

manuscripts have been deliberately omitted, following the national legislation of Member States. This reflects the reality that manuscripts are intended for subsequent reproduction and not intended to be contemplated as unique works of art.[54] Consequently authors are able to benefit from reproduction and performance and do not need to rely on a resale right for their income. The insertion of the words "works intended to be viewed" underlines this argument. The amended Recital 15 makes clear that original manuscripts and works of applied art are to be excluded. No explanation is provided as regards the applied art exclusive; the exclusion is probably due to the fact that works of applied art are usually mass produced and that most existing *droit de suite* provisions expressly exclude them.

The originality requirement performs two functions. First, it is usually the deciding factor as to whether or not copyright subsists in a particular work. A *droit de suite* can only apply to a copyright work; a point that is never expressly stated. Secondly, originality limits the *droit de suite* to the initial work excluding reproductions of this initial work. The Commission has recognised the need to define "original".[55] This poses great difficulty in bringing together the "author's own intellectual creation" requirement of the civil law countries with the U.K.'s lower standard requirement that the work is not copied and originates from the author. In a series of copyright directives the E.U. has employed the civil law concept and the U.K. has been forced to adopt this version of originality in its implementing legislation.[56] However, in the proposed Directive the commission has taken a different approach. The proviso in Article 2 contains two limbs given in the alternative. If either one of them is satisfied the work is "original" for *droit de suite* purposes. The limbs are:

"provided they are made by the artist himself"

On a literal interpretation it would appear that even a work that did not meet the criteria for copyright could attract a *droit de suite* payment. To take an obvious example, a work that was made by an artist but copied from another artist's work. The new work would fail to earn copyright

---

[54] European Parliament Report, Committee on Legal Affairs and Citizens' Rights, February 3, 1997, A4–0030/97 (henceforth referred to as the "European Parliament Report"), 19.

[55] Memorandum *ibid.*, para. 5.

[56] The E.U.'s on going programme of harmonisation has already resulted in six Directives being adopted and the proposed *Droit De Suite* Directive under consideration, which have or are about to have an impact on the U.K.'s Copyright Law. In addition to the proposed *Droit De Suite* Directive four of the other Directives have a direct bearing on the concept of originality: the Semiconductor Chip Protection Directive 1987 (EEC Directive 87/54/EEC), led to the Semiconductor Products (Protection of Topography) Regulations 1987 now modified and replaced by the Design Right (semiconductor Topographies) Regulations 1989 which unlike the 1987 Directive and 1987 Regulations does not contain the "author's own intellectual creation" originality definition; the Protection of Computer Programs Directive 1991 (E.C. Directive 91/250/EEC), implemented in the U.K. by the Copyright (Computer Programs) Regulations 1992; the Term Directive (see p. 170, n. 18 above), implemented by the Duration of Copyright and Rights in Performances Regulations 1995, (S.I. 1995 No. 3297) in regard to photographs; and the Database Directive 1996 (Directive 96/9/EC [1996] O.J. L77/20); implemented in the U.K. by the Copyright and Rights in Databases Regulations 1997 (S.I. 1997 No. 3032).

on the grounds that it was copied but would meet the *droit de suite* requirement that it was made by the artist himself. It is doubtful that the Commission intended such an illogical outcome.

"are copies considered to be original works of art according to the relevant legal provisions in each Member State"

The Commission has therefore, despite its stated intent noted above, made no attempt to define original and has left the matter to individual Member States. In drafting a harmonising Directive the Commission has left one of the most important definitions unharmonised. This unsatisfactory position has resulted from the dropping of the second limb of the proviso contained in the first draft of the proposed Directive without adequate consideration of an alternative definition to take its place. This limb read:

"are copies considered to be original works of art according to professional usage in the Community"

This begged the question as to what is "professional usage"? Who is included in this profession? Painters, photographers, dealers, academics and commissioners of work? While it would be insufficient for one of these professionals to consider a work to be an original, would two be sufficient? Artists would have a clear interest in maintaining that their work is original through their professional usage. Conversely, dealers would have an interest in establishing that the work is not original. The end result may be increased uncertainty and, where high value work is involved, litigation with a battle between the expert witnesses. The only professional usage that counts is that within the Community. An avant-garde method of producing artistic works which may be considered original in, say, New York, may not be considered original within the Community. The Commission acknowledged that no such "professional usage" exists at Community level and dropped this criterion.

The provision also opened up the possibility for copies to be originals. While addressing the problem of limited edition works, by generously bringing them within the ambit of *droit de suite*, it blurred the distinction between true originals and copies—secondary or pseudo originals. Neither the Berne Convention nor the French or German legislation satisfactorily deals with this problem. The argument for not including limited editions in the first *droit de suite* law, the 1920 French Law, that such editions would rarely meet the sales price threshold for *droit de suite*, is no longer valid today. In the U.S. Federal Copyright Code a "work of visual art" is given an extensive definition:

a painting, drawing, print, or sculpture, existing in a single copy, in a limited edition of 200 copies or fewer that are signed and consecutively numbered by the author, or, in the case of a sculpture in multiple cast, carved, or fabricated sculptures of 200 or fewer that are consecutively numbered by the author and bear the signature or other identifying mark of the author.[57]

The U.S. Copyright Office has recommended that any future federal *droit de suite* should apply to works falling within this definition with the modification that works in limited editions should only apply to 10 or fewer copies.[58] The Commission's first draft contained no limit on the number of editions that may be considered original; it was left to professional usage to decide. The Commission has now addressed this problem by expressly including a limit of 12.[59]

The first limb of the originality proviso is unnecessary. It is difficult to envisage an "original work" that is not "made by the artist himself". Even a computer generated work is authored or "made" by the person who undertakes the arrangements necessary for the creation of the work.[60] It is also difficult to imagine copies that are considered to be original works of art under a Member State's legislation that are not "made by the artist himself".

The clear intention is that the *droit de suite* should apply to the same subject matter in every Member State.[61] Harmonisation would be assisted by adopting a uniform definition of originality. The "author's own intellectual" creation approach adopted in the majority of the harmonising Directives would have served this purpose and had the additional benefit of further harmonising the originality criterion across E.U. copyright legislation.

B. Type of sales

The approved Directive would apply the *droit de suite* to "any resale of the work by public sale, in a commercial establishment or with the involvement of a seller or dealer".[62] This is a change from the proposed Directive which expressly excluded transactions effected by individuals acting in their private capacity. Transactions between private individuals are excluded reflecting the need to avoid the practical problems stemming from the difficulty of monitoring such operations.[63] This is narrower than the Berne Convention provision which applies to "any sale" following the first sale. A more significant change is that the Committee have attempted to exclude promotional sales by excluding the "first transfer of ownership between sellers or between a seller and a final purchaser, provided such a transaction takes place within three years of

---

[57] Copyright Law of 1976, as amended, s.101(1). This is also the definition adopted in the Visual Artists Rights Act of 1990. Despite its detail, this definition has its critics, see L. DuBoff, "What is Art? Towards a Legal Definition", (1990) 12 *Hastings Comm/Ent L.J.* 303.
[58] U.S. Copyright Office's Report, 151.
[59] European Parliament Minutes, Article 2 as amended by Amendment 18.
[60] Copyright Designs and Patents Act, s. 9(3).
[61] Recital 15.
[62] Article 1.
[63] Memorandum Ch. V, p. 21, para. 1.

the seller having acquired the work".[64] This is ambiguous as it implies that each professional seller regardless of when the work is acquired has three years in which to dispose of a work before attracting a *droit de suite*. The intention must be that professional sellers have three years from the date of acquiring the work *from the artist* to disposes of a work (emphasis added) before the *droit de suite* bites. This would reflect the common practice of the art world in which professional sellers (dealers and gallery owners) purchase unsold works of new artists.

The difficulty of monitoring non-auction sales is illustrated by the non collection of *droit de suite* payments in respect of non-auction sales following the 1957 revision in France which brought such sales within the *droit de suite* for the first time.[65] In order to be able to include all commercial sales some form of notification procedure needs to be established. This could be in the form of a central register, either national or European Union wide, with a seller having to register a sale for a value equal or greater than the *droit de suite* threshold. Penalties for non registration, akin to those for non payment of tax, would aid compliance.

C. Threshold

The level at which the approved *droit de suite* bites is left to Member States to decide but must not exceed ECU500 (about £330).[66] Not having a threshold would result in disproportionately high collection and administration costs.[67] The minimum threshold in the first draft was set at ECU1,000, which is the average amount currently in force.[68] The minimum was lowered to "ensure that new and lesser-known artists" would benefit.[69] This threshold may prove to be too low to be viable. The viability will be further pressured if a Member State adopts an even lower threshold. The reason for this apparent flexibility is to allow Member States the opportunity to "further the interests of young artists".[70] This seems to derogate from the harmonising function of the Directive, though it is stated in Recital 10 that differences which do not affect the functioning of the internal market do not need to be eliminated. It is felt by the Commission that works of low value are not likely to affect trade appreciably and could be "justified on manifest social grounds".[71] Regular cross border sales to evade a lower threshold may prove profitable by some dealers, undermining both the purpose of the lower threshold and the functioning of the internal market, albeit on a small scale. Thus, a uniform threshold would be preferable. An alternative threshold basis is proposed in the next section.

---

[64] Article 1.
[65] See page 20 above.
[66] Article 3. Exchange rate 1 ECU = £0.66 sterling (£1 = ECU1.5109) as at February 16, 1998.
[67] Recital 14.
[68] Memorandum Ch. V, p. 21, para. 7.
[69] European Parliament Report p. 18.
[70] Recital 14.
[71] Memorandum Ch. V, p. 22, para. 8.

D. Calculation basis and the rates of collection

A new Article 3a has been inserted in the approved Directive stating that the purchase price shall be net of "taxes, restoration costs and any other costs that do not arise from the creation of the work". There is no elaboration of what these "other costs" may include but it is clear that the overall effect of such deductions will be to reduce the amount of resale royalties due—reducing the burden to the purchaser and the benefit to the artist. Basing the right on the net sale price reflects the Commission's acknowledgement of the effectiveness of this basis as shown by experience gained at national level.[72] The increase in value approach was rejected as it would cause considerable regulatory difficulties and that the royalty should be payable by reason of the work's exploitation, irrespective of its success.[73] This is in line with the approach adopted in France and Germany and is allowed by the Berne Convention.

Article 4 proposes a tapering scale of rates based on three price bands. A basic rate of 4 per cent applies to the sale price between ECU1,000–ECU50,000. This, the Commission states, is the average of the rates adopted by the various Member States.[74] A mid rate of 3 per cent applies to sale prices between ECU50,000–ECU100,000. For sale prices in excess of ECU100,000 a rate of 1 per cent For example, the *droit de suite* for a work sold for ECU500,000 would be ECU7,460; calculated as follows:

First ECUs 1,000 (@ 0 per cent) = 00 plus

Between ECUs 1,000—50,000 (49,000 @ 4 per cent) = 1,960 plus

Between ECUs 50,000–100,000 (50,000 @ 3 per cent) = 1,500 plus

Between ECUs 100,000–500,000 (400,000 @ 1 per cent) = 4,000.

The mid 3 per cent rate in the first draft of the Directive applied between ECUs 50,000–250,000 and the sale price above ECU250,000 attracted a 2 per cent rate. The ECU500,000 sale would have earned a *droit de suite* ECU12,960.[75] Thus by amending the bandings and a percentage rate the Commission has considerably reduced the size of payments for high value sales. The reason for the amendments is to keep the payments below the costs "entailed by transferring the sale to New York or Zürich".[76]

There is a lacuna in the proposed Directive. The minimum threshold must not exceed ECU500 but a resale right is not charged until a sale

---

[72] Recital 14.
[73] Memorandum Ch. V, p. 21, para. 6.
[74] *ibid.*, p. 22, para. 9.
[75] 1,960 (49,000 @ 4 per cent) plus 6,000 (200,000 @ 3 per cent) plus 5,000 (250,000 @ 2 per cent).
[76] European Parliament Report, p. 21.

price of ECU1,000 is reached. Article 4(2) attempts to address this. It states, "Should a lower threshold than ECU1,000 be established, the Member State shall set the applicable percentage, which may not be lower than 4 per cent." A Member State is compelled to set a threshold that does not exceed ECU500. The lacuna would be more easily removed by increasing the threshold to ECU1,000 or by lowering the starting point of the 4 per cent rate to ECU500. There is another fundamental flaw with the scale and apportionment. Sale prices that just cut above the threshold level would result in minuscule *droit de suite* payments that probably would not merit their administrative and collection expenses. For example, assuming the threshold was set at ECU1,000 a sale price of ECU1100 would result in a *droit de suite* of ECU4.[77] A more satisfactory approach would be to extend the 4 per cent band to start from zero and adopt a payment threshold of ECU40, below which the *droit de suite* would not be paid. A sale price of ECU1100 would then attract a *droit de suite* payment of ECU44, making collection more worthwhile. An even more satisfactory approach would then be to increase the payment threshold to ECU100, thereby ensuring that collection is worthwhile and greatly reducing the proportion that is swallowed up by administrative costs. The effect would be that a sale price of at least ECU2,500 would be required for a *droit de suite* payment. From the previous section, it is recommended that this threshold is applied throughout the E.U.

A radical idea not discussed by the Commission is to consider having a maximum threshold payment. This would be in line with the regressive nature of the scale and be in keeping with the desire not to award vast sums of money to already successful and wealthy artists.[78] If the maximum threshold sale price was set at ECU1,000,000 this would provide a maximum *droit de suite* payment of ECU12,460 for all sale prices equal to or in excess of this threshold.[79] In addition to the prevention of further adding to the wealth of the already wealthy artists, it would also counter the major economic arguments against a *droit de suite*. Internationally mobile high value sales would not be driven away from the E.U. market to non *droit de suite* markets as a capped *droit de suite* of ECU12,460 would represent a relatively small proportion of the total selling costs.

The overall effect is that under the Directive's scale, artists producing works selling for lower prices would receive a proportionately higher *droit de suite* than artists producing higher value works; thus assisting the young and less established artists.

It is important not to set these rates too high so as to encourage sales outside the Community Consideration was given to charging Community exports with the *droit de suite* but this idea was dismissed because of the practical difficulty of policing them.[80] This may also offend the

---

[77] 100 @ 4 per cent.
[78] Such a threshold is applied in the Public Lending Right for authors. See p. 149, n. 3 above.
[79] 1,960 (49,000 @ 4 per cent) plus 1,500 (50,000 @ 3 per cent) plus 9,000 (900,000 @ 1 per cent).
[80] Memorandum Ch. V, p. 22, para. 11.

TRIPS agreement.[81] The rates must balance the interests both of "artistic circles", presumably the artists, and of the art market.[82] However, it appears that the balance is tipped in favour of the latter as the rate is only a fraction of the dealers commission.

Despite the above discussion, the whole idea of having a scale of rates is questionable. The French experience has shown preference for a single rate when the sliding scale was scrapped in 1957. Germany also employs a single rate. The administrative difficulties will be accentuated, at least until monetary union is realised, by the rates having to be converted into fifteen different currencies. A single rate of 5 per cent would simplify the calculation and administration. As 5 per cent is a higher percentage than that envisaged by the Commission, the maximum sales price suggested above can be reduced to ECU500,000.

The proposed Directive's payment can be compared to the payment resulting from the *droit de suite* suggested above.

A comparison can be made between the payments resulting from the *droit de suite* suggested above, the first draft of the proposed Directive and the approved Directive. For the purpose of comparison and to remove the uncertainty regarding the approved Directive's minimum threshold it will be assumed that a threshold of ECU1,000 will be set.

The payments under the Directives start at a very low level, far below that which is economical to collect; whereas under the suggested scheme they start at ECU125, an amount that is worth collecting. Also, at this ECU2,500 starting point an artist will receive ECU125, which is more than double the amount he would under the Directives. Although, until a sale price of ECU250,000 the payment increases exponentially under the Directives, the artist still receives considerably more under the suggested provision. At this level he receives ECU12,500 as opposed to ECU4,960 or ECU7,960. A doubling of the sale price to ECU500,000 doubles the payment of the suggested provision, reaching the maximum payment of ECU25,000. At this level the artist would receive almost twice that of the proposed Directive and more than three times that of the approved Directive. Between a sale price of ECU2,500 and ECU500,000 the artist is far better off under the suggested provision. Also, works of this value are not the ones the London art market fears will be driven away. Sales below ECU2,500 can be ignored as being *de minimis*. Sales at this low level may be aided by the lack of a *droit de suite* but equally, the payment under the Commissions provision may be seen as being too insignificant to dwell in the mind of a seller.

Both Directives continue to produce ever increasing payments as the sale price increases. They do not match the suggested payments ceiling until a sale price of well over two million ECUs is reached for the approved Directive or over a million for the proposed Directive. Then payments continue to rise. The heirs of Piccasso stand to make

---

[81] Agreement on Trade-Related Aspects of Intellectual Property Rights (1984), Article 4.
[82] Recital 19.

ECU102,460 for a work selling at 10 million ECU. This would represent a relatively small (1.2 per cent) but still considerable saving if the seller chose to sell his work outside the E.U. This is almost half as much as the original proposal would have produced (ECU202,960, 2.3 per cent). Under the suggested provision, such a multi-million ECU sale would attract the same payment, ECU25,000, as the work selling for ECU500,000. This is almost insignificant representing a mere 0.25 per cent of the painting's sale price, hardly proving an incentive to export the work for sale outside the E.U.[83]

Sale Price (ECU)	Proposed Directive's Payment (ECU)	Approved Directive's Payment	Suggested Provision's Payment (ECU)
1,000	nil	nil	nil
1,100	4	4	nil
2,500	60	60	125
5,000	160	160	250
10,000	360	360	500
20,000	760	760	1,000
50,000	1,960	1,960	2,500
100,000	3,460	3,460	5,000
250,000	7,960	4,960	12,500
500,000	12,960	7,460	25,000
750,000	17,960	9,960	25,000
1,000,000	22,960	12,460	25,000
2,000,000	42,960	22,460	25,000
5,000,000	102,960	52,460	25,000
10,000,000	202,960	102,460	25,000

[83] On November 10 1997 *The Dream* by Picasso fetched $48.4 million (£28.5 million or ECU42.1 million) at auction at Christie's in New York; Picasso's Dream Revives Art Market, *The independent*, November 12 1997, p. 11. If the sale had taken place with the E.U.'s approved *droit de suite* applying then the heirs of Piccasso would have stood to make ECU486,460 (just over 1 per cent) on the sale and under the original proposed *droit de suite* would have stood to make a staggering ECU970,960 (fractionally over 2 per cent). A seller faced with a *droit de suite* payment of around half a million ECU (or around one million ECU under the proposed Directive) would be unlikely to hesitate in locating the sale outside the EU to avoid this substantial payout. However under the suggested provision the *droit de suite* payment of ECU25,000 represents a mere 0.05 per cent of the total sale price.

E. Person liable for payment

The royalty is to be paid by the seller which may be a person or an undertaking.[84] Although in theory, a buyer could pay, the seller is liable for the payment in all existing *droit de suite* provisions.

F. Persons entitled to receive royalties

The artist and, after his death, "his legal heirs" shall receive the royalty.[85] Thus, as under the Berne Convention, it is left to national legislation to determine how the right devolves on the artist's death. This means that the French law may continue to prohibit testamentary dispositions while the German law may continue to permit them. The explanation for not harmonising this measure is that the laws of succession do not affect the functioning of the internal market. The Commission also cited the subsidiarity principle as a reason for not intervening in this area of Member States' law.[86] The Directive does not deal with joint artists. One must therefore assume that this is another matter left for national legislation.

G. Collection procedure

Authors are responsible for the management of the sums paid and may arrange for collective management.[87] Originally the proposed Directive stated that it is for Member States to determine the arrangements for collecting and distributing royalties for both its own nationals and other Member State nationals. This follows the Berne Convention's provision, and reflects the desire of the Commission to permit flexibility in the management of the right. The options envisaged by the Commission include the right being managed by a public authority, a national collecting society or collecting societies, or by the owner of the right himself.[88] The change in emphasis from the State to the author removes any obligation on the State to set up a collecting authority or to pursue any other courses of actions such as issuing guidelines. Whichever approach is adopted by the artists in each Member State, nationals and other Member State nationals must be treated equally.[89]

A modification can be made to the collection rate suggested above to allow an amount to fund the administration of the scheme. For example, for sale prices above ECU20,000 1 per cent of the payment could be diverted to a collecting society; thus the artist would receive 4 per cent

---

[84] Recital 20.
[85] Article 6.
[86] Memorandum Ch.V, p. 22, para. 13; Recital 22.
[87] Article 6(2).
[88] Memorandum Ch. V, p. 22. para. 14; Recital 23.
[89] As per judgment of the Court of Justice, October 20 1993, Joined Cases C–92/92 and C–326/92. *Collins v. Imrat Handelsgesellschaft GMbH* [1993] E.C.R. 545.

instead of 5 per cent. An artist would still receive the full 5 per cent for sales below ECU20,000. The established artists would be subsidising the administration of payments to the less established artists and thus help to further one of the objectives of the *droit de suite*. Any excess could be used to promote art in schools or as grants for unestablished artists.

H. Right to obtain information

It is now proposed that an artist or his agent may obtain any information from the management of commercial establishments or of public sales and sellers and commercial dealers, that "may be necessary in order to secure payment of the sum payable under the artist's resale right" for three years following the date of the transaction.[90] This time period is a welcome improvement on the ambiguous one year period contained in the proposed Directive. However, a prudent artist would be advised to make annual requests for information to all the dealers known or considered likely to deal in the artist's work. Where an artist wishes to exercise this right, to establish the identity of an anonymous seller, for example, the seller's agent may attempt to maintain a low profile of the transaction so as not to bring it to the artist's attention within this limitation period. The effect may be to deprive the artist of the information right in the cases in which it is most needed.

The value of the limitation period must therefore be questioned. If it is just to protect dealers from an ongoing liability to provide information then it is also aiding the reluctant dealer to evade a *droit de suite* payment. The right to information may expire after three years but the right to payment does not. A more acceptable limitation to prevent abuse is to limit the exercise of the right to collecting societies, as per the German provision.

I. Third-country nationals

Reciprocal treatment applies for third-country nationals.[91] From the wording of the Article it appears that the third-country must offer the right to nationals of all Member States to receive reciprocity. This is in line with the Berne Convention.[92]

The E.U. may benefit by applying the right to third-country artists irrespective of reprocity. If the right was limited to E.U. artists then it can be argued that auctioneers and art dealers would prefer to sell works by third-country artists,[93] to the detriment of E.U. artists. Thus, granting the *droit de suite* to as many third-country artists as possible would be beneficial to E.U. artists in addition to the obvious benefit to third-

---

[90] Article 9.
[91] Article 7.
[92] Article 14ter.
[93] See P. Katzenberger, "The *Droit de Suite* In Copyright Law" (1973) 4 I.I.C. 361, at 377.

country artists. Third-countries considering the introduction of a *droit de suite*, such as the U.S. for the same reason, can assume that their artists will benefit from the *droit de suite* abroad.

From the first enactment of the *droit de suite*, in France, Belgium and Germany, special arrangements applied to foreign artists depending upon whether a reciprocity agreement existed between the countries involved. This was relaxed in France in 1956 when the *droit de suite* was made available to all artists who had participated in French artistic life and had resided in France for at least five years.

J. Inalienability

The Directive defines the *droit de suite* as an inalienable right.[94] If it was not made inalienable then the right could be bought and sold with the work to which it attaches and be rendered totally ineffective. The proposed Directive made no mention on whether or not the *droit de suite* was waivable. If an artist was permitted to waive his right then one can envisage pressure from a dealer being exerted to exercise the waiver. In the U.S., the Californian provision expressly prohibits a waiver unless it is for an amount greater than the royalty rate.[95] The Copyright Office has suggested that a Federal *droit de suite* should also be made non-waivable.[96]

This omission in the proposed Directive may not have been deliberate as the Commission's intention, clearly stated in the Memorandum, is that the "effectiveness of the right is necessarily conditional on the right's inalienability and the impossibility of waiving it".[97] For this reason the approved Directive expressly states that the right "cannot be given up prematurely or otherwise".[98] The objective of the Commission is now with legal force.

K. Implementation, duration and revision clauses

It is proposed that Member States implement the Directive by January 1, 1999.[99] The right shall last for the period laid down in the Term Directive—life of the author plus 70 years from the end of the year in which the author died.[1] It is afforded full copyright status in this respect.

A revision clause is included.[2] It is expressed that proposals to adjust the minimum threshold and the rates of the royalties to "take account of changes in the sector" shall be considered.[3] Presumably, periodic adjust-

---

[94] Article 1.
[95] California Civil Code S.986(a).
[96] U.S. Copyright Office Report, 151–155.
[97] Memorandum Ch.V, p. 22, para. 3.
[98] Article 1.
[99] Article 11.
[1] Directive 93/98/EEC, Article 9.
[2] Article 10.
[3] *ibid.*

ments may have to be made to account for inflation. However, it may also be seen as demonstrating less than full confidence in the banding structure.

VIII. U.K. 2: The Response To Proposed Directive

The proposed Directive has forced the Government to reconsider the *droit de suite* once again.

A. Arguments against a U.K. *droit de suite*

The Government has maintained its firm opposition to the introduction of the *droit de suite*. It has consistently defended the findings of the Whitford Report, now 20 years old, stating that "no new factors had emerged" and "nothing had changed".[4] Neil Smith, the Secretary to the British Art Market Federation, not surprisingly, agrees that the situation has not changed significantly since the Whitford Report.[5] The Minister for Trade and Industry prior to the recent elections, Lord Fraser, affirmed the Conservative Government's robust stance: "we do not accept the Directive . . . this measure is ill-directed and the sooner it is confined to some dusty shelf for eternity the better."[6] Despite the change in Government on May 1, 1997, there is no indication that the new Government is any less hostile to the introduction of the *droit de suite*.[7]

I. The Whitford Objections Reconsidered[8]

a) Inefficacy

The amount of income deriving from a *droit de suite* would depend on the frequency of sales of the artist's work. Thus, the point made by the Whitford committee that whether any substantial income derived from the right would be a matter of "sheer chance" rings true. "Occasionally the widows of a 'Henry Moore' will make a killing—but no other."[9] An artist seeking to provide for his heirs would be advised to leave them a few paintings and not rely on the uncertainties of a *droit de suite*.

b) Procedural and Administrative Difficulties

The difficulties envisaged by Whitford can be illustrated by examining the experience in other Member States. Smith contends that the French

---

[4] J. Ibbotson, "*Droit de Suite*—Why the E.C. Directive Should be Supported" [1996] 63 Copyright World 21 (Ibbotson)", 22.
[5] Smith, 26.
[6] Hansard, H.L. 11 Dec. 1996, Col. 1178.
[7] Tony Scott of the Copyright Directorate, Department of Trade and Industry, confirmed that the position remained "unchanged"; telephone conversation May 16, 1997.
[8] See page 26 above. For ease of comparison between the original findings of the Whitford Committee and the situation today, the same headings are used.
[9] *ibid.*

system is inefficient pointing out that, despite the vast sums paid to the heirs of famous artists such as Matisse and Picasso, one of the main collecting societies, SPADEM, had filed for bankruptcy "as the amount collected was not sufficient to meet its own running costs".[10] SPADEM has now ceased to exist. Collection costs, according to Smith, as a proportion of sums collected are put at about 40 per cent for Denmark and 68 per cent for Sweden.[11] However, this must be put in context. Sweden introduced the *droit de suite* in 1996 and it is only to be expected that teething problems would cause high initial collection costs.

c) Economic Effect

The British market will suffer the greatest consequences of a E.U. *droit de suite*. London accounts for 60 per cent to 70 per cent of the European art market. Smith estimated that the value of the British market which would be subject to a *droit de suite* amounted to £300 million in 1995, with over 50 per cent of the sellers coming from outside the E.U. The price sensitivity of the international art market leads sellers to opt for the locations where they "can get the best price and where formalities are not too cumbersome."[12] The introduction of a U.K. *droit de suite* would stop works entering the British market; "galleries will go out of business or reduce their operations so drastically that they will no longer be able to provide much of a launching pad for up and coming artists."[13] Lord Fraser referred to his Department's unpublished report which reveals that the introduction of the right could "lead to the British art market losing earnings of up to £68 million with some 5,000 jobs going."[14] Smith alleges that a 17 per cent fall in U.K. art imports for 1995 could be attributed to the imposition of VAT, as well as the realisation that more lucrative profits could be earned elsewhere.

The health of the market is dependant on the artists, middlemen (auction houses and dealers), and purchasers. Each is interdependent upon the others. A *droit de suite* would first harm auction houses and dealers, then consequently artists, and eventually purchasers would suffer.

2. Other Objections

In addition to the objections raised by the Whitford Committee several further objections to the introduction of the *droit de suite* exist. Four E.U. Member States, Austria, Ireland, the Netherlands, as well as the U.K. do not have a *droit de suite*. According to Lord Fraser, a more satisfactory way of achieving harmonisation would be to abolish the right within the

[10] *ibid.*, 26.
[11] *ibid.*, 27.
[12] *ibid.*
[13] *ibid.*, 26.
[14] Hansard, H.L. Dec. 11, 1996, Col. 1177.

E.U.[15] Also, many countries which have a *droit de suite* in their legislation have not implemented.[16]

Another objection stems from the different approach to copyright existent in the U.K. and other common law countries which contributes to the general reluctance to adopt a *droit de suite*. Civil law countries, employing an authors' right system, have a different perspective.[17]

Some commentators argue that an artist's income is to be derived from a once and for all sale of his work and is not akin to the writer's income consisting of an author's right to receive a royalty from each copy of his work sold.[18] They also contend that the historical justification for the starving artist is no longer valid.

In formulating a *droit de suite* provision a subjective judgement as to the meaning of "art" is inevitable. In the E.U.'s proposed provision this judgement has been exercised to the detriment of jewellery designers, furniture builders and architects.

There already exists a method of enabling an artist to receive a percentage of the price of a work when it is resold. An artist could include a clause in the first sale contract binding a purchaser to pay a percentage of the sale price, to the artist, on the subsequent sale of the work and to bind the new purchaser to a similar clause. In the U.S. this clause is contained in a "Projansky contract", named after the lawyer who first drafted such a contract.[19]

B. Arguments for a U.K. *droit de suite*

I. The Whitford Objections Reconsidered

The Whitford Report is now 20 years old and its findings, based on research conducted in the 1970s, have to be re-evaluated in the light of both the changes and developments that have occurred over the last two decades and the experience of *droit de suite* in other countries.

a) Inefficacy

The inherent nature of copyright favours the successful author. It is therefore to be expected that the most successful artists (or writers and composers) will receive large royalty payments while less successful ones

---

[15] Hansard, H.L. Dec. 11, 1996, Col. 1178.
[16] In 1985 of the thirty countries (as well as the state of California) reported as having *droit de suite* legislation 17 countries had not implemented the right; Executice Committee of the International Union for the Protection of Literary and Artistic Works and Intergovernmental Committee of the Universal Copyright Convention, *Droit De Suite*: Drafting Principles Concerning the Operation of this Right, Paris, June 10, 1985, B/EC/XXIV/13.
[17] See further Shapiro.
[18] Victor Ginsburgh, Professor of Economics at Brussels University, Art Newspaper, May 1996, referred to and supported by Smith, 27.
[19] See further L. DuBoff, *The Deskbook of Art Law*, (Oceana, New York, 1977), 1131; and D. Cochrane, *This Business of Art*, (Watson—Guptill Publications, New York, 1978), 50.

receive much smaller payments. Furthermore, all copyright related rights depend on exploitation of the work which may also be a matter of "sheer chance". It is therefore unjust to raise this objection only in regard to *droit de suite*.

b) Procedural and Administrative Difficulties

Whitford reported that artists were not organised and could not voice a collective opinion on the right. In September 1996 there were 32 artists and authors organisations representing around 20,000 artists backing the Artists' Campaign for Resale Rights.[20] The allegation that the right is economically unworkable can be refuted by the possibility of an efficient artists collecting society administering right using a computerised management system. Accurate and up to date data can be supplied by auction houses and dealers, most of which have computerised their sales data. The use of computers by both parties would now make this a relatively straight forward and inexpensive operation. Evidence from Denmark shows that a collecting society can be run efficiently. The Danish collecting Society, Copydan Billedkunst, which consisted of just one member of staff and a computer database, was able to distribute an average of about £70,000 a year during 1991 and 1993, despite the recession.[21] Figures given for the amounts collected in Germany and France ranged from £3.5 million to £6 million illustrating the potential effectiveness of their respective provisions.

c) Economic Effect

Concern was expressed over the need for European harmonisation and that "the current residual problems consist of, or are exacerbated by Britain's reluctance to conform".[22] The 1951 Gregory Report shared the view first espoused in the 1909 Copyright Committee Report (which led to the Copyright Act 1911) that:

> it would be a great advantage if the British law were placed on a plain and uniform basis, and that that basis were one which was common, so far as it is practical, to the nations which join in the [Berne] Convention.[23]

This statement is now 88 years old but still holds true today and could be brought up to date by replacing the word "Convention" with words "European Union". In a perfect world there would only be one set of uniform laws covering copyright and its related rights. The adoption of a European *droit de suite*, if argument for it can be made out, would be a step closer to this goal.

---

[20] Ibbotson, 22.
[21] "Artists' Campaign for Resale Rights" [1993] 32 C.W. 16.
[22] *ibid*.
[23] Report of the Copyright Committee (Cmnd. 8662) (1952), 2.

Economic arguments now tend to dominate the discussion. Art market representatives postulate over the "wholesale transference of the market to countries where the right does not exist, bringing with it the suggestion of mass unemployment to auction houses and galleries and the threat of lost revenue to the treasury."[24] The art market is already affected by its own changes—VAT, Capital Gains Tax, Inheritance Tax, import and export taxes, export licences, regulation of the market, social insurance contributions, commission levels, levels of expertise, and a changing economic climate. The 1980s boom in the international art market was followed by a dramatic decline in the early 1990s. The current gradual recovery has mirrored the economic fortunes of most Western economies.

The anti *droit de suite* lobby consists almost exclusively of the auction houses and dealers, fearing their profits would be adversely affected. A 1991 Fine Art Trade submission to the European Commission argued that auctioneers and dealers could not afford to pay a small percentage to artists.[25] However, in 1992 Sotheby's increased its buyers' commission by 5 per cent (more than the proposed *droit de suite* rate) to 15 per cent. During 1995 Christie's profits increased by 3 per cent and Sotheby's increased its sales by 25 per cent (to $1.67bn).[26] It is also worth bearing in mind that a *droit de suite* would only apply to works of art still in copyright and many of the sales would not be affected.

There is grave concern that art sales destined for the U.K. market may transfer to Switzerland or the USA, both non *droit de suite* countries. Evidence for this concern is the decline of the Paris market since the 1920 French provision. This, however, can be attributed to other factors such as the emergence of American buyers, who prefer to purchase in their native language and therefore favour London or New York to Paris. Other factors include transportation costs (which can be doubled if an unsold work is re-imported), insurance, export licences, and taxes. Despite having a *droit de suite*, the French market still remains considerably larger in terms of both works sold and of revenues earned than the neighbouring Swiss market.[27] New York's dominance as the world centre for art sales and London's number two position can not be attributed solely to their lack of *droit de suite* provisions.[28] Self perpetuating expertise and reputation play a considerable part in maintaining their positions.

Even if this argument had some validity, the introduction of a E.U. *droit de suite* may prompt the U.S. to consider the introduction of a

---

[24] Ibbotson, 22.

[25] Stephenson Harwood, U.K. Fine Art Trade Working Party 1991 submission to the E.C.

[26] A. Thorncroft, Higher Demand For Art And Jewels Lifts Christies 32 per cent, Financial Times, March 13, 1996, 29.

[27] There were 21439 recorded auction sales in Switzerland valued at SF306,572,460 (£139,870,195) between 1/1/90–24/10/96. The respective figures for France were 8,8727 sales valued at FF7,023,268,510 (£778,037,372). Art Sales Index 1990–1996, CD—ROM, Art Sales Index Limited, I Thames Street, Weybridge, Surrey KT13 8JG. ("Art Sales Index").

[28] 120,305 reported auction sales took place in the U.S. between 1/1/90–24/10/96 valued at $4,827,212,264 (£2,959,886,960) and 174,968 sales in the U.K. valued at £1,882,497,717. Art Sales Index.

Federal *droit de suite* provision; thus removing the whole foundation of this objection. An indication that this occur was made by the U.S. Congress when it considered the 1992 U.S. Copyright Report.

Economic Evidence

The IFO Institute for Economic Research study commented that they were unable to obtain reliable data; "it was . . . impossible to obtain such data. Experts in the field point out that the art market has always been a secretive domain."[29] The U.S. Copyright Office, in putting together its report rejecting the introduction of a *droit de suite*, did not conduct an empirical study and its report contains very little empirical evidence. Despite the Australian Copyright Council's extensive data collection and analysis its findings were inconclusive, other than to suggest "that there is sufficient basis to support further detailed study".[30]

d) Whitford Today

A spokesman for the Artists' Campaign for the Resale Right wrote in 1993 that:

> [t]he concerns voiced by Whitford were either not credible or were no longer relevant in light of subsequent events. Artists . . . had not been properly informed or consulted, and such consultation as had taken place seemed to have been very limited and selective; things had changed dramatically since the issue was last addressed ten or more years ago, and artists are now aware of how morally compelling the arguments are for resale rights, and can demonstrate that such rights would have been both "logical and practical".[31]

2. Other (Non Whitford) Considerations

The Artists' Campaign for the Resale Right argues that the "artist starving in a garret" is not pure myth as even today the majority of artists have to supplement their income in other ways.[32] This is supported by the findings of the Australian Copyright Council Report which showed that while the average income for male artists was marginally lower than average weekly earnings, the figure for female artists was only 45 per cent of average weekly earnings.[33] Comment was passed that the adjective "starving" could be applied to female artists.[34]

---

[29] Hummel, Becker, Humber and Krojager, The *droit de suite* (IFO Institute for Economic Research, Munich, 1995), p. 3, para. 1.3.
[30] Australian Copyright Council Report, 74.
[31] P. Nathan, "Artists' Campaign for Resale Rights" [1993] 32 Copyright World 16, 16.
[32] Ibbotson, 22.
[33] Australian Copyright Council Report, 53.
[34] *ibid.*

The "increase in value" theory may be as relevant today as it was in the beginning of this century. A number of high profile sales in the U.S. have highlighted the substantial profits made by astute dealers while the artists received relatively little for their initial and only income making sale. One of the earliest reported examples is the 1948 sale by Grant Woods of his *Daughters of the American Revolution* painting to a dealer who shortly after resold the work making a three hundred per cent profit.[35] This led Wood to insist on a contractual clause granting him a fifty per cent share of the profits on subsequent resales of his work; an early forerunner to the Projansky contract. The 1973 New York auction sale of Robert Rauschenberg's assemblage entitled *Thaw* by taxicab magnate and art collector Robert Scull made headline news. Scull had purchased the work in 1958 for $900 and the 1973 sale fetched $85,000.[36] It was this sale that started the *droit de suite* debate in the U.S. More recently a work sold by artist James Rosenquist for $500 was subsequently resold for a staggering $274,000.[37]

The Projansky contract is dependant on the purchaser accepting it.[38] As the bargaining position is almost always weighted in favour of the purchaser a sale may be made without the acceptance of such a term. Privity of contract would prevent an artist from enforcing a Projansky contract against a subsequent purchaser, thus it may only prove effective for the first resale. The result has been that few buyers have signed a Projansky contract.[39] It is therefore not a workable alternative to a *droit de suite*.[40]

IX. Conclusion

Does a sophisticated legal system need a *droit de suite*? The original justifications for the introduction of *droit de suite*, the concept of which was born in 1893 and was first realised with the enactment of the 1920 French law, have now to be seen in a contemporary light. If these historical justifications are no longer valid and there is no new or additional justification for a contemporary *droit de suite* then it should not be introduced. In having as its objective the removal of disparities

[35] Grant Wood Paints George Washington and a Cherry Tree, Life, 19.2.1948.
[36] In a much publicised incident following the auction Rauschenberg confronted Scull and complained "I've been working my ass off just for you to make that profit!", Roger Ricklefs, "Artists Decide They Should Share Profits on Resale of Paintings", (1974) 11.2 Wall Street Journel 1.
[37] The Great Debate Over Artist's Rights, Washington Post, 22.5.1988, F4, col. 2. The $48.4 million sale of Picasso's *The Dream* on November 10, 1997 (see p. 182 n. 83 above) earned the estate of the sellers a profit in excess of 500 per cent. The price at which the sellers had originally purchased the painting was not disclosed but the auction of 58 paintings from part of the modern art collection of Victor and Sally Ganz raised a total of $207. The total original investment in art by the Ganz family was less than $2 million.
[38] See page 60 above.
[39] Goetzl (1989), 257.
[40] For further comment of the proposed introduction of a *droit de suite* in the U.K. see: A. Williams, "*Droit de Suite*: not so sweet" [1992] 136(20) S.J. 496; Campaign For Resale Rights Continues [1994] 43 Copyright World 16.; R. Fry, "Slow Progress for Resale Royalty" [1995] 55 Copyright World 28; and R. Fry, "Commission Launches *Droit de Suite* Initiative" [1996] 60 Copyright World 9.

between Member States which distort competition and interfere with the free movement of goods the European Commission has put forward a new justification for the existence of a *droit de suite*. It is questionable whether this harmonisation of law necessarily justifies the introduction of a *droit de suite* as harmonisation could also be achieved by removing *droit de suite* from the Member States in which it exists. However, the removal of an existing right is more difficult than the introduction of a new right and consequently the E.U. has tendered to harmonise upwards; the Term Directive being prime example.

Of all the justifications the equality of treatment theory has the greatest potential to merit the introduction of a *droit de suite*. A *droit de suite* enables artists to fully participate in the success of their work placing them on a par with authors and composers. If this is the objective then the case for the existence of the right can be made. A *droit de suite* should not exist simply for the purpose of harmonisation.

An explanation for the different approaches taken in attempting to justify a *droit de suite* between the French Parliament and the European Commission may lie in the differences in attitude underlying the French authors' right system and the common law's copyright system. The starting point of the former as its very name asserts is the right of the author. The author is king. The artist as author has a natural right to the complete exploitation of their work. In contrast, the starting point of the copyright system is the economic exploitation by the owner, not necessarily by the creator, of the work. The European Commission, of what is still essentially a economics driven organisation, has found an economic justification for the *droit de suite*. The rights of artists are of secondary importance to the removal of disparities that may distort trade between Member States. It just so happens that in the case of *droit de suite* artists will benefit as a by-product of the Commission introducing a harmonised *droit de suite* to achieve its objective. The different justifications underline the change in emphasis from the authors' right approach to the copyright (economic) approach.

The *droit de suite* has been considered as being a lost child of the *droit d'auteur* and the legislature had hardly seemed to care.[41] However, the British legislator is about to be forced to care. Under Article 110A of the Treaty of Rome, with majority voting and the U.K. being the only Member State opposed to the measure, the Parliamentary stage may prove to be little more than a formality and the adoption of the Directive then inevitable. A British veto will be totally ineffective and there will not be the possibility of the U.K. receiving special treatment as with her opt-out clause written into the Social Chapter. The British Government should wake up to this reality and instead of its stubborn, no compromise stance should consider attempting to play a leading role, reflecting London's position in the market, in the adoption of a *droit de suite* but on terms that will not harm the U.K. or the E.U. market. The Government

---

[41] R. Plaisant (1988), 157.

should realise that the debate has moved on beyond the existence question and involve itself in the drafting of the substantive provision.

The amendments made to the proposed Directive are a welcome stride forward in achieving a workable *droit desuite* but with further fine tuning a more effective and less harmful provision is achievable. The further amendments advocated in this article are to:

- Adopt a uniform definition of originality.
- Include a notification requirement.
- Increase the minimum threshold and its basis.
- Include a maximum threshold.
- Prevent Member States from setting their own thresholds.
- Replace the four band scale with a single uniform rate.
- Consider introducing an administrative levy on higher payments.
- Remove or extend the limitation period on the information right.
- Clarify the position of works by joint authors.

A *droit de suite* drafted as suggested may also provide the catalyst for a worldwide *droit de suite*, perhaps to be embodied in an updated mandatory Article 14ter of the Berne Convention.

7. A Case Study in Cultural Imperialism: The Imposition of Copyright on China by the West

Robert Burrell

Lecturer in law, King's College London. LL.B, LL.M (London). Formerly Lecturer in Law, University of Wales, Aberystwyth. He has published in the *Common Market Law Review* and is a contributor to the forthcoming edition of *Copinger on Copyright*. He is in the course of co-authoring a work, with Allison Coleman, on exceptions to copyright.

A Case Study in Cultural Imperialism: The Imposition of Copyright on China by the West*

Introduction

Since the late 1980s China has been under intense pressure from Western Governments to introduce "adequate" protection for foreign copyright works. China has responded to this pressure by passing various statutes and regulations and by joining the major international copyright conventions. Yet Western Governments remain dissatisfied, arguing that the Chinese Government has often acted in bad faith, turning a blind eye to widespread and well organised piracy, even as it promulgated new legislation. By and large this official explanation for the continuing "problem" of copyright piracy in China has been uncritically adopted by the media, with the result that China has been caricatured as a "freeloading" nation which needs to be forced into accepting international legal norms.[1]

This essay does not directly take issue with the dominant view of China as a pirating nation. Rather, this essay looks at the way Western countries have gone about trying to persuade China to adopt and enforce copyright legislation. In the case of the United States the methods of persuasion adopted have been those of "aggressive unilateralism," that is, it has relied almost exclusively on the use of threats and cajolements.[2] It will be argued that the use of such tactics rests on a number of assumptions and has a number of consequences. Most importantly, the use of such tactics assumes that Western models of intellectual property are universally applicable. Objections to the adoption of a Western model of intellectual property based on cultural norms or economic objectives are dismissed as attempts at obfuscation or procrastination. Thus alternative models, which might be able to achieve functional equivalence, are dismissed out of hand. It will be argued that this approach can be criticised for a variety of reasons.

---

* My thanks go to Benga Bamodu, Emily Haslam, Perry Keller, Shane Kilcommins and Craig Lind.
[1] For example, see "Pirates of Peking", *The Times*, Feb. 8, 1995; but compare "West cries piracy while pillaging Chinese Labour," *The Guardian* Feb. 17, 1995. For an historical overview of the extent to which reporting from China has tended to reflect Western policy see Becker, "Ideological bias in reporting China", in Porter (ed.), *Reporting the News from China* (Royal Institute of International Affairs, London, 1992). More generally, see Chomsky and Herman, *Manufacturing Consent: The Political Economy of the Mass Media* (Pantheon, New York 1988).
[2] In general, Europe has tended to support American aims whilst calling on both sides to show more flexibility, but has insisted that China extend benefits given to American nationals to European citizens. See Endeshaw, *Intellectual Property in China* (Singapore, Acumen, 1996), pp. 32, 48, 85, 86. Our attention will be primarily focused on American policy as this has set the pace of reform and the tone of China's response.

First, this approach fails to respect other voices and other traditions, and instead posits the moral superiority of a value system which is far more recent than the tradition it seeks to condemn. Equally, this approach rejects out of hand the Chinese Government's ideological difficulties with the notion of intellectual property rights. In contrast to this way of thinking, this essay will attempt to show that the Chinese Government was justified in having concerns about the impact of introducing intellectual property rights and that there were reasons why such concerns were particularly pronounced in the case of copyright protection. By ignoring such concerns the West has acted in a high-handed and arrogant fashion.

Secondly, there is a potential conflict between the West's demand that China introduce strong intellectual property protection and China's desire for economic and technological development, in that China could attempt to close the gap between itself and the developed world through the unrestricted copying of foreign technology. In anticipation of the argument that China's reluctance to protect foreign intellectual property is therefore justified, some commentators have called for a right to intellectual property to be recognised as an inalienable human right, thereby seeking to exclude "policy" based justifications for Chinese hesitance. When examined more closely, however, such calls are unconvincing and serve to obscure more substantive moral and ethical issues.

Thirdly, when the West's motives are examined in more detail, it is possible to object to the approach that has thus far been adopted on the grounds that it lacks integrity. Integrity, as an aspect of political morality, requires governments to speak and act coherently. Integrity therefore demands that the language of justice is not adapted or abandoned so as to meet political goals. By thereby requiring us to apply the same standards to everyone, the principle of integrity ensures that we do not arbitrarily discriminate between groups and individuals. As such integrity is an important, but distinct, aspect of the more general requirement that we treat others with respect.[3]

Fourthly, and most seriously, the West has encouraged China to introduce criminal sanctions for copyright infringement. Not only does this lack integrity in the sense considered above, it has also exposed China's population to the risk of grave human rights abuse. This suggests that western governments are more concerned with property rights than with the more fundamental rights of China's population.

More generally, the aim of this essay is to draw attention to the extent to which cultural differences, economic aspirations and related ethical issues should be taken into account by those advocating world-wide protection for intellectual property. Whilst there has been at least some recognition that there are ethical issues involved in granting intellectual

---

[3] See further, Dworkin, *Law's Empire* (Fontana, London, 1991) pp. 176–224. Although Dworkin ties his theory of adjudication to integrity, it is a broader principle which survives a rejection of the more controversial aspects of his theory of law such as the "one right answer" thesis. Also see Raz, *The Morality of Freedom* (Clarendon, Oxford, 1988), p. 212.

property protection for certain types of subject matter (such as patents for genetically modified organisms) or in new environments (such as in cyberspace), this essay attempts to show that simply advocating protection for the "settled core" of intellectual property rights can raise a number of ethical issues.

Before turning to consider the above issues in more detail, however, it is first necessary to enter two caveats. First, although frequent reference will be made to "ethical" issues and concerns it should not be assumed that a particular theory of ethics is being advanced here.[4] Thus the aim of this essay is not so much to justify the conclusions that are reached on the issues that are identified, but rather to flag them as concerns that will have to be taken into account if we are to develop a morally defensible ethic of intellectual property. Indeed, some commentators have argued that forcing China to comply with Western intellectual property standards may have a number of desirable consequences. For example, the Intellectual Property Rights (IPR) Agreement of March, 1995 has the potential to lead to greater openness in matters of legislation and censorship.[5] Moreover, one commentator has argued that the protection of intellectual property rights has an important psychological dimension for China, in that it has required full participation in the international community and has required serious consideration to be given to the role of the market in the regulation of society and the nature of commodities that can enter the marketplace.[6] Such arguments are undoubtedly important and would have to be taken into account in order to construct a comprehensive picture of the effects of advocating strong intellectual property protection. So far, however, such arguments have, at best, provided an *ex post facto* justification for policies grounded in economic and domestic political concerns.

Secondly, and more importantly, although it will be argued that the West's, and particularly the United States', policy towards China has

---

[4] For example, a demand that we listen to other voices and that we treat others with respect is perhaps most obviously justified in terms of a postmodern ethic of "alterity." (See Douzinas and Warrington, *Justice Miscarried* (Harvester Wheatsheaf, Hemel Hempstead, 1994), in particular, at pp. 160–166). Yet concern for others also forms an important part of non-individualistic forms of liberalism. (See Raz, *The Morality of Freedom* (Clarendon, Oxford, 1988).) Equally, it would be possible to justify this demand on the rather more self-serving grounds that we must listen to other voices to ensure that received opinion is constantly challenged so that we do not fall into error. (See Mill, *On Liberty* (London, Penguin, 1985) pp. 75–118).

[5] For a summary of the effect of the 1995 agreement see "US—China IPR Agreement," [1995] March, *East Asian Executive Reports* 4. Prior to this agreement, a common complaint from American copyright owners was that the censorship system was being used to delay the release of films and music albums, sometimes indefinitely. Under the terms of the 1995 agreement China will have to decide on matters of censorship within 60 days, and should normally do so within 10 days, an obligation which clearly has much wider political implications. In addition, China has an obligation under the terms of this agreement to publish all rules and regulations relating to intellectual property, with the effect that internal guidelines will no longer have the force of law. This is important because a long standing obstacle to legal reform in China has been the continued existence of so called "secret legislation." This seems, therefore, to provide a rare example of where the adoption of legal standards acceptable to the West has forced China to adopt some (very) limited political liberalisation.

[6] See Dicks, "The Chinese Legal System: Reforms in the Balance," (1989) 119 *The China Quarterly* 540, in particular, at 554.

been unethical in certain respects, this should not be taken as an argument for excusing China's own appalling human rights record. Nor should scepticism about attempts to present intellectual property as an inalienable human right or a defence of cultural rights and the right to development be conflated with arguments for cultural sovereignty in respect of all rights and freedoms. The demand that we respect other traditions means that we have to handle human rights issues sensitively, it does not mean that we have to abdicate all responsibility for the well-being of foreign citizens.

I. Culture, Capitalism and the Struggle for History

In this first section attention will be focused on the extent to which copyright can be said to conflict with traditional Chinese values, current ideology and legitimate economic goals. It will be argued that when such issues are taken into account, the Chinese leadership was justified in wanting to take a slower, more measured, approach to copyright reform. In order to explore these questions in more detail it is necessary to trace the history of copyright protection in China. The historical narrative that this entails is itself interesting in that it discloses examples of Western Governments acting in ways which would now be almost universally regarded as unacceptable. This perhaps indicates that we should be slow to formulate aggressive policies based on our current values and understandings.

Authors and censors in imperial China

China was almost certainly the first country in the world to impose restrictions on the unauthorised copying of books and certain other types of work, beginning with an edict of the Emperor in A.D. 835, during the Tang dynasty. This prohibited the reproduction of calendars and other works connected with astronomy. These restrictions were subsequently expanded in the early part of the eleventh century (during the Song dynasty) as a response to the invention of type printing, which was seen as a potential threat to Imperial power.[7] In order to meet this threat, publishers were required to register their works with the local author-ities, seemingly to ensure that they could be censored.[8] Variants on this system of registration lasted into the early years of this century.

---

[7] For a detailed account of the history of paper making and printing in China see Tsien Tsuen-Hsuin, "Paper and Printing" Pt. 1, Vol. 5 in Needham (ed.), *Science and Civilization in China* (Cambridge UP, Cambridge, 1985).
[8] See Zheng Chengsi, "Printing and Publishing in China and Foreign Countries and the Evolution of the Concept of Copyright (I)," [1987] 4 *China, Patents and Trade Marks* 41; Alford, "Don't Stop Thinking About Yesterday . . . Why There was No Indigenous Counterpart to Intellectual Property in Imperial China," (1993) 7 *Journal of Chinese Law* 3; Alford, *To Steal a Book is an Elegant Offense* (Stanford UP, Stanford, 1995) pp. 9–29.

There has, however, been a degree of dispute over the importance which should be attached to these Imperial restrictions. The traditional view has been that they were an early form of copyright protection, the inevitable response to the invention of printing, matched some six centuries later by developments in Europe.[9] This account has since been challenged by Alford, who points to the non-proprietary nature of the restrictions in Imperial China, the lack of any specific remedies against copyists of privately owned works and, most importantly, the emphasis placed on reinterpreting the past in Chinese culture and the resulting absence of a firm notion of plagiarism.[10] On this view the printing restrictions in Imperial China were grounded in a belief that rulers had a duty to stop their subjects from being misled by "incorrect" ways of thinking, rather than stemming from a desire to protect the labour and expenditure of authors and publishers.

One complicating factor is a lack of evidence as to how the registration system operated in practice. Certainly there were cases of private publishers successfully seeking redress from local officials and some publishers would place a notice on copies of a work, claiming the exclusive right of reproduction.[11] Moreover, Zheng Chengsi has argued from a Marxist perspective that to the extent that Chinese culture failed to support property based restrictions on the reproduction of works, this was because the forces of (re)production (*i.e.* printing and the financial system) were insufficiently developed to create more than a manageable tension between the dominant modes of expression and the property system.[12]

To some extent the debate could perhaps also be classified as a semantic one, in that the Western concept of copyright has emerged only recently.[13] As a result, most commentators have not been content to begin an historical analysis of the development of copyright with the British Statute of Anne, 1710,[14] normally considered to be the world's first copyright act. Rather, they have gone back to look at the spread of the system of printing privileges, which originated in Venice in the latter part of the fifteenth century.[15] These privileges, derived from the royal

---

[9] For example, see Zheng Chengsi, *Chinese Intellectual Property and Technology Transfer Law* (Sweet & Maxwell, London, 1987) p. 86; "Printing and Publishing in China and Foreign Countries and the Concept of Copyright (II)", [1988] 1 *China, Patents and Trade Marks* 47; Nimmer and Geller (eds.), *International Copyright Law and Practice* (Matthew Bender, New York, 1996) p. CHI 15.

[10] Alford, *To Steal a Book is an Elegant Offense.* Also see Wen Fong, "The Problem of Forgeries in Chinese Painting," [1962] *Artibus Asiae* 95; Zurchër, "Imitation and Forgery in Ancient Chinese Painting and Calligraphy", (1955) 1 *Oriental Art: New Series* 141, in particular, at 142.

[11] Zheng Chengsi, "Further on Copyright Protection in Ancient China", [1996] 4 *China Patents and Trademarks* 62; Copinger, *The Law of Copyright in Works of Literature and Art*, (4th ed.), (Stevens & Haynes, London, 1904) p. 675.

[12] Zheng Chengsi, "Further on Copyright Protection in Ancient China", [1996] 4 *China Patents and Trademarks* 62 at 63.

[13] *cf.* Skinner, "Meaning and Understanding in the History of Ideas," [1969] *Past and Present* 3 at 12, "The second historical absurdity generated by the methodology of the history of ideas is the endless debate—almost wholly semantic, though posing as empirical—out whether an idea may be said to have 'really' emerged at a given time and whether it is 'really all there'."

[14] 8 Anne c. 19.

[15] The Venetian system of privileges and their subsequent spread throughout Europe is considered by Rose, *Authors and Owners* (Harvard University Press, London, 1993), pp. 9–30.

prerogative, appear much closer to the system of registration in Imperial China, particularly as they too became rapidly associated with censorship.[16] Nor did the passage of the Statute of Anne mark such an obvious break with the past, rather the new Act became associated with, and helped to develop, emerging discourses concerning the nature of property and notions of authorship.[17] This continuity between the privilege system and copyright was particularly marked in Germany, where the transition to a true copyright system was not completed until 1870.[18]

Nevertheless, the argument remains important in that it affects the way we view subsequent developments in China. On the traditional view, demands for the protection of copyright are entirely in line with Chinese history and culture. The failure of China's registration system to develop along European lines can be explained in purely structural terms, by pointing, for example, at the lack of a developed system of finance in Imperial China or the relatively low levels of literacy.[19] The result of this approach is that as China's economy develops, its adoption of a copyright system is seen as part of an almost inevitable process.

The attraction of the more recent view is that it allows for a much more sophisticated analysis, one that can account for the effect of cultural values, such as the way in which authorship was perceived by Confucianists.[20] As a result, it is possible to see copyright as foreign to, and capable of conflicting with, Chinese culture. To the extent that these traditional values survive in present day China then, on this view, existing policy towards intellectual property protection is objectionable, in that it treats those aspects of political culture which conflict with Western models of protection solely as obstacles which need to be overcome. Ultimately, this approach "threatens to undermine, if not totally destroy, the values that indigenous systems ascribe to intellectual property and the manner in which they allocate rights to intellectual goods."[21] It is only by our accepting the legitimacy of other notions of cultural productivity that we can come to respect other voices and other traditions. Nor, as is sometimes suggested, does this call for other cultures to be respected necessarily involve presenting those other cultures as static or homogenous. Thus, in the case of Imperial China, we

---

[16] This seems particularly true of France, where an Ordinance of 1566 provided for death by hanging or strangulation for the publication of unauthorised works. See Davies, *Copyright and the Public Interest* (VCH, Weinheim, 1994), p. 17.

[17] See Rose, "The Author as Proprietor: *Donaldson v. Beckett* and the Genealogy of Modern Authorship," in Sherman and Strowel, *Of Authors and Origins* (Clarendon Press, Oxford, 1994).

[18] Davies, *Copyright and the Public Interest*, p. 105.

[19] For a more general consideration of how these factors may have affected China's subsequent development see Kennedy, *The Rise and Fall of the Great Powers* (Fontana, London, 1989) pp. 9–10.

[20] Much has been made in this context of one of the most famous sayings attributed to Confucius, "The Master said: 'I transmit but do not create. Being fond of the truth, I am an admirer of antiquity'." (*Analects*, Book 7, Chap. 1). See Dawson, (trans.) *The Analects* (OUP, Oxford, 1993) p. 24. In particular, see Alford, "Don't Stop Thinking About Yesterday . . . Why There was No Indigenous Counterpart to Intellectual Property in Imperial China," (1993) 7 *Journal of Chinese Law* 3.

[21] Gana, "Has Creativity Died in the Third World? Some Implications of the Internationalization of Intellectual Property," (1995) 24 *Denver Journal of International Law & Policy* 109 at 142.

can note that there were those who attacked the production of "forged" paintings and who opposed treating the paintings of antiquity with undue deference.[22] Still less does this approach value maintaining differences for their own sake. Rather, this approach seeks to recognise that other countries may legitimately want to draw upon their *predominant* cultural values when formulating legal protection for intellectual creations and that the legal regimes that result from this process are in no way ethically inferior to those in the West. On the contrary, at a time when dominant notions of intellectual property are being challenged by people operating on the electronic frontier and when even the European Commission is predicting that technological developments will mean that "the concept of originality will develop in a less personal and more relative direction",[23] it may be that China's emphasis on social creation and production contains a useful insight into alternative ways of thinking about the subject matter of intellectual property rights.

Furthermore, even if we were to accept the rather more sophisticated argument that those facets of traditional Chinese culture which seemed to conflict with copyright protection were a consequence of the failure of the Chinese economy to develop beyond a certain point, we might still come to the conclusion that Western policy has been misguided.[24] In particular, there would seem to be little point in trying to force China to adopt a system of property relations which will inevitably emerge with the development of China's economic "base". Moreover, insofar as Marx saw property rights as an aspect of the legal system he would have expected the precise form of those rights to have been shaped, at least in part, by cultural factors.[25] Yet, as we shall see, China has been precluded from engaging in the sort of legal experimentation that might have resulted in the creation of a copyright law "with Chinese characteristics".

In order to pursue our enquiry further, however, it is necessary to return to the historical narrative we have been following.

Gunboats, socialism and cultural impediments

The first pressure on China to adopt a modern copyright law resulted from the Commercial Treaties of 1903 signed with Japan and the United

---

[22] Consider, for example, the attack on predominant artistic values made by Chao Hsi-ku (ca. 1250), "why must we seek [aesthetic enjoyment] far-way in hoary antiquity, beyond the reach of our eyes and ears?" quoted in Zurchër, "Imitation and Forgery in Ancient Chinese Painting and Calligraphy," (1955) 1 *Oriental Art: New Series* 141 at 141.

[23] *Copyright and Related Rights in the Information Society*, Com(95) 382 Final, p. 27.

[24] Indeed, Zheng Chengsi has remained critical of American policy, see Zheng Chengsi, "Further on Copyright Protection in Ancient China," [1996] 4 *China, Patents and Trademarks* 62 at 64.

[25] For a Marxist property rights have a pre-legal aspect in that they inevitably reflect the predominant productive forces. For example, see Marx, *The German Ideology* in Maclellan (ed.) *Karl Marx: Selected Writings* (OUP, Oxford, 1977), in particular, at pp. 161–164. But contrary to the way Marx is often caricatured he did not believe that the economic base mechanistically determines every aspect of the superstructure. Rather, the forces of production provide "the universal light with which all the other colours are tinged and modified through its peculiarity:" Marx, "Introduction to the critique of political economy," quoted in Parel and Flanagan (Eds), *Theories of Property* (Wilfred Laurier UP, Waterloo, 1979), p. 292.

States.[26] To understand the nature of these treaties, it is first necessary to appreciate the position China found itself in following the imposition of the Treaty of Nanking on China, by the British, in 1842.[27] Described as "an unprecedented example of a unilateral treaty"[28] the Nanking agreement was to mark the beginning of a period in which China would be forced to grant increasingly wide privileges and concessions to a number of countries, including Britain, France and, somewhat later, Japan. These concessions even included the creation of extraterritorial courts, with the power to administer their respective systems of justice, hence the existence of bilateral treaties between the Western powers for reciprocal protection of intellectual property rights within China.[29] Thus, although the 1903 treaties did provide reciprocal protection for Chinese copyrights, they were negotiated at a time when China was deprived of full sovereignty. The first true copyright law passed in 1910, at the very end of the Qing dynasty, must also be seen in this light.[30]

The governments which followed the 1911 revolution retained an interest in updating Chinese copyright law, at least initially in order to placate the West, hoping that this would in turn lead to a restoration of full sovereignty. In all a further three Acts were passed prior to 1949. All three went a long way towards providing a Western style copyright system, but it is worth noting that a registration requirement was retained throughout.[31] In addition, it should be remembered that the governments of this period were never able to consolidate their grip on the country, making the application of these laws somewhat sporadic.

Shortly after the creation of the People's Republic of China in 1949, all pre-existing laws were repealed,[32] but at first it appeared as though a new copyright law would be swiftly enacted, modelled along Soviet lines.[33] The first step towards a new law was taken in 1950 at a meeting of the first National Publications conference, which adopted a document

[26] Reproduced in Macmurray, *Treaties and Agreements with and Concerning China 1894–1919* (OUP, New York, 1921), pp. 413, 429. For a commentary on the effect of these treaties see Allman, *Handbook on the Protection of Trade Marks, Patents, Copyrights and Trade Names in China* (Kelly & Walsh, Shanghai, 1924).
[27] The Treaty of Nanking was imposed on China after its defeat in the Opium War. The Opium War was sparked by British Merchants who were smuggling huge quantities of opium from India into China. See further, Fay, *The Opium War 1840–1842* (University of North Carolina Press, Chapel Hill, 1975).
[28] Wu, *Chinese Government and Politics* (The Commercial Press, Shanghai, 1934), p. 334.
[29] See Macmurray, *Treaties and Agreements with and Concerning China 1894–1919*, pp. 502, 735, 927. Also see Copinger, *The Law of Copyright in Works of Literature and Art* (4th ed.) p. 676.
[30] For a discussion of this Act see Nimmer and Geller (eds.), *International Copyright Law and Practice* pp. CHI5–CHI7.
[31] See Zheng Chengsi, *Chinese Intellectual Property and Technology Transfer Law*, p. 87.
[32] By article 17 of the Common Programme 1949, confirming a decision to that effect taken by the Central Committee of the Chinese Communist party earlier that year.
[33] For an overview of the Soviet system of intellectual property see Butler, *Soviet Law* (Butterworths, London, 1988), pp. 197–199, 387–388; Stewart, *International Copyright and Neighbouring Rights* (Butterworths, London, 1983) Chap. 19. As to its early development, see Levitsky, "The Beginnings of Soviet Copyright Legislation," (1982) 50 *Legal History Review* 49.

which set out the general principles of copyright protection.[34] By 1957 the Ministry of Culture had drafted two further documents intended to form the basis for a full copyright system. These were never implemented due to the intervention of the Anti-Rightist Campaign, launched in the autumn of that year, and then subsequently the Cultural Revolution. As a result, China was without a genuine law of copyright from 1949 until the present law came into force on June 1, 1991. During this period emphasis was placed on the Marxist idea that authors and artists are involved in social activities and that it would therefore be inappropriate to reward them for their creative genius (rather than for their labour), a notion of authorship which found fertile ground in Chinese culture. It would be wrong, however, to assume that authors were not afforded any legal protection between 1949 and 1991. Loeber has pointed out that administrative regulations provided some protection for a domestic authors moral rights, whilst labour law dealt with an author's right to remuneration.[35]

The main impetus for the current law was international pressure, particularly from the United States. An important first step was the signing in 1979 of the Agreement on Trade Relations between the United States and the People's Republic of China. Under the terms of this agreement China agreed to provide protection for U.S. patents, trade marks and copyrights. In the case of patents and trade marks progress was rapid, with the enactment of a trade marks law in 1982 and a patents law in 1984. At first it appeared as though a copyright law would follow equally swiftly, but despite references to copyright and author's right in other legislation,[36] and the enactment of a number of provisional regulations—which reaffirmed authors' administrative rights—progress remained slow.[37]

From this brief historical survey we can see that prior to 1991 some protection had been given to authors for over eighty years, whilst restrictions on the unauthorised publication of works had been in place for more than a millennium. Any attempt to trace the development of the concept of authorship, or the history of printing, would undoubtedly have to take this into account. Yet in terms of how copyright is normally perceived—as a property right which flows naturally from the creation of a work—we can see that China only had such a system very briefly

---

[34] "Decisions Concerning the Improvement and Development of Publishing." For the effect of this document and other administrative regulations see Zheng Chengsi, *Chinese Intellectual Property and Technology Transfer Law* pp. 88–109; Nimmer and Geller (eds), *International Copyright Law and Practice* pp. CHI7–CHI10.

[35] Loeber, "Copyright Law and Publishing in the People's Republic of China," (1977) 24 U.C.L.A. Law Review 907.

[36] *E.g.* Article 2, Inheritance Law, 1985; Article 94, General Principles of Civil Law, 1986. The latter used copyright (*banquan*) and author's right (*zhuzoquan*) interchangeably, a position now confirmed by Article 51 of the Copyright Law, 1990.

[37] As to the effect of the provisional regulations, see Nimmer and Geller (eds.), *International Copyright Law and Practice*, pp. CHI9–CHI10.

(between 1910 and 1949), and that was during a period of prolonged political instability. In addition, we can see that the laws of this period were largely the result of foreign dominance, they were laws "learnt at gun point."[38]

More generally, we can see that the dominant non-proprietary notions of creativity and authorship of classical Chinese culture are, if anything, likely to have been reinforced in the years of leftist dominance. This gulf in cultural values was further reinforced by an ideological difficulty which lies in the very notion of intellectual *property*. For any avowedly communist regime, notions of property inevitably raise interconnected issues of economics, law and ideology.[39] The ideological problem is more acute in the case of copyright, than in the case of patents and trade marks, as registration is seen as having a much more restricted role, thus limiting the control of the state.[40] This perhaps explains why the Chinese Government seemed reluctant to extrapolate from its experience in relation to the protection of foreign patents. Predictably, the West has proved uninterested in such ideological concerns, but it must be remembered that China, as a sovereign nation state, has the right under international law to determine its own economic order.[41] To the extent that China is a non-capitalist nation pursuing goals which may, at times, be diametrically opposed to the interests of foreign capital, then China is entitled to give a great deal of thought to rights which may run counter to this prevailing ideology.[42]

Taken together with the aggressive manner in which the United States pressed its demands (for example, by threatening to withdraw China's

---

[38] See Alford, *To Steal a Book is an Elegant Offense*, Chap. 3.
[39] The ideological debate seems to have revolved around the question of whether it is appropriate to treat copyright works as commodities, bearing in mind the level of China's socialist development. For example, see Shen Rengan, "On the Assumption of the Nature of Commodities by Literary and Artistic Works *vis-à-vis* Copyright Protection," [1990] 3 *China Patents and Trade Marks* 61 (arguing that it is appropriate for China to treat intellectual property rights as commodities).
[40] For example, the Universal Copyright Convention provides that in the case of foreign works, placing the symbol © together with the name of the copyright proprietor and the year of publication is sufficient to comply with any formalities imposed by a Contracting State in respect of its own nationals (UCC, Art III). Moreover, even where registration systems have been employed, the theory has tended to be that the property right does not actually flow from the act of registration. Rather, registration has been seen as confirming a pre-existing property and as providing the owner with a greater range of remedies.
[41] See Jennings and Watts (eds), *Oppenheim's International Law*, (9th ed. Longman, London, 1992), p. 337. Also see Emmert, "Intellectual Property in the Uruguay Round—Negotiating Strategies of the Western Industrialized Countries," (1990) 11 *Michigan Journal of International Law* 1317.
[42] There has been a tendency in the West since the early 1980s to present Chinese politics in non-ideological terms: see Becker, "Ideological bias in reporting China," in Porter (ed.), *Reporting the News from China*, p. 78. Recent academic literature, however, has focused on the continuing importance of ideology. For example, see Feng Chen, *Economic Transition and Political Legitimacy in Post-Mao China: Ideology and Reform* (State University of New York Press, Albany, 1995), "China's political system remains an ideological one that requires a theoretical basis for all major policies to sustain the system's legitimacy. Ideological constraints on economic policies at the early stage of reform were significant, and they continue to be relevant as reform moves on" at p. 2.

most favoured nation status),[43] the effect of the absence of the cultural notions which would underpin copyright legislation and the history of foreign dominance has been to produce a crisis of legitimation.[44] That is to say, the vast majority of the population do not see these laws as enforcing important interests. As a result, there is no public acceptance of the need for such laws and they do not see activities which infringe them as morally wrong.[45] Thus in the perhaps rather more familiar language of Hartian jurisprudence, we can say that the vast majority of the population do treat such laws as having an "internal aspect."[46] This seems to remain the case, despite the use of an ambitious program of public legal education to raise awareness of copyright issues.[47]

Chinese difficulties were still further compounded by the political situation in China. Clearly no Chinese leader could be seen bowing to pressure from the United States without being in danger of undermining his own position, a difficulty which goes some way towards explaining much of the brinkmanship which has characterised the negotiations between China and the United States on this issue.

Bearing these problems in mind it is hardly surprising that a genuine dispute emerged over how best to serve the needs of a vast developing country, "with the only distinct existing culture able to challenge the West in terms of longevity, sophistication and number of adherents."[48] One aspect of this debate was the extent to which alternative arrangements, best suited to China's culture and needs, should be sacrificed in favour of complying with international norms. The United States, however, insisted that China should join the Universal Copyright Convention, and preferably the Berne Convention as well, and that it should formulate copyright legislation accordingly. The American Government was particularly dismissive of suggestions that a new international convention might be formulated in order to allow China to join the international copyright community. This is despite the fact that the Universal Copyright Convention was created in the 1950s primarily in

---

[43] See further, Kim, *China and the World: Chinese foreign relations in the post cold war era*, (3rd ed.), (Westview, Oxford, 1994) "In China the most favoured nation issue pressed upon a sensitive nerve of national pride; public interest in it, as in China-U.S. relations generally, dwarfed that in the United States. The possibility that the United States might 'reject' and 'punish' China by withdrawing the status activated the negative pole of that deep-seated ambivalence towards American power and culture that many, particularly well educated Chinese, have long felt" p. 86.

[44] For a consideration of the obstacles to legitimacy faced by the 1993 Chinese Trade Mark Law see Carter, *Fighting Fakes in China* (Intellectual Property Institute, London, 1995), pp. 35–44. More generally, see Dozortsev, "Trends in the Development of Russian Civil Legislation During the Transition to a Market Economy," (1993) 19 *Review of Central and East European Law* 513, in particular, at 520–522. Also see Kahn-Freund, "On Uses and Misuses of Comparative Law," (1974) 37 M.L.R. 1, who notes that it is the use "of foreign models as instruments of social or cultural change which raises most sharply the problem of transplantation".

[45] See Carter, *ibid*. Even in the West there is a degree of public resistance to the enforcement or intellectual property laws, as can be seen most clearly in relation to home taping.

[46] Hart, *The Concept of Law*, (2nd ed., Clarendon, Oxford, 1994), pp. 56–57.

[47] As to popular legal education in China, see Chen, "The Developing Legal System in China," (1983) 13 *Hong Kong Law Journal* 291.

[48] Pendleton, "Chinese Intellectual Property—Some Global Implications for Legal Culture and National Sovereignty," [1993] 4 *European Intellectual Property Review* 119 at 120.

Burrell

order to draw the United States into the copyright fold.[49] American negotiators did not seem to find it awkward that China was being pushed into joining the Berne Convention when, despite international pressure, America had resisted doing so for more than a century.[50] Nor did they seem prepared to acknowledge that although America has finally joined the Berne Convention, in certain respects the Convention has still not been properly implemented.[51]

Economics and inalienable rights

So far we have focused on the social, cultural and ideological factors which gave the Chinese Government good cause to delay the implementation of copyright reform and which cast doubt on the legitimacy of the West's approach. In addition, however, there were economic reasons for the Chinese Government to proceed with caution.

China's key economic reason for caution was a fear of the effects of extending protection to works of a technical nature, such as industrial drawings and, above all, computer programs. There was a very real concern that such protection might hinder economic development, either by restricting access to materials or by creating a trade imbalance with the developed world.[52] This was combined with a fear that American corporations would be able to use newly acquired rights to gain control of emerging markets in China, particularly as regards the market for computer software. On the other hand, it was hoped that unrestricted access to technical works might allow China to bridge the technological gap between China and the developed world, thereby allowing the Party to meet one strand of one of its key policy objectives.[53] The Chinese Government was also understandably sceptical of American arguments that strong intellectual protection was necessary in order to provide an incentive for the production and importation of new works and that without such protection economic development would be impeded. In particular, this argument seemed to be belied by the fact that the United States and, more recently, other East Asian countries had gone through periods of rapid economic growth whilst refusing to protect foreign copyright works.

---

[49] See Lahore, *Copyright and Designs*, (Butterworths, Sydney, 1996), para. 56, 165; Cornish, *Intellectual Property: Patents, Copyright, Trade Marks and Allied Rights* (2nd ed., Sweet & Maxwell London, 1989), p. 252.
[50] See Barnes, *Authors, Publishers and Politicians: The Quest for an Anglo-American Copyright Agreement 1815–1854*, (Routledge & Kegan Paul, London, 1974), p. 50 "As a country, nineteenth century America was akin to a present-day underdeveloped nation which recognizes its dependence on those more commercially and technologically advanced, and desires the fruits of civilization in the cheapest and most convenient ways".
[51] Most obviously, the United Sates has refused to provide express provision for an author's moral rights. Cf. Berne Convention for the Protection of Literary and Artistic Works, Art. 6bis.
[52] See Pendleton, *Intellectual Property in the PRC* (Butterworths, Singapore, 1986), pp. 39–43.
[53] Since 1978 China has pursued a policy of "the four modernisations." This policy seeks to narrow the gap between China and the developed world in four key areas, namely, defence, agriculture, industry and science and technology. See further, Feintech, *China's Four Modernisations and the United States* (Foreign Policy Association, New York, 1981) Chapter. 2.

At first, the economic aspects of the dispute between China and the West may seem to have little connection with the ethics of the West's approach. However, when such issues are examined more closely, we can see that at the heart of this aspect of the dispute lies a disagreement over the extent to which a developing nation is entitled to "misappropriate" the intellectual property rights of foreign nationals in order to meet its economic objectives. This, in turn, explains why some commentators have tried to present a right to intellectual property as an inalienable human right. On the assumption that such rights "trump" economic goals,[54] these commentators conclude that "it should be considered inconsistent with general public international law to deny an adequate protection of intellectual property only on the basis of the exercise of sovereignty."[55]

Some support for the view that a right to intellectual property should be recognised as an inalienable human right can be gained from Article 27(2) of the Universal Declaration of Human Rights, which provides "everyone has the right to the protection of the moral and material interests resulting from any scientific, literary or artistic production of which he is the author."[56] In effect, however, this attempt to present a right to intellectual property as an inalienable human right is little more than a jurisprudential sleight-of-hand, which seeks to close off arguments as to the merits of allowing developing countries to make free use of foreign intellectual property.[57] Attempts to present rights to intellectual property as inalienable human rights are also heavily dependent on the mythology of intellectual property, that is, they depend on a vision of a transformative genius whose contribution to society merits special recognition and protection. Such attempts look rather less convincing when compared to the commercial, formulaic nature of many copyright works and when placed in the context of the widespread corporate ownership and collective administration of intellectual property rights.[58]

Moreover, it is to be doubted whether those advocating a human rights based justification for intellectual property in this context would be prepared to accept some of the consequences that would seem to flow from employing this justification more generally. For example, a human rights based justification might force us to re-examine the role of the patent system or the way in which we treat works created in the course of employment. Nor is such a justification as difficult to counter in this

---

[54] Dworkin, *Taking Rights Seriously* (Duckworth, Guildford, 1994) p. xv.

[55] Hilf and Opperman, "International Protection of Intellectual Property: a German proposal" in Chowdhury, Denters and de Waart (eds.), *The Right to Development in International Law* (Martinus Nijhoff, Dordrecht, 1992) p. 291.

[56] Also see Emmert, "Intellectual Property in the Uruguay Round—Negotiating Strategies of the Western Industrialized Countries," (1990) 11 *Michigan Journal of International Law* 1317.

[57] Similarly, it precludes arguments that the West owes the developing world a debt for "the brain drain." See further, Bulajic, "International protection of intellectual property in the context of the right to development," in Chowdhury, Denters and de Waart (eds.), *The Right to Development in International Law.*

[58] Also see Rose, *Authors and Owners*, p. viii.

context as is perhaps sometimes supposed. On the contrary, it is equally possible to present the "right to development" as an inalienable right vested in the Chinese people.[59] We would then be left without any way of choosing between these competing claims.[60] One possible way out of this apparent deadlock would be to attempt to prioritise between different "generations" of rights. For example, a right to intellectual property could be categorised as a first generation right on the grounds that it subsists in individuals and can be seen as being morally prior to Government action or intervention. By contrast, a right to development would normally be categorised as a third generation right, primarily because it is seen as subsisting in groups or societies as a whole and because "development" will often be dependent upon sustained and comprehensive Government intervention.

It is submitted, however, that attempts to distinguish between different generations of rights are unhelpful. In particular, this division between different generations of rights seeks to prioritise "negative" liberty over "positive" liberty, but this is an approach which many countries, and socialist countries above all, reject.[61] From this perspective the designation of first, second and third relates to the historical order in which these rights came to be recognised, rather than to any moral priority between the different generations. Trying to present a right to intellectual property as a first generation right also throws light on the tension which exists at the very heart of the notion of negative liberty. Negative liberty is typically seen as marking out areas in which an individual should be free from Government intervention. Yet in complex industrialised societies the protection of such rights depends upon an interconnected system of statutes and regulations, courts and law enforcement agencies, which in turn require taxes to be levied and collected.[62] Thus, as Bentham argued, rights guaranteeing negative liberty are more aptly described as "securities" which are recognised and guaranteed by the state.[63] Whilst it might still be possible to draw some distinction between rights to positive and negative liberties based on the level of intervention required to support their existence, such a distinction looks unconvincing in the

---

[59] As to the right to development in international law, see Garcia-Amador, *The Emerging International Law of Development* (Oceana, New York, 1990); Snyder and Slinn (eds), *International Law of Development: Comparative Perspectives* (Professional Books, Abingdon, 1987).

[60] This type of intractable dispute provides a key component of the communitarian critique of liberalism. For example, see Macintyre *After Virtue*, (2nd ed., Duckworth, London, 1985), p. 6 "The most striking feature of contemporary moral utterance is that so much of it is used to express disagreements; and the most striking feature of the debates in which these disagreements are expressed is their interminable character. I do not mean by this that such debates go on and on and on -although they do- but also that they apparently can find no terminus. There seems to be no rational way of securing moral agreement in our culture."

[61] For the classical statement of the difference between these two types of liberty and for a critique of positive liberty see Berlin, *Four Essays on Liberty* (OUP, Oxford, 1969). Also see Rawls, *A Theory of Justice* (Clarendon, Oxford, 1972), in particular, at pp. 60–61.

[62] See Rosen, *Thinking about Liberty*, Inaugural Lecture delivered at University College London, November 29, 1990, in particular, at p. 9. Also see Raz, *The Morality of Freedom* (Clarendon, Oxford, 1988) pp. 18–19.

[63] Rosen, *ibid.*, p. 8.

case of intellectual property rights, as such rights are heavily reliant upon complex bureaucratic structures. This is most obviously true of rights which are dependent upon registration, but even rights which arise without formality (such as copyright) require governmental support and a sophisticated system of adjudication.[64]

If arguments about abstract rights are therefore unhelpful in this context, it seems far more satisfactory to focus on the substantive moral and economic issues which surround the use of foreign intellectual property by developing countries. This involves recognising that developing countries have a legitimate interest in having unlimited access to foreign technology, whilst the pirating of films, books and sound recordings can ensure that these works are available to consumers at reasonable prices. In return for adopting a developmental strategy that respects foreign intellectual property rights, Western Governments should offer other types of aid and alternative trade concessions. Thus intellectual property owners who complain (with some justice) that it is not their responsibility to provide developmental aid should also focus on ensuring that Western governments make other types of aid available.

Summation

We have seen that in addition to conflicting with traditional Chinese values, American policy has interfered with China's political sovereignty, including China's legitimate desire for development. In addition, this policy has involved considerable hypocrisy, as America resisted giving adequate protection to foreign authors for many years, during which time America emerged from its period as a developing nation.

2. Scaremongers and Scapegoats: The Origins of Aggressive Unilateralism

Thus far we have focused on how Western policy was received in China. In this section attention will be turned to concentrate on why strong protection for intellectual property has become such a dominant feature of the United States' foreign policy. We will see that the adoption of this policy had much to do with political expediency. This in turn casts further doubts on the morality of the West's approach.

The United States of America first moved towards adopting a new trade policy in 1985. This new policy, commonly referred to as aggressive unilateralism, received sustained legislative support culminating in the passage of the Omnibus Trade and Competitiveness Act 1988, which introduced the super and special 301 procedures. Aggressive unilateralism is characterised by demands for unilateral liberalisation and reform and these demands are supported by the threat of trade sanctions. The

---

[64] See Suchman, "Invention and Ritual: Notes on the Interrelation of Magic and Intellectual Property in Preliterate Societies," (1989) 89 *Columbia Law Review* 1264 at 1272.

motivation for this policy was said to be that American firms were increasingly being discriminated against because foreign governments were engaging in unfair trade practices, even as America opened up its domestic market to foreign competition. This discrimination was in turn said to have implications for American competitiveness, employment and the trade and budget deficits.[65] A demand for strengthened intellectual property protection rapidly became associated with aggressive unilateralism, in part as a response to estimates that as much as six per cent of all world trade is in goods that infringe intellectual property rights.[66] In addition, a refusal to protect foreign intellectual property rights provided tangible evidence of the "unfairness" suffered by American corporations, as compared to rather more amorphous complaints about socio-economic barriers to free trade and hidden government agendas.

However, although there were undoubted economic reasons for the targeting of countries who were seen to be engaging in unfair trade practices and although there was a genuine sense of injustice in some quarters, it seems that both Congress and the President were anxious to be seen to be doing something to promote the economy in an era of "zero sum politics."[67] Thus although there had been a policy favouring strong intellectual property rights for many years, it is only since the mid 1980s that this policy has received substantial attention or resources.[68] By focusing on the supposed wrongdoings of America's trading partners it was hoped that public attention would be deflected away from the structural difficulties the American economy was experiencing at the time and the effect an overvalued dollar was having on exports.

The administration also believed that if the President did not seem to have a coherent plan to solve America's economic woes Congress might try to recover the powers to regulate foreign commerce which are vested in it by the Constitution,[69] but which have in effect been delegated to the executive since the early 1930s.[70] Moreover, by appearing sympathetic to export interests it seems that the administration hoped to be able to rally the support of these interests against the protectionist lobby in Congress. Both the Reagan and Bush administrations were ideologically opposed to the introduction of import quotas and the like. But there was a lobby, consisting of domestic industries and labour organisations that were being badly affected by foreign imports, that was pressing Congress to introduce measures to protect American investment and jobs. The hope

---

[65] In general see, Bhagwati and Patrick, *Aggressive Unilateralism: America's 301 Trade Policy and the World Trading System* (University of Michigan Press, Ann Arbor, 1990); Bayard and Elliot, *Reciprocity and Retaliation in U.S. Trade Policy* (Institute for International Economics, Washington, 1994).

[66] As calculated by the International Chamber of Commerce, cited in Davies, *Copyright and the Public Interest*, p. 175.

[67] See Davidson, *The Postreform Congress* (St. Martin's Press, New York, 1992).

[68] For an account of the evolution of the U.S. position see Uphoff, *Intellectual Property and U.S. Relations with Indonesia, Malaysia, Singapore and Thailand* (South East Asian Program, New York, 1991).

[69] U.S. Constitution, Article I, Section 8, "Congress shall have Power To regulate Commerce with foreign Nations."

[70] Bayard and Elliot, *Reciprocity and Retaliation in U.S. Trade Policy*, p. 25.

was that if the export sector was healthy then an export lobby would emerge that would oppose the introduction of measures that were likely to lead to retaliatory action and possibly a full scale trade war.[71]

The Reagan and Bush administrations were similarly opposed to the introduction of an industrial policy, which was increasingly being credited for the success of the Japanese and other East Asian economies. Such a policy, which would have involved considerable government interference in the economy, was anathema to Republican administrations wedded to *laissez-faire* economics. Aggressive unilateralism allowed the economic success of East Asian nations to be explained in terms of their having engaged in unfair trade practices, thereby deflecting attention away from the constructive role government intervention had played in the success of these economies.[72]

Within this milieu of political manoeuvrings mention must also be made of the role of the intellectual property industries who campaigned to get their concerns to the top of the political agenda. In part their campaign was successful because it was well organised and well funded, but it was given added attention because many of the industries concerned are located in important electoral areas such as California. This latter factor, combined with the need to be seen to be taking effective action, meant that industry estimates of the economic consequences of piracy were never vigorously challenged.

In addition to the rather self-serving motivations that have so far been identified, it also appears that the policy of aggressive unilateralism was motivated by two more general political concerns. First, some within Congress were quite open about the need to press for strong protection for intellectual property rights in order to maintain America's technological superiority.[73] In this respect there was the potential for a direct conflict between America's desire for strong intellectual property protection and the desire of developing countries to close the gap between themselves and the developed world. The second general motivation relates to a belief in the force of trade as a civilising influence. Here the belief was that forcing a country to open its markets and making it abide by international intellectual property standards, would help ensure that country's integration into the world economy. This in turn would make military aggression seem a much less attractive prospect, particularly as such global integration would raise awareness of the rest of the world, thereby reducing tensions and suspicions.[74] Such a justification must

---

[71] *ibid.*, pp. 52–53; Uphoff, *Intellectual Property and U.S. Relations with Indonesia, Malaysia, Singapore and Thailand*, pp. 8–9, 11–12.
[72] See Uphoff, *ibid.*, p. 8.
[73] See Boyard and Elliot, *Reciprocity and Retaliation in U.S. Trade Policy*, p. 2.
[74] See Endeshaw, *Intellectual Property in China* (Acumen, Singapore, 1996) p. 47. Such a belief has a long tradition in liberal political theory, for example, see Constant, *"De la liberté des anciens comparée à celle des modernes,"* (1819) in Fontana (trans.), *Constant: Political Writings* (Cambridge UP, Cambridge, 1988), p. 314, "Commerce [in ancient times] was a lucky accident, today it is the normal state of things, the only aim, the universal tendency, the true life of nations. They want repose, and with repose comfort, and as a source of comfort industry. Every day war becomes a more ineffective means of satisfying their wishes. Its hazards no longer offer to individuals benefits that match the results of peaceful work and regular exchanges."

have seemed particularly attractive as regards China, where there was a degree of lingering distrust, particularly in relation to its intentions towards Taiwan.

Overall, therefore, we can see that there were numerous reasons why America adopted the policy of aggressive unilateralism, but that it had much to do with domestic political factors. As regards foreign policy objectives, it is inconceivable that disputes over intellectual property would have been allowed to sour relations with China in the late 1970s and early 1980s (when the United States was seeking to foster links with China in order to create a further bulwark against the USSR).[75]

Yet in contrast to the primarily political motives we have identified, American complaints about piracy in China have invariably been framed in the language of justice or fairness—the "theft" of American intellectual property by Chinese pirates is unfair. On one level this simply suggests that we should treat American protestations of outrage and calls for the recognition of rights to intellectual property as inalienable human rights with caution. On another level, however, this inconsistency casts further doubt on the morality of the American approach. We have already observed that integrity, as a demand of political morality, requires Governments to speak and act on the basis of a coherent set of principles. This in turn involves two sub-principles. First, in order to act with integrity an individual (or in this case a Government) must actually believe in the principles he or she espouses and must attempt to provide honest explanations and justifications for his or her actions.[76] This does not of course mean that we cannot also have political reasons for supporting a just conclusion, but it does mean that we should be honest about our motives and that we should act out of conviction. Ultimately, this aspect of integrity rests on the belief that those who act immorally but out of a mistaken belief that their actions are correct, are in some way less morally culpable than those who act in a way that they know to be wrong or those who act amorally. Integrity assumes that "we can recognize other people's acts as expressing a conception of fairness or justice or decency even when we do not endorse that conception ourselves."[77] Secondly, integrity requires that we try and adopt a coherent set of principles. In this way integrity ensures that we apply the same standards of justice to everyone, it ensures that we treat others with equal concern and respect.

When we look at American policy as regards intellectual property in China we can see that it lacks integrity in both the senses we have identified. As regards the first aspect, we have seen that political motives

---

[75] See Endeshaw, *Intellectual Property in China*, above n. 74, p. 32. More generally, see Shambaugh, "Patterns of Interaction in Sino–American Relations," in Robinson and Shambaugh (eds.) *Chinese Foreign Policy* (OUP, Oxford, 1994), pp. 202–3; Middleton, "U.S. Policy Towards Moscow and Beijing in an Era of Declining Détente," in Stuart and Tow (eds), *China, the Soviet Union and the West* (Westview Press, Boulder, 1982).

[76] See Guest, *Ronald Dworkin* (Edinburgh UP, Edinburgh, 1992), pp. 81–82.

[77] Dworkin, *Law's Empire* (Fontana, London, 1991), p. 166.

have been dressed up in the language of justice and fairness. As regards the second aspect, we can see that American policy has lacked principled coherence over time, in that America is now advocating a stance that it previously rejected. The demand that a state acts with integrity over time may be a rather more difficult and controversial idea. However, if we accept that our membership of a community imposes associative obligations and responsibilities on us, then we cannot deny that we are responsible for the actions of our community personified, even if those actions took place some time ago.[78] Such associative obligations and responsibilities apply with particular force to officials in circumstances where they have a personal nexus with the actions of the community. Thus officials cannot simply say that a previous policy was pursued by an entirely different set of individuals.

The obvious reply to all of the above points is that to expect America to have adopted a wholly principled stand as regards the international protection of intellectual property rights demonstrates a startling ignorance of *realpolitik*. Yet it is precisely this sort of machiavellian argument which casts doubt on the integrity of the West's approach and which entitles us to give serious consideration to developing countries' cultural, economic and ideological agendas.

3. The Use and Abuse of Criminal Sanctions: the 1994 Decision of the Standing Committee of the National People's Congress

Of the four objections to the West's approach that we initially identified, we have explored the arguments that Western policy has failed to respect the unique traditions and distinctive political character of a large developing country, it has conflicted with China's right to economic and technological development and it has lacked integrity. This section explores the final objection that we initially identified, namely, that Western policy towards intellectual property protection has at times had serious adverse consequences for China's population. To explore this objection further, this section focuses on the consequences of the decision taken in 1994 to introduce criminal sanctions for copyright infringement. This decision merits such special treatment because, as we shall see, it provides an example of where Western policy towards intellectual property protection has run counter to basic human rights concerns. In this respect Western policy has not only lacked integrity in the sense that has already been considered, it has also made the West a potential accomplice to grave human rights violations.

---

[78] See *ibid.*, pp. 167–175; 195–216. In this way Dworkin explains the seemingly counterintuitive (from the perspective of classical liberalism) phenomenon that we can feel responsible for the past actions of our community even though we ourselves were in no way personally responsible for those actions. Thus, for example, "it is not absurd to suppose that Germans have special responsibilities because the Nazis were German too" or that Britons should feel responsible for the consequences of Empire.

Background

Following intense diplomatic pressure, the Standing Committee of the 7th National People's Congress[79] finally enacted a copyright law on September 7, 1990. This Act came into force on June 1, 1991. It must, however, be read in conjunction with the Implementing Regulations for the Copyright Law issued by the State Council,[80] which came into force on the same day. In addition, a separate set of computer software regulations were promulgated by the State Council on June 4, 1991. These became effective on October 1, of that year. This legislation draws rather more heavily upon the continental *droit d'auteur* tradition of protection for authors, than upon the Anglo-American copyright tradition. For example, the Copyright Law contains fairly generous moral rights provisions. In common with the position in France such rights are perpetual in duration.[81] At times, however, the older socialist attitude towards authors appears to have reasserted itself. For example, the law allows for authorship (and not just ownership) to vest in legal persons in relation to works which are "created at its will, under its sponsorship and upon its responsibility."[82] Although provisions allowing for legal persons to be treated as authors are fairly common within the Anglo-American approach, *droit d'auteur* regimes are normally only prepared to treat natural persons as authors. The continuation of the socialist approach to authors is also to be seen as regards remuneration for Chinese authors, with the copyright administration department being empowered to lay down recommended levels of payment.[83]

Initially China remained outside the major international copyright conventions. As a result, foreign works could only attract copyright by virtue of a bilateral agreement or by first publishing the work in China. Despite the existence of a relevant bilateral agreement between China and the U.S., the American Government remained dissatisfied and urged China to join the Berne Convention. The American Government also disliked China's separate system of protection for computer software, which required software to be registered as a precondition to bringing an action for infringement. As such this system was seen as being too reliant on the perceived vagaries of Chinese bureaucracy.

---

[79] The Standing Committee of the National People's Congress is China's main legislative body. See further, Chen, *An Introduction to the Legal System of the People's Republic of China* (Butterworths, Hong Kong, Asia, 1992) pp. 58–9; Wu Naito, "NPC: The Supreme Power of the People," [1990] *Beijing Review*, Sept. 3–9, 10–16, 17–13, pp. 13–22, 13–18, 19–23.

[80] In accordance with Article 53 of the Copyright Law. The State Council is the chief executive body of the PRC. An English translation of the Implementing Regulations is available at [1991] December *East Asian Executive Reports* 22.

[81] See further, Zheng Chengsi, "The Berne Convention and the Moral Rights in the Chinese Copyright Law," [1992] 4 *China, Patents and Trade Marks* 68.

[82] Article 11, Copyright Law of the People's Republic of China, 1990 (Official translation).

[83] Article 27 of the Copyright Law provides, "Standard scale of remunerations for the use of works shall be laid down by the copyright administration department under the State Council in conjunction with the departments concerned. Where otherwise agreed upon in the contract, remuneration may be paid in accordance with the terms of the contract." (Official translation). Also see, "People's Republic of China: Statutory Scheme of Copyright Remuneration," (1994) 25 I.I.C. 310.

216

Continued American dissatisfaction led to renewed tension between the two countries. Following "several tense and vitriolic rounds of negotiation" a Memorandum of Understanding was signed on January 17, 1992.[84] Under the terms of this agreement China agreed to protect foreign computer programs as literary works. China further agreed to accede to the Berne Convention for the Protection of Literary and Artistic Works and to modify its law accordingly. In order to meet its new obligations China issued the International Copyright Treaties Implementation Rules, which became effective as of September 30, 1992. China officially joined the Berne Convention on October 15, 1992 and the Universal Copyright Convention on October 30, 1992.

The decision to introduce criminal sanctions

Although the signing of the Memorandum of Understanding brought China within the international copyright community, piracy of copyright works remained a widespread phenomenon in China. By 1994 the U.S. was again applying considerable diplomatic pressure (including the use of the threat of trade sanctions) on the Chinese Government. One of the ways in which it was believed such piracy could be reduced was through the provision of criminal sanctions and hence, in a desire to appease the United States, the Standing Committee of the National People's Congress issued legislation to that effect in July 1994.[85]

These new rules took effect as an amendment to the Criminal Code and introduced criminal liability for the unauthorised copying and distribution of certain categories of work, including those which are most attractive to commercial pirates, namely, computer programs and sound and video recordings.[86] Liability is dependent upon a finding of knowledge as to the facts of the offence which, according to the general principles of Chinese criminal law, will include a finding of recklessness.[87] In addition to the *mens rea* requirement the defendant must have made a "relatively large amount of illegal income," or there must be "other serious circumstances." If these conditions are met the defendant can be sentenced to up to three years imprisonment and may also be fined. Alternatively, if the defendant has made "a huge amount of illegal income," or where "there are other specially serious circumstances," the defendant will be sentenced to between three and seven years imprisonment and may still face a fine.

As already stated, I believe that the pressure for the introduction of criminal sanctions for copyright infringement in China was misplaced,

---

[84] See "Memorandum of Understanding on intellectual property signed by USA and PRC," [1992] 3 E.I.P.R. D-46.
[85] An English translation, together with a brief commentary, is available at [1994] 6 Ent.L.R. 230.
[86] There is also a catchall provision in Article 1(1), although the precise effect of this is unclear, *ibid.*, at 231.
[87] Chen, *An Introduction to the Legal System of the People's Republic of China* p. 188.

and the subsequent introduction of such sanctions to be objectionable. More specifically, the introduction of criminal sanctions can be criticised on three grounds. The first, and most straightforward, objection relates to the wording of the 1994 legislation. By relying on vague and undefined terms such as "huge" and "specially serious" the Standing Committee has created the potential for considerable inconsistency in the application of these provisions,[88] an inconsistency which is serious given the draconian nature of the penalties (particularly the minimum three year sentence for the more serious offences).[89] Clearly responsibility for the drafting of the legislation lies with the Chinese, although bearing in mind their general approach to legislative drafting one could hardly say the result was unforeseeable.[90] On the other hand, the hurried manner in which the decision had to be taken can only have exacerbated the problem.

The second objection to the introduction of criminal sanctions in these circumstances is of a conceptual nature. According to a traditional "liberal" understanding, the principal role of the criminal law is to regulate serious anti-social behaviour, as perceived by a majority of the members of any given society. Accordingly, the criminal law is seen as protecting society against the rogue individual. In addition, our traditional understanding would suggest a second pre-condition, this time aimed at the potential criminal, which requires that most people will have a sufficient understanding of the acts prohibited by the law to allow them to avoid any potential liability. Yet it has long been recognised that this traditional understanding fails to explain the existence of a whole range of offences within Western societies. This is particularly, although not exclusively, true of so called regulatory offences, such as offences aimed at individuals who have failed to give information to government departments.[91] In these areas we are therefore forced to look for different justifications for the criminalisation of certain behaviour. One such suggestion is that we should begin to "reconceive criminal law as a form of public law, both in the sense that it is involved in rendering certain kinds of publicly relevant behaviour accountable, and also in the sense that criminalising practices generate and deploy a wide range of public powers, in both formally public and private bodies and officials."[92]

As to offences against intellectual property, it must be doubted whether the public's understanding and appreciation of the significance

---

[88] Some clarification has now been provided by the Supreme People's Court in its circular, "Interpretation of Some Issues for Applying the Resolution on Copyright Crimes," but much uncertainty remains. See further, Nimmer and Geller (eds), *International Copyright Law and Practice* pp. CHI 58–CHI 59.

[89] Compare this, for example, with the maximum two year prison sentence under U.K. law: Copyright Designs and Patents Act 1988, s.107(4)(b).

[90] See Tanner, "The Erosion of Communist Party Control over Lawmaking in China," (1994) 138 *The China Quarterly* 381.

[91] See Ashworth, *Principles of Criminal Law* (Clarendon Press, Oxford, 1991) Chaps. 1–3.

[92] Lacey, "Contingency and Criminalisation," in Loveland (ed.), *The Frontiers of Criminality* (Sweet & Maxwell, London, 1995), p. 25.

of intellectual property rights is anywhere, let alone in China, sufficient to justify the intervention of the criminal law on the traditional model. To this we can add a number of important practical difficulties, which would also normally weigh against any decision to criminalise certain behaviour, perhaps the most important being that "any criminal law regulation of this field would necessarily be fragmented, sporadic and unco-ordinated."[93] The solution to these difficulties, as tentatively suggested by Firth, is to recognise that the criminalisation of offences against intellectual property is a paradigm of the operation of the criminal law as a sub-branch of public law.[94]

The problem with the above solution in the Chinese context is that there is a much sharper division between "serious unlawful acts," regulated by the criminal law, and "general unlawful acts," regulated by administrative, civil or economic law.[95] In other words, China already recognises the need for broad social regulation, going beyond that provided by the mainstream criminal law, but it achieves this through different mechanisms. The most important of these mechanisms is the system of administrative penalties, imposed by the relevant authorities, which can include a severe fine or a limited deprivation of liberty, subject to the possibility of judicial review.[96] As the Implementing Regulations for the Copyright Law already included such penalties,[97] the pressure to introduce criminal sanctions seems very difficult to justify, and would seem to result from a failure to consider the existing provisions in light of Chinese jurisprudence.

The third objection relates more generally to the ethics of the West encouraging China to employ its criminal justice system. It seems outrageous that China, rated by Amnesty International as having one of the worst human rights records of any country in the world,[98] should be persuaded by the West to use a criminal system which is characterised by political interference and which in practice lacks even basic procedural safeguards. The West purports to be concerned about human rights violations in China but, as we have seen, a fundamental feature of such rights is that they take priority over political goals. Yet the West is itself prepared to foster policies which may run counter to such concerns

---

[93] Firth, "The Criminalisation of Offences Against Intellectual Property," in Loveland (ed.), *ibid.* p. 127.

[94] *ibid.*, p. 148.

[95] Chen, *An Introduction to the Legal System of the People's Republic of China*, p. 166; more generally see pp. 166–168, 204–205.

[96] *ibid*, p. 167. The abuse of this system of administrative penalties has itself been responsible for a pattern of human rights violations. Thus even if the West were to advocate the use of such penalties rather than the use of criminal sanctions, it might still be possible to object to the West's approach for the reasons set out below.

[97] Chap 6, Implementing Regulations for the Copyright Law of the People's Republic of China, 1991. Revised rules as to these administrative penalties were passed on 28 January 1997, and became effective on February 1, 1997. See [1997] 6 *China Law & Practice* 9.

[98] Amnesty has produced a number of reports, particularly since 1989. Some examples are *Prisoners of Conscience and the Death Penalty* (1984), *Torture in China* (1992) and *China: No one is safe* (1996). More generally as to the operation of the criminal justice system in China, see Leng and Chiu, *Criminal Justice in Post-Mao China* (State University of New York Press, Albany, 1985).

when its own political interests are at stake. In this respect it can again be said that the West's policy has lacked integrity. Moreover, there would not seem to be any obvious reason to suspend our usual judgment that moral responsibility attaches to those who incite others to act immorally. Thus the West can and should be held responsible for those who are deprived of their liberty for long periods of time for offences they do not fully comprehend through the operation of a deeply flawed criminal justice system. Furthermore, if the experience of the criminalisation of trade mark offences in China is followed, then it may be that the West will become implicated in still more serious abuses. Thus far it has been reported that at least 14 defendants have been sentenced to death for producing counterfeit goods.[99] In the two cases that have been reported in the West the defendants were sentenced under the provisions of the Criminal Code prohibiting speculation, rather than under the specific offences relating to trade marks.[1] It may well be that copyright infringement will also be held by the Chinese courts to amount to speculation, and will thus lead to a death sentence. Such a sentence in China often means public humiliation or public execution,[2] execution to order (so that the requirements of organ donors can be met) and a host of other well-documented abuses.[3]

Thus, although the introduction of criminal sanctions for the infringement of copyright might meet the immediate concerns of American corporations, it is open to serious doctrinal and ethical objection. In the longer term, pressure to use the criminal law to combat piracy re-focuses responsibility upon the Chinese state, and whilst this might have the desired effect in the short term, ultimately what is really needed for the adequate protection of intellectual property rights is the creation of a rights culture, in which the owners of such rights will seek redress, either individually or collectively, as through a collecting society, for example.[4]

4. Lessons for the future: the need for a new approach towards developing countries

Since 1994 Sino-American relations as regards intellectual property matters seem to have settled into a strange pattern, with periods of brinkmanship characterised by the use of threat and counter-threat,

---

[99] Carter, *Fighting Fakes in China*, p. 63.
[1] See the cases of Luo Deming, [1993] 1 *China Law & Practice* 20 and Wei Shulin, [1993] 10 *China Law & Practice* 24.
[2] Such spectacles have been largely done away with in the modern penal complex of Western societies and are widely regarded as unacceptable. For an account of the transformation from a corporal to a carceral modality of punishment in Western societies, see Foucault, *Discipline and Punish* (Penguin, London, 1991).
[3] See n. 98, above.
[4] A number of commentators have emphasised the importance of the creation of a rights culture for effective legal reform in China. For example, see Han Yanlong, "Legal Protection of Human Rights in China," in Smith (ed.), *Human Rights: Chinese and Dutch Perspectives* (Kluwer, Hague, 1996), in particular, p. 93; Alford, *To Steal a Book is an Elegant Offense*, p. 117.

being followed by periods of uneasy compromise marked by the signing of a new bi-lateral agreement.[5] Over this period piracy does seem to have diminished as a result of Government intervention,[6] but whether this will remain the case once the attention of the central Government shifts elsewhere is as yet unclear. Even if there is a long term improvement in levels of enforcement in China and even if intellectual property rights do eventually come to be more widely accepted, Western policy will have been slow to achieve its objectives. At the same time Western policy has closed off possibilities for legal experimentation and, in the case of criminal sanctions, has exposed China's population to the risk of serious human rights violations. Moreover, in order to achieve even this limited success, the United States has had to exert a disproportionate amount of its diplomatic influence solely on intellectual property matters. As a result, other policy objectives, and human rights issues in particular, have been largely neglected.[7]

Where, then, lies the way forward? It would clearly be unrealistic to expect the developed world to ignore widespread piracy, particularly when a developing country begins to export large quantities of pirated goods. Yet all too often policy choices are framed in terms of a false dichotomy between doing nothing and adopting an aggressive stance on trade issues. The challenge, therefore, is to develop a new, morally defensible approach towards intellectual property in the developing world. Such an approach will have to be firmly grounded in respect for other voices and other traditions. It will have to respect developing countries sovereignty and their desire for economic, technological and cultural development.

Any new approach will require Western countries to act with much more humility and to accept that they have often fallen short of the standards they now seek to universalise. They must avoid exaggerated demands for the recognition of intellectual property as an inalienable human right and each country must strive to speak with one voice and to act with integrity. Striving to speak and act with integrity may also cause attention to be focused on some of the important differences of approach to copyright protection that exist within the developed world.[8] An awareness of these differences may in turn make non-Western forms of

---

[5] Two further agreements have been signed since 1994. The Intellectual Property Rights Agreement of March 1995 takes the form of a general letter and an action plan and should be read as an extension to the 1992 Memorandum of Understanding. Unlike the Memorandum of Understanding, however, this document is primarily aimed at dealing with problems of enforcement, rather than being focused upon substantive legal issues. The 1996 Agreement has a narrower focus and concentrates on software and audio-visual products. See further, "U.S.-China IPR Agreement," [1995] March, *East Asian Executive Reports* 4; Clark, "Sino-U.S. IPR accord still fails to clarify market access issue," [1996] 7 *China Law & Practice* 54.

[6] See Wheare, "Intellectual Property: China's Unrewarded Efforts?" [1996] 6 *China Law & Practice* 38.

[7] A similar point is made by Alford, *To Steal a Book is an Elegant Offense*, p. 120.

[8] Most obviously, there are differences between the Anglo-American copyright approach and the continental *droit d'auteur* approach, but even within these traditions there are important variations between different countries. For example, France provides perpetual protection for an author's moral rights, whilst in Germany protection expires at the same time as economic rights.

intellectual property protection seem less unacceptable. The West should also reconsider the unified approach it has adopted towards copyright and intellectual property more generally. At present the West tends to insist that developing countries should extend protection to all works protected by copyright in the West, from technical manuals and computer programs to popular music. Whilst, as we have seen, developing countries have an interest in ensuring that works of popular culture are available at reasonable prices, their interest in copying such works is less important than their interest in copying works which impact directly on their economic and technological development.

Thus it would be preferable if the West were to distinguish between works of popular culture and more technical works when calling on developing countries to protect foreign copyrights.

A morally defensible approach will also require the West to find much more imaginative ways of persuading developing countries to adopt and enforce *appropriate* forms of intellectual property protection. For example, it has been suggested that developed countries could unilaterally extend protection to works created by the nationals of countries who do not protect foreign works. Royalties or profits generated by such works could then be paid into a blocked bank account, with the funds to be released when reciprocal protection for foreign nationals is granted by the country in question.[9] However, such a strategy could now only be applied to a handful of countries, as in the majority of cases the problem is primarily one of enforcement, often because developing countries have genuine difficulties in finding the resources to combat piracy. In these cases the West needs to help provide the necessary resources and needs to offer training to legal personnel and officials.[10]

At the same time, attempts to persuade developing countries to adopt and enforce appropriate forms of intellectual property protection need to be matched by incentives for companies to transfer technology to the developing world. At present the international legal environment within which such transfers take place is heavily biased towards the interests of multinational corporations.[11] Moreover, it needs to be recognised that direct technology transfers may be unsuccessful because the recipient country lacks the expertise and the infrastructure to take advantage of the technology as it is used in the West. Resources therefore need to be channelled into developing more appropriate "intermediate" technologies.[12]

---

[9] See Laddie, Prescott and Vitoria, *The Modern Law of Copyright* (Butterworths, London, 1994), para. 4.10, p. 267.

[10] To this extent Europe's recent attempts to distance itself from the United States' policy towards China are to be welcomed. In May 1996 the European Union's Trade Commissioner, Leon Brittan, signed an agreement under the terms of which Europe will provide legal and administrative training for judges and officials. See further, Wheare, "Intellectual Property: China's Unrewarded Efforts?" [1996] 6 *China Law & Practice* 38.

[11] Blakeney, *Trade Related Aspects of Intellectual Property Rights* (Sweet & Maxwell, London, 1996), p. 169.

[12] *ibid.*, p. 171. And see McRobie, "Intermediate Technology: Small is Successful," (1979) Vol. 1, No. 2, *Third World Quarterly* 71.

Arguably, the first steps towards a new ethically defensible approach have already been taken, with the signing in June 1992 of the Rio Convention on Biological Diversity.[13]
This agreement establishes the principle that a country has the right to exercise control over its genetic resources. A country which grants access to its genetic resources therefore has the right to the "fair and equitable sharing of the benefits arising out of the utilization" of those resources, including through the "appropriate transfer of relevant technologies."[14] The Convention also imposes an obligation on developed countries to ensure that such transfers take place.[15] As developing countries have over eighty per cent of the world's genetic resources, it should be they who benefit most from this agreement. The potential importance of the Convention was perhaps best expressed, however, by the United States Patent and Trademark Office in June 1992, which in a press release explaining why the U.S. did not originally sign the Convention, asserted that the Convention "would coerce, rather than encourage, transfer of technology from the U.S. private sector to developing countries outside of the free market system."[16]
Nevertheless, despite the potential importance of the biodiversity Convention, it is too early to judge what its practical impact will be and some of the obligations it imposes are ambiguous. It is therefore beholden upon those formulating policy in the West to ensure that the Convention is implemented in accordance with its underlying rationale of seeking to maintain biological diversity through the fair distribution of benefits accruing from the exploitation of genetic resources.
More generally, the principle of equitable treatment is one which needs to be extended to other areas. For example, the developed world needs to provide adequate protection for expressions of folklore. This can only be achieved by ensuring that the creators of expressions of folklore (or the community as a whole where that would better reflect that community's understandings of cultural creation) have the right to share in the profits that are made by exploiting such works. Creators and/or communities must also have the right to prevent the tourist industries from producing insensitive Western imitations of expressions of folklore.[17] Similarly, it needs to recognised that disagreements about the ownership of historical artefacts which have been removed from developing countries are not merely arguments about who should have control over the "physical

---

[13] See further, Straus, "The Rio Biodiversity Convention and Intellectual Property" (1993) 24 I.I.C. 602; Verma, "TRIPS and Plant Variety Protection" [1995] 6 E.I.P.R. 287. More generally, see Correa, "Biological Resources and Intellectual Property Rights" [1992] 5 E.I.P.R. 154.
[14] Rio Convention on Biological Diversity, Art. 1.
[15] ibid., Art. 16(3).
[16] See Straus, "The Rio Biodiversity Convention and Intellectual Property" (1993) 24 I.I.C. 602 at 607. The U.S. signed the Convention in June 1993.
[17] See further, Golvan, "Aboriginal Art and the Protection of Indigenous Cultural Rights" [1992] 7 E.I.P.R. 227; Xu Chao, "Legal Protection for Expressions of Folklore in China," [1997] 1 China Patents & Trademarks 55. Also see Sherman "From the Non-original to the Ab-original: A History" in Sherman and Strowel (eds.), Of Authors and Origins.

remains of the past," they are also arguments about who should control our perceptions of history.[18] Demands for the restitution of important pieces and calls for compensation must therefore be considered sympathetically.[19] In this way both sides can begin to provide mutual protection for all forms of cultural expression and not just for those limited forms of creativity which are enshrined in Western intellectual property laws. It is only when the principle of equitable treatment has been accepted that other cultures and other voices will be treated with the respect and concern to which they are entitled.

[18] See Warren, "A Philosophical Perspective on the Ethics and Resolution of Cultural Properties Issues" in Messenger (ed.), *The Ethics of Collecting Cultural Property* (University of New Mexico Press, Albequerque, 1989).
[19] Also see Greenfield, *The Return of Cultural Treasures* (Cambridge U.P., Cambridge, 1989), p. 307 "With time, the view that certain major treasures selected under fixed criteria ought to be returned may not be regarded as the pipedream of misguided liberals and scholars, nor as the abandonment of national self-interest, nor as a precipitate action which will cause the ultimate absurdity—the return of everything".

8. Unfair Competition and Ethics

Anselm Kamperman Sanders

Senior Lecturer in Trade and Intellectual Property Law at Maastricht University. LL.M (Tilburg University, The Netherlands), 1991. PhD (QMW, London), 1995, where he was Research Fellow, sponsored by a Marie Curie Fellowship (E.C. Human Capital and Mobility). His editorial and advisory board membership comprises the *Maastricht Journal of European and Comparative Law*, and *Intellectual Property Quarterly*. He has published in *E.I.P.R., Managing Intellectual Property, Intellectuele Eigendom en Reclamerecht*, and *PIP*. He is the author of the book *Unfair Competition Law—The Protection of Intellectual and Industrial Creativity* (Clarendon Press, Oxford, 1997), and has recently contributed a piece entitled "Exhaustion of Trade Mark Rights" to the *Molengrafica European Private Law* series (Deventer, Kluwer, 1977).

Unfair Competition and Ethics

Introduction

At face value ethical considerations do not play a role in unfair competition law when it concerns the protection of intellectual and industrial creativity.[1] This area of law deals with competition, where economic considerations and arguments are used to establish and justify the instances in which an action should lie. In this article aims to describe the way in which arguments of economic efficiency have been translated in ethical and moral legal rules, as well as the way in which ethical and moral rules have shaped and may yet shape the law of unfair competition in its further development.

Economic Efficiency as a Vantage Point

To exemplify the economic basis of unfair competition law, it is useful to look at the most common situation to which it provides a remedy.[2] Stamping out the creation of confusion in the marketplace is the prime example of ensuring market efficiency, so that consumers can make informed choices about their purchasing decisions. The resulting market transparency leads to a reduction in transaction costs.[3] Allowing a situation of confusion to go unchecked would merely lead to wasteful competition and insecure consumers, which are both undesirable phenomena as they do not further the increase of welfare in the free market economy. Morality does not come into play other than in the determination that the creation of confusion is tortious because the causing of harmful effect on the market is a wrong. When considering the broader concept of unfair competition, economic arguments become even more dominant in defining the elusive "unfairness".[4] The economic consideration that innovative marketers require lead time protection against

---

[1] See in general Kamperman Sanders, *Unfair Competition Law The Protection of Intellectual and Industrial Creativity*, (Clarendon Press, Oxford, 1997); Only, *Richterrecht und Generalklausel im Recht des Unlauteren Wettbewerbs: ein Methodenvergleich des englischen und des deutschen Rechts*, (Köln Heymann, 1997); for France see Passa, *Contrefaçon et Concurrence Déloyale*, (Litec Paris, 1997).

[2] For a description of acts of unfair competition see *Protection Against Unfair Competition*, (WIPO Geneva, 1994); *Model Provisions on Protection Against Unfair Competition*, (WIPO, Geneva, 1996); WIPO (ed.), *Introduction to Intellectual Property—Theory and Practice*, (Kluwer International, London, 1997) 243–82.

[3] See Akerlof, "The Market for 'Lemons': Quality Uncertainty and the Market Mechanism", (1970) *Q.J.E.* 488; Diamond, "The Public Interest and the Trademark System", (1980) 62 *J.P.O.S.* 528; Cornish and Phillips, "The Economic Function of Trade Marks: An Analysis With Special Reference to Developing Countries", (1982) 13 *I.I.C.* 41; Economides, "The Economics of Trademarks", (1988) 78 *T.M.R.* 523; Landes and Posner, "Trademark Law: and Economic Perspective", (1989) *I.P.L.R.* 229; Kamperman Sanders, "Unfair Competition Law—Some Economic Considerations", in Sterling (ed.), *Intellectual Property and Market Freedom*, PIP Vol. 2, (Sweet & Maxwell, London, 1997).

[4] *Mogul Steamship Co. v. McGregor Gow & Co.* (1889), 23 Q.B.D. 598, *per* Fry L.J. at 615:
"To draw the line between fair and unfair competition, between what is reasonable and unreasonable, passes the power of the courts."

copying is not only a dominant consideration underpinning patent protection,[5] but also an important principle when considering the protection against parasitic behaviour and copying of business assets and achievements. In their quest to provide the doctrine of misappropriation with a doctrinal basis, various academics[6] have argued for the economic principle of asymmetric market failure to be the determining factor in deciding whether an action in unfair competition should lie. Market failure can be described as a situation in which creators are not rewarded for their economic efforts because their achievements are not protected. This makes it economically more attractive to copy than to create, resulting in creators producing fewer innovative works than the public would be willing to pay for. This market failure is asymmetric when one party, the creator, faced market barriers and the other, the copyist, does not.

How Economic Efficiency is Transformed into Ethical Precepts

Protection against asymmetric market failure on the basis of unfair competition law is therefore no more than restoring an economic optimum, of which the disturbance is deemed wrongful. Economic market efficiency, rather than ethical considerations therefore appear to underlie unfair competition law. We must not forget, however, that economic efficiency, or the lack thereof, has social implications for competitors and consumers alike. Economic desirability may be the basis for legal norm against which the behaviour of a market participant is to be tested, but a moral and ethical stance on behaviour which is detrimental to economic efficiency may quickly overtake the underlying economic reality. Economic efficiency is translated into a norm of proper business conduct, or *boni mores*, through which the policy goals of society are to be effectuated. In South Africa, where public policy has been accepted.[7] as the determining factor in the establishment of wrongful business conduct, Van Dijkhorst J. described this phenomenon as:

> "[T]he general sense of justice of the community, the *boni mores*, manifested in public opinion. In determining and applying this norm in a particular case, the interests of the competing parties have to be weighed, bearing in mind also the interests of society, the public weal.

---

[5] The other being public disclosure. See Kaufer, *The Economics of the Patent System*, (Chur, Harwood Academic Publishers GmbH, 1989).
[6] Gordon, "Asymmetric Market Failure and the Prisoner's Dilemma in Intellectual Property", 17 *U.D.L.R* 853–69 (1992); Reichman, "Legal Hybrids between the Patent and Copyright Paradigms", 94 *Col. LR* 2432 (1994); Karjala, "Misappropriation as a Third Intellectual Property Paradigm", 94 *Col. LR* 2594–609 (1994); Samuelson, "Assertive Modesty", 94 *Col. LR* 2579–93 (1994); Samuelson, Davis, Kapor, Reichman, "Manifesto Concerning the Legal Protection of Computer Programs", 94 *Col. LR* 2308–2431 (1994).
[7] Van Heerden and Neethling, *Die Reg aangaande Onregmatige Mededinging*, (1983, Durban, Butterworths); Van Aswegen, "Policy Considerations in the Law of Delict", 56 T.H.R.H.R 171 (1993).

> As this norm cannot exist *in vacuo*, the morals of the market place, the business ethics of that section of the community where the norm is to be applied, are of major importance in its determination."[8]

This quote is indicative of the way in which rules of economic efficiency have been translated into a general norm of proper business conduct. A general norm of *boni mores*, be it accepted in case law or contained in legal statute, needs to be embedded in the legal system in order to establish a coherent legal system.[9] As a consequence other normative rules will determine the place of general norm in the legal system, as well as its scope. When testing a real life situation against the general norm, it is inevitable that these other normative rules will have an impact on the way in which the general rule is applied. The influence of considerations other than those of economic efficiency[10] is most clear in those jurisdictions in which unfair competition law has been codified.[11] It is then the task of the judiciary to apply a general norm of fair business conduct in a credible way in providing their judgments with a rationale that is consistent with other legal norms, both ethical and economical and the sense of justice in the community. At this point ethical standards are introduced to support a judgment that serves to maximize welfare in society. The ethical norms remain in the public conscience, the economic efficiency argument does not. The inclusion of ethical norms in statute regulating market behaviour has in fact become the rule, rather than the exception.[12] Apart from this natural conversion of principles of economic efficiency into ethical business norm, it is also interesting to look at the peripheral ethical norms that shape the law of unfair competition, and may also be relied upon to support protection against unfair competition

---

[8] *Atlas Organic Fertilizers (Pty.) Ltd v. Pikkewyn Ghwano (Pty.) Ltd and Others*, 1981(2) S.A. 173 (T.P.D.) at 188 per Van Dijkhorst J.

[9] Wintgens, "Some Critical Comments on Coherence in the Law", in Brouwer, Hol, Soetman, Van der Velden, and De Wild (eds.), *Coherence and Conflict in Law*, (Zwolle, Kluwer/Tjeenk Willink, 1992) especially at 109–37.

[10] Hughes, "The Philosophy of Intellectual Property", 77 *Geo.L.J.* 287, at 306 (1988):
"[t]here is a very simple reason why the legal doctrines of unfair competition and trade secret protection are inherently orientated towards the value-added theory: they are court-created doctrines and people rarely go to court unless something valuable is at stake. When intellectual property is created more systematically, such as through legislation, the resulting property doctrines seem less singularly oriented toward rewarding social value."

[11] Compare in this respect the situation in France and Germany. See Passa, *Contrefaçon et Concurrence Déloyale*, n. 1 above; and Hefermehl, "Die Konkretisierung der wettbewerblichen Generalklausel durch Rechtsprechung und Lehre", in Beier, Kraft, Schricker, and Wadle (eds.), *Gewerblicher Rechtsschutz und Urheberrecht in Deutschland, Festschrift zum hunderdjährigen Bestehen der Deutschen Vereinigung für gewerblichen Rechtsschutz und Urheberrecht und ihrer Zeitschrift*, (1991, Munich, VCH), 897–937.

[12] Shell, "Substituting Ethical Standards of Common Law Rules in Commercial Cases: An Emerging Statutory Trend", 82 *Nw.ULR* 1198–1254 (1988), who notes that the trend in U.S. legislation is to incorporate sweeping general clauses, such as 'good faith' in statutory provisions. At 1223–4:
"In short, the broad definitions of 'unfair' or 'deceptive' conduct relegate traditional contract and tort categories to the status of helpful, but not dispositive, analytic tools in the inquiry of commercial liability."

Ethics as a Distinct Basis of Unfair Competition

Ethical norms do not only result from the application of principles of economic efficiency, they also mould the law of unfair competition. Leaving aside the commonly accepted category of the creation of confusion, other ethical considerations may be taken into account when considering whether an act of unfair competition has taken place. The terms "free riding" and "parasitic behaviour", when applied to the copying of the achievements of others commonly evoke a sense of injustice. Where some jurisdictions provide a remedy against this perceived unethical behaviour, others do not. In France, for example, intervention in the market is accepted to enforce standards of ethical business conduct.[13] This may be exemplified by the case *Société Mars Alimentaire v. Société Aegean Trade CT and Istanbul Gida Dis Ticaret AS,*[14] where a claim for *concurrence parasitaire* was accepted and a company was enjoined from copying a marketing concept consisting of a packaging configuration concept of chocolate bars. When market leader Mars changed its triple bar set to 300g, Aegean followed suit immediately. The Parisian Court of Appeal ruled that action in such a parasitic way from the success of a competitor was a wrong.[15] In the U.K., on the other hand, such ethical considerations are excluded from common law liability, as the dictum in *Hodgkinson & Corby Ltd and Another v. Wards Mobility Services Ltd* shows:

> "Some think that copying is unethical; others do not. Often the copyist of today becomes the innovator of tomorrow. Copying is said by some to be part of the lifeblood of competition, the means of breaking *de facto* market monopolies and keeping down the price of articles not protected by special monopolies such as patents or registered designs. Others say that copyists are parasites on innovators. None of this matters. Certainly it is not the law that copying as such is unlawful: the common law (and I am concerned with the common law) leans against monopolies. Appeals were made to such notions as 'riding on the back of Roho', or 'taking Roho's market'. Indeed evidence was led that Ward's salesman actually said that 'Ward's were riding on the back of Raymar in order to achieve better sales of their cushion.' [. . .] But it does not matter. Even if it was said, it does not amount to

---

[13] See Claus, "The French 'Law of Disloyal Competition'", [1995] 11 E. I. P. R. 550; Passa, *Contrefaçon et Concurrence Déloyale,* n. 1 above, 13–78.

[14] [1993] PIBD n° 550 III–522, [1993] 12 E. I. P. R. D-282 (CA Paris). See in this respect also *S. A. Lego v. SARL Tomy* [1995] GRUR Int. 505, [1996] IIC 729 (Cass.).

[15] *ibid.*

"[E]n réalité Istanbul et Aegean ont entendu ainsi, pour vendre un produit semblable à celui antérieurement commercialisé par Mars depuis soixante ans selon la documentation, démarquer les présentations de l'entreprise qui détient 42 per cent du marché européen (Le Nouvel Économiste du 13 avril 1990) afin de tenter de profiter de succès de ce concurrent; que cette pratique parasitaire est fautive."

For a critical appraisal of this case see Kamperman Sanders, *Unfair Competition,* n. 1 above, 28–30, and 206–7.

anything relevant. You can ride on the back of a competitor by deceiving customers or by honest competition. One is unlawful, the other is not . . ."[16]

In *International News Service v. Associated Press*,[17] the U.S. Supreme Court considered the behaviour of INS, a West Coast publisher, who appropriated from AP, its East Coast competitor who ran the stories earlier due to time differences, news on the first world which was news he could not report on himself, because he was banned from the war area on grounds of suspected German sympathies. It was held that INS, in appropriating AP's stories, had usurped the fruits of another's labour, precisely at the point where the profit is to be gained. According to Callmann[18] this judgment introduced a concept of ethical business conduct into the law which is based on the principle of unjust enrichment.

Unjust enrichment as it is now codified in various jurisdictions,[19] or recognised in case law,[20] is a principle which has it origins in Roman law, where Pomponius formulated the principle that on the basis of natural justice no one should be enriched at the expense of another.[21] Poponianus' principle did not create a new action, but served as a general principle of justice.[22] In this sense it is different from Aristotle's position on corrective justice,[23] which describes the restitutionary remedy to a situation of which the cause is unknown. Aristotle does not describe the wrong that should trigger correction.[24] It has been argued that the principle of restitution can serve as a basis for establishing liability in cases involving the copying of business assets similar to those protected under intellectual property regimes.[25] The wrong which should trigger

---

[16] [1995] F.S.R. 169, *per* Jacob J.

[17] 248 U.S. 215 (1918).

[18] "He Who Reaps Where He Has Not Sown: Unjust Enrichment in the Law of Unfair Competition", 55 Harv. L.R. 595, at 597 (1942).

[19] See Kamperman Sanders, *Unfair Competition Law*, n.1 above at 124–5 for examples of Swiss, Italian, U.S. law, at 125–8 for German law, and at 129–30 for Dutch law.

[20] *ibid.* at 128–9 for examples of French case law, and at 130–4 for the more complex situation in English law. See in this respect also Goff and Jones, *The Law of Restitution*, (4th ed., Sweet & Maxwell, London, 1993).

[21] Pomponius in Justinian, *Digesta* (D. 12,6,14):
"Nam hoc natura aequum est, neminem cum alterius detrimento fieri locupletiorem."

[22] Dawson, *Unjust Enrichment—A Comparative Analysis*, (Little, Brown and Co. Boston, Mass., 1951), at 3–5, where he states that Pomponius' statement expresses both and aspiration and a standard for judgment.

[23] Aristotle, *Nicomachean Ethics*, (trans. Ross, Clarendon Press, Oxford, 1980), Bk. V, Chap. 4, 115–17:
"The judge tries to equalise things by means of a penalty, taking away from the gan of the assailant . . . It makes no difference whether a good man has defrauded a bad man or a bad man a good one . . ., the law looks only to the distinctive character of the injury, and treats the parties as equal."

[24] See Posner, "The Concept of Corrective Justice in Recent Theories of Tort Law", 10 J.L.S. 187–206 (1981), at 191–3; Coleman, "Corrective Justice and Wrongful Gain", J.L.S. 421–40 (1982); see, however, Wright, "Substantive Correctve Justice", 77 I.L.R. 625 (1992), who states that notions of wrong can be distilled from Aristotle's writing as a whole.

[25] Gordon, "On Owning Information: Intellectual Property and Restitutionary Impulse", 78 U.L.R. 149 (1992).

this correction is established on the basis of knowledge on the part of the defendant that the plaintiff expects to be compensated for the use of the asset he has developed. The claimant has to make sure that the prospective copyist is made aware of the fact that the producer of the original expects compensation. This should be achieved through tagging of the asset.[26] When considering the scope of protection, however, it is important to determine which assets can attract protection under this regime. This can either be achieved by relying on economic rationale, such as economic market failure,[27] or on the principle of unjust enrichment as an independent action, as opposed to restitution for a wrong. Liability in unjust enrichment can be established on the basis of subtraction; a situation in which something of value has passed from the plaintiff to the defendant.[28] This situation may occur in three instances. The first is when the plaintiff has made clear he does not want to transfer benefits to the defendant, or when he has specified the conditions under which he wants a transfer to occur. This first category ties in with the practice of tagging described earlier. The second arises when the defendant has come upon a benefit and chooses to acquiesce. The third is when a defendant has actively set out to obtain the benefit from the plaintiff, most likely by copying. In all instances it has to be demonstrated that the defendant has been enriched at the expense of the plaintiff. The most common way of demonstrating this is by showing that it was imperative for the defendant to acquire the benefit he has now received for free, or that the defendant has realised financial gain subsequent to the copying and use of the asset. In all three instances there also needs to be detriment to the plaintiff. In cases involving the copying of intellectual and industrial creativity, this requirement will usually be satisfied by a competitive nexus between the parties involved, but the plaintiff's loss and the defendant's gain do not have to equal to one another.[29] As such the principle of unjust enrichment could be employed to provide an ethical doctrinal base in certain unfair competition cases involving parasitic behaviour.[30]

Where norms of business behaviour that find their genesis in arguments of economic efficiency are mixed with other ethical norms, such as unjust enrichment, it is also possible to take away objections that can be raised against the establishment of rights on the basis of economic analysis alone. When a judge has to decide a case where the rights of the parties are not pre-determined by an intellectual property regime, reliance on economic analysis alone is highly suspect, as principles of

---

[26] Encryption technology will increase in importance as a means to instill knowledge in infringers, as reflected in the WIPO Copyright Treaty 1996 Article 12, and WIPO Performances and Phonograms Treaty 1996, Article 19.

[27] Gordon, "Asymmetric Market Failure and the Prisoner's Dilemma in Intellectual Property", n. 6 above .

[28] See Birks, *An Introduction to the Law of Restitution*, (Clarendon Press, Oxford, 1989), at 23.

[29] *ibid.* at 132; Goff and Jones, *The Law of Restitution*, n. 20 above, 35–9.

[30] For a proposition along these lines see Kamperman Sanders, *Unfair Competition Law The Protection of Intellectual and Industrial Creativity*, n. 1 above, 121–53, with practical examples at 186–210.

economic efficiency, public policy, and the general sense of justice of the community may not coincide.[31] Without ethical norms such a system of justice would not be acceptable to society.

Conclusion

At face value arguments of economic efficiency dominate the field of unfair competition law. The need for coherence in the legal system requires that these rules of economic efficiency be translated in common ethical norms of business conduct. In doing so it is possible for other ethical norms within the legal system to seep into the law of unfair competition. The example of the incorporation of the principle of unjust enrichment demonstrates the need for this mixing of norms, so that undesirable effects from the sole pursuit of economic efficiency can be avoided.

---

[31] Hol, "Balancing Rights and Goals", in Brouwer, Hol, Soeteman, Van der Velden, and De Wild (eds.), *Coherence and Conflict in Law*, n. 9 above, 91–106, at 101 and 103:
"When is it difficult to find out who was given an entitlement to what, is not the judge playing politics when he is deciding the case? When he is, should he choose the principle of the maximization of wealth? . . . Corrective justice demands giving each his due what was wrongly taken. What is his due is protected by rights. However, when wrong is equated with efficiency, there is a chance that those rights will not be protected, when they should. That is because rights in economic analysis have no independent meaning, but are seen as a mere function of wealth maximisation."

INDEX

(All references are to page numbers)